Programming The Raspberry Pi Pico
In C

Harry Fairhead

I/O Press
I Programmer Library

Harry Fairhead, Programming The Raspberry Pi Pico In C
ISBN:9781871962680
First Edition
First Printing, April 2021
Revision 0

Published by IO Press   www.iopress.info
In association with I Programmer   www.i-programmer.info
and with I o T Programmer   www.iot-programmer.com

The publisher recognizes and respects all marks used by companies and manufacturers as a means to distinguish their products. All brand names and product names mentioned in this book are trade marks or service marks of their respective companies and our omission of trade marks is not an attempt to infringe on the property of others.

In particular we acknowledge that Raspberry Pi and Pico are registered trademarks of the Raspberry Pi Foundation.

For updates, errata, links to resources and the source code for the programs in this book, visit its dedicated page on the IO Press website: iopress.info.

Preface

The Pico is a remarkable microcontroller. It has a power and sophistication that would have been unthinkable just a short time ago. For the sort of jobs it is ideal for, it has plenty of processing power and enough memory to make tasks that would have once required careful planning, relatively easy. Instead of struggling with the machine, you can now focus on getting a good implementation of your algorithms.

This said, it has to be admitted that to enjoy all of its power and sophistication there is no better language than C. It wastes none of the power and it gives you what you need to get at the new features. However, getting started with the Pico with C isn't as simple as getting started with MicroPython. You have to find a way to create programs and you have to set things up so that program testing and debugging is easy.

I have settled on VS Code as my preferred IDE and it is a good choice to use with the Pico SDK. I take the approach that you need to get set up in VS Code and debugging as quickly as possible. So, rather than explain how to get command line things working, we go straight to a workable IDE-based environment. I hope this approach makes getting started with Pico C programming easier than alternatives.

The rewards of getting a good IDE working are many and once you have things working you can concentrate on making use of the Pico, which has so many resources that a comprehensive account would fill a book twice this size. In order to make things fit in the space available I have limited myself to explaining what you need to know to get a good understanding of the basics. Topics not covered are Direct Memory Access (DMA), using the second core, power-saving states, the interpolator and the hardware divider. All of these topics are "second level" in the sense that you generally only need them after you have mastered everything else. There clearly is scope for a second volume of this book!

I have covered the use of the PIO (Programmable I/O), however, because it is one of the key advantages of using the Pico, as it allows you to delegate interaction with external hardware to a peripheral. The PIO isn't the solution to every problem, but it is very useful, challenging and a lot of fun. You will find out about the PIO in a dedicated chapter and then use it to implement a "driver" for the DHT22 and the 1-Wire bus.

This book doesn't teach you C, but you really only need a basic level of understanding of the language. All examples are written in a very simple style that avoids the use of constants and functions that might obscure the meaning. You can easily refactor any of the examples into a set of functions that suit your particular purpose and programming style.

If the Pico has a drawback, it is that it doesn't have a network connection. To solve this problem there is a chapter on using the low cost ESP8266 as a WiFi client and web server. The two devices together make the Pico a true IoT device.

This is not a projects book, although there isn't much left for you to do to round out the embryonic projects that are used as examples. Instead it is about understanding concepts and the acquisition of skills. The hope is that by the end of the book you will know how to tackle your own projects and get them safely to completion without wasting time in trial and error.

Thanks to my tireless editors Sue Gee and Kay Ewbank. I may know what a comma is for in C, but my understanding of its role in natural language is severely limited. Errors that remain, and I hope they are few, are mine.

For the source code for the programs in this book, together with any updates or errata, links to resources including recommendations for obtaining electronic components, visit its dedicated page on the IO Press website: iopress.info.

You can also contact me at harry.fairhead@i-programmer.info.

Harry Fairhead
April, 2021

Table of Contents

Preface   **3**

Chapter 1
The Raspberry Pi Pico – Before We Begin   **13**
    The Pico And Its Family..14
    What To Expect..16
    What Do You Need?..16
    Community...20
    Summary..21

Chapter 2
Getting Started   **23**
    Getting Started In C..23
    Pico On Pi..25
    Pico On Windows..26
    Blinky Using VS Code...27
    Download And Debug Using A Pi 4..32
    Debug Using PicoProbe For Windows..35
    Automatic Project Creation...39
    What Is Missing?...40
    Summary..41

Chapter 3
Getting Started With The GPIO   **43**
    Pico Pins..43
    Basic GPIO Functions...45
    Blinky Revisited...46
    Summary..48

Chapter 4
Simple Output   **49**
    Basic GPIO Functions...49
    Working With Multiple GPIO Lines...50
    How Fast?..52
    Including Pauses...54
    Fixed Time Delay...57
    Phased Pulses..58
    Overrides..60
    Summary..61

Chapter 5

Some Electronics   **63**

Electrical Drive Characteristics....................................63

Driving An LED...64

LED BJT Drive...66

A BJT Example..67

MOSFET Driver..70

MOSFET LED..71

Setting Drive Type..72

Setting Output Mode..74

Basic Input Circuit - The Switch.................................74

Debounce...76

The Potential Divider...76

Summary..78

Chapter 6

Simple Input   **79**

GPIO Input..79

Basic Input Functions..80

The Simple Button..81

Press Or Hold..84

Serial Data...85

How Fast Can We Measure?...86

The Finite State Machine...87

FSM Button...89

FSM Hold Button..91

FSM Ring Counter..92

Summary..95

Chapter 7

Advanced Input – Events and Interrupts   **97**

Events...97

Interrupts Considered Harmful?.................................98

Hardware Events...99

An Edgy Button...101

Measuring Pulses With Events...................................102

Interrupts...104

How Fast Is An Interrupt?..107

Race Conditions and Starvation................................107

Responding To Input...110

Summary..111

Chapter 8
Pulse Width Modulation   **113**

Some Basic Pico PWM Facts...113
Pico PWM Initialization...115
PWM Configuration...116
Clock Division...119
A Frequency and Duty Cycle Function...122
Using PWM Lines Together...123
Changing The Duty Cycle...126
Working With The Counter...127
Using PWM Interrupts..128
Uses Of PWM – Digital To Analog..130
Frequency Modulation...133
Controlling An LED...134
PWM Input..137
A Configuration Struct..140
What Else Can You Use PWM For?..141
Summary..142

Chapter 9
Controlling Motors And Servos   **143**

DC Motor...143
Brushed Motors...144
Unidirectional Brushed Motor..146
Unidirectional PWM Motor Controller..148
Bidirectional Brushed Motor..150
Bidirectional Motor Software...154
Using A Single Full H-Bridge As Two Half H-Bridges.................156
Controlling a Servo...157
Brushless DC Motors..160
Stepper Motors...163
Stepper Motor Driver..166
Stepper Motor Rotation – Using Timers......................................172
Summary..178

Chapter 10

Getting Started With The SPI Bus   **179**

SPI Bus Basics...179

Pico SPI Interfaces...182

The SPI Functions..182

Using the Data Transfer Functions....................................185

A Loopback Example...186

Using The CS Line..188

The BME280 Humidity, Pressure and Temperature Sensor..........190

Problems..196

Summary...197

Chapter 11

A-To-D and The SPI Bus   **199**

Pico ADC..199

The MCP3008 SPI ADC..204

Connecting To The Pico..206

Basic Configuration..206

The Protocol..207

Some Packaged Functions..210

How Fast...211

Summary...212

Chapter 12

Using The I2C Bus   **213**

I2C Hardware Basics...214

The Pico I2C..216

The I2C Functions..216

Slow Read Protocols...222

A Real Device..223

First Program...225

The I2C Protocol In Action...227

Reading The Raw Temperature Data....................................227

Processing The Data..229

Reading Humidity...230

Checksum Calculation...231

Complete Listing..232

Summary...234

Chapter 13
Using The PIO 235

PIO Basic Concepts..236
Configuring GPIO for PIO Output..236
PIO Blinky...238
Clock Division And Timing...241
Writing Loops..243
Data To The PIO...244
Output To GPIO...246
Side Effects...251
Input..253
Edges...256
Advanced PIO..258
Summary...259

Chapter 14
The DHT22 Sensor Implementing A Custom Protocol 261

The DHT22..261
The Electronics..264
The Software..265
DHT22 Using the PIO – Counting..270
DHT22 Using the PIO – Sampling..276
Complete Listing..278
Summary...281

Chapter 15
The 1-Wire Bus And The DS1820   **282**
The Hardware..282
Initialization..283
Writing Bits...285
A First Command - Writing Bytes.......................................287
Reading Bits...288
Computing The CRC...290
The DS18B20 Hardware..292
Initialization..294
Initiating Temperature Conversion.....................................295
Reading The Scratchpad...296
Getting The Temperature..296
A Temperature Function...297
The Complete Program...298
A PIO DS18B20 Program...301
The Complete Program...307
Other Commands...310
Summary...313

Chapter 16
The Serial Port   **315**
Serial Protocol..315
UART Hardware...317
Setting Up the UART..318
Data Transfer..320
Reading and Writing Characters and Strings..........................322
Stdio..323
Working With Small Buffers...324
Summary...326

Chapter 17
WiFi Using The ESP8266   **327**
    The Amazing ESP8266..327
    Connecting the ESP8266 ESP-01.......................................328
    AT Commands...329
    Attention!...330
    Some Utility Functions...334
    Configuring WiFi...335
    Connecting to WiFi...337
    Getting a Web Page...338
    A Web Server...341
    Complete Listing Of Web Server...345
    Summary...350

Chapter 18
Direct To The Hardware   **351**
    Registers...351
    Single-Cycle IO Block...353
    The SDK Set Function..355
    Example I - Events...356
    Example II PAD - Pull, Drive and Schmitt.........................358
    Digging Deeper..361
    Summary...362

Chapter 1

The Raspberry Pi Pico - Before We Begin

The Raspberry Pi Pico is a bold step for the Raspberry Pi world. It isn't a full System On a Chip (SoC), but a microcontroller - a small system with a minimal operating system designed to be used to control and connect to other devices. Its uses range from controlling washing machines to making games that use buttons and lights. Unlike the Raspberry Pi Zero, which is often used as a microcontroller, you can program it without having to struggle with Linux drivers and system commands. Perhaps more importantly, you don't have to fight against the multi-tasking behavior of Linux which makes getting timing right difficult. Programming the Pico means you know exactly what is happening and when and timing becomes so much easier. It doesn't mean it's a solved problem, but it is easier. However, not having an operating system also brings its own problems and if you are used to working with the Pi Zero, say, you might well find that there are times when you would like to make a Linux call to solve a problem. My opinion, and I hope yours too once you have read on, is that overall for the type of task the Pico is suited to, not having an operating system is a big plus point.

As to comparing the Pico to alternative microcontrollers, its big advantage is that it is powerful. It has a fast processor with enough memory to get most jobs done. It also has a great many built-in peripherals and can talk to devices such as the PWM, I2C, SPI, UART and ADC without much trouble and, with the help of the innovative PIO (Programmable I/O), just about anything else, including custom interfaces and the 1-Wire bus.

The PIO is a special feature of the Pico that is worth knowing about sooner rather than later. It is a processor in its own right and while it is restricted to only a handful of instructions it is targeted at the very specific job of working with pulsed input and output. This means that you can often write a fairly simple program to enable the PIO to code and decode any protocol that is or isn't already supported. For example, in Chapter 14 we implement a 1-Wire bus protocol and so extend the Pico

to working with this popular class of device. It doesn't just stop at new protocols. For example, if you find a I2C or SPI device that doesn't quite fit into the very loose specifications of these two protocols, or goes beyond them in some way, then you can implement custom versions. Going beyond the very practical, it is worth saying that programming the PIO is great fun and very educational. It gives you an insight into how assembly language works in general.

At the moment the only negative aspect of the Pico is that it doesn't have WiFi on board. This means that, out of the box, it can't be used as an IoT (Internet of Things) device as it can't connect to the Internet. However this is easily fixed. In Chapter 17 we discover that it is simple and cheap to add an ESP8266 WiFi device via a single serial interface.

A very important point about the Pico is that it is widely available. This might seem like a strange thing to say, but the Raspberry Pi Zero is still restricted to one per customer and, as such, not really a good candidate for moving from a prototype to a commercial product. The Pico can be bought in any quantity and so can the chip it is based on. As such, it is suitable for a project that might graduate to a fully finished end product.

This is a sketchy overview of what the Pico is all about. In the rest of the chapter we look at the details of the Pico and the things you need to get started.

The Pico And Its Family

The Pico is based on the RP2040 processor chip which was designed by Raspberry Pi specially for the Pico. It is based on the ARM Cortex M0 and runs ARM machine code. The processor is available as a chip that can purchased to build your own implementation of a Pico-like device. Many other well known hardware companies, notably Arduino, have done just this and, if you want a Pico, you aren't restricted to just the Raspberry Pi Pico, there are other choices. Some are very small and some have extras on board:

These alternatives to the Pico are easy to use because they operate just like the Pico. You can program them using the same SDK and the same environment. The only differences might be that the smaller form factors expose fewer hardware lines so you might not be able to use everything you can use on the full Pico. In the remainder of this book the programs target the Raspberry Pico, but they should just work or be easily modifiable for any device that used the RP2040.

The key points about the Pico hardware are:

- Dual-core Arm Cortex M0+ processor, flexible clock running up to 133 MHz
- 264KB of SRAM, and 2MB of on-board Flash memory
- USB 1.1 with device and host support
- Low-power sleep and dormant modes
- Drag-and-drop programming using mass storage over USB
- 26 × multi-function GPIO pins
- 2 × SPI, 2 × I2C, 2 × UART, 3 × 12-bit ADC, 16 × controllable PWM channels
- Accurate clock and timer on-chip
- Temperature sensor
- Accelerated floating-point libraries on-chip
- 8 × Programmable I/O (PIO) state machines

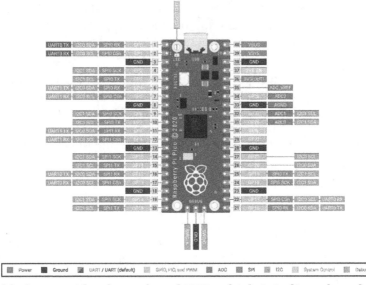

You could also consider the on-board LED, which is indicated on the diagram, as a key feature – it may be small, but it is very useful in getting started and testing.

What To Expect

There are no complete projects in this book – although some examples come very close and it is clear that some of them could be used together to create finished projects. The reason for this is that the focus is on learning how things work so that you can move on and do things that are non-standard.

What matters is that you can reason about what the processor is doing and how it interacts with the real world in real time. This is the big difference between desktop and embedded programming. In the desktop world you don't really care much about when something happens, but when you are programming a physical system you care very much.

This is a book about understanding general principles and making things work at the lowest possible level. This knowledge isn't always necessary when you are working on a relatively slow system in, say, MicroPython, but it is always helpful for understanding what is going on when things go wrong. When you are working directly with the hardware, speed matters and so does knowing what is happening.

All of the examples are as basic as possible and the code is designed to be as easy to understand as possible. In most cases this means avoiding the use of constants that appear to come from nowhere and functions that make it difficult to see the basic steps. Also error handling is reduced to a bare minimum – simple programs look complicated if you add error handling code. Of course, there is no reason not to refactor these examples into something that looks more like production code and the effort in doing this is much less than getting the basic programs working in the first place.

Rather than go through multiple possible configurations for a development environment, this book uses VS Code from the start. All of the setup and programming instructions are in terms of using VS Code. If you want to work in a different way then the documentation has instructions, but working with VS Code is a lot simpler and more powerful than using the command line.

What Do You Need?

Well – a Pico at least! In fact you would be well advised to buy at least two Picos, especially if you are going to be programming using a PC, Mac or general Linux machine. The Pico is small and lacks an operating system, so running all of the software you need to create programs on it needs another machine – the development machine. The choice here is between all the other possible computers and a Raspberry Pi 4 or 400. Using a Pi as the development machine has some big advantages - so much so that you can consider it the standard and recommended way of doing things. The reason is that the Pi has its own GPIO connections which makes it possible to download programs and debug programs running on the Pico without having to buy anything extra. The software installation instructions for the Pi are also simpler than for other machines. If you don't want to work directly with a Pi then you can still program from the comfort of your desktop machine by using remote desktop to the Pi 4.

If you do opt to use a Pi 4 or 400 as your development system then you only need to buy a single Pico as you don't need an extra one to do debugging. However, given the error-prone nature of this sort of physical computing, I would still suggest buying more than one Pico, although I have never damaged one since I have been working with them.

If you opt to use a PC, Mac or general Linux system then you really do need to buy two Picos. The reason is that these machines do not have GPIO connections and this makes it impossible to install easy download and debug connections. The easiest solution in this case is to use a second Pico to act as a debug probe. The second Pico connects to your desktop machine via USB and to the Pico you are working with via a basic three-wire debug connection. You also need to download some special PicoProbe software onto the first Pico, but all of this is described in more detail in the next chapter. What matters at the moment is that you know that you will need two Picos to do development if you are using a PC, Mac or general Linux machine.

This isn't quite true as the Pico has a "drag-and-drop" way of loading programs using just a USB connection. This is much advertised as the easy way to get started, but in fact this is really all it is. Dragging-and-dropping programs means that you don't need a second Pico to act as a download and debug probe. You simply connect the Pico you are using to the desktop machine via USB and power it on while holding down the reset button. This makes it appear as folder on the desktop machine and you can drag-and-drop a program into the folder and it will start running. The problem is that no debugging facilities are provides and the time wasted in restarting and dragging-and-dropping to the Pico is such that it very quickly becomes irritating and an impediment to getting anything done. If you are going to program anything more than a "Hello World" style "Blinky", you need to use a full debug connection and this should be considered the essential way to work.

If you are not using a Pi 4/400 to develop and debug programs you need a second Pico to act as a debugging device.

There is also the problem of how to connect to the Pico. As it comes, the Pico has no pins soldered to its PCB. For development you either need to buy a slightly upgraded Pico with pins already soldered or you need to solder your own. As well as the 40 pins on both sides of the Pico, you also need to solder three pins to the debug port at the edge opposite the USB port. Many off-the-shelf "kits" tend to forget this, so it is worth checking that the debug port is fitted or that you have three extra pins to solder yourself. Also notice that if you are using a prototyping board to connect to the pins, you need to solder the debug pins on the other side of the Pico so that they are accessible while the Pico is plugged in:

As to additional hardware over and above the Picos, you will need a solderless prototype board and some hookup wires – known as Dupont wires. You will also need some LEDs, a selection of resistors, some 2N2222 or other general purpose transistors and any of the sensors used in later chapters. See the Resources page for this book on the I/O Press website for links. It is probably better to buy what you need as you choose to implement one of the projects, but an alternative is to buy one of the many "getting started" kits. You will probably still need to buy some extra components, however.

A solderless prototype board and some Dupont wires

While you don't need to know how to solder, you will need to be able to hook up a circuit on a prototyping board. A multimeter (less than $10) is useful, but if you are serious about electronic projects, investing in a logic analyzer (less than $100) will repay itself in no time at all. You can get small analyzers that plug in via a USB port and use an application to show you what is happening. It is only with a multichannel logic analyzer that you have any hope of understanding what is happening. Without one and the slight skill involved in using it, you are essentially flying blind and left to just guess what might be wrong.

A Low Cost Logic Analyzer

Finally, if you are even more serious, then a pocket oscilloscope is also worth investing in to check out the analog nature of the supposedly digital signals that microcontrollers put out. However, if you have to choose between these two instruments, the logic analyzer should be your first acquisition.

It is worth noting that the Pico can generate signals that are too fast to be reliably detected by low-cost oscilloscopes and logic analyzers, which work at between 1MHz and 25MHz. This can mean that working with pulses much faster than $1\mu s$ can be difficult as you cannot rely on your instruments. There are reasonably priced 200MHz and 500MHz logic analyzers and one of these is certainly worthwhile if you are serious about hardware. It is worth knowing that both instruments can mislead you if you try to work with signals outside of the range that they can work with.

It is also assumed that you are able to program in a C-like language – Java, C#, Python are all similar to C and, of course, so is C++. There isn't space in this book to teach C programming, but the programs are easy enough to follow and any out-of-the-ordinary coding is explained. If you want to learn C in detail, see *Fundamental C:Getting Closer To The Machine*, ISBN: 9781871962604.

Community

If you get stuck the best place to ask for help is in the Pico forums or, second best, Stack Overflow. There are lots of people ready to help, but notice that programming the Pico in C is beyond the scope of most developers and you need to filter out attempts to be helpful by people who misunderstand your question. The quality of answers varies from misleading to excellent. Always make sure you evaluate what you are being advised in the light of what you know. Be kind and supportive of anyone offering an answer that indicates that they misunderstand your question.

You also need to keep in mind that the advice is also usually offered from a biased point of view. The Python programmer will give you an answer that suits a system that uses Python and electronics beginners will offer you solutions that are based on "off-the-shelf" modules, when a simple alternative solution is available, based on a few cheap components. Even when the advice you get is 100% correct, it still isn't necessarily the right advice for you. As a rule never follow any advice that you don't understand.

Summary

- The Pico is a remarkably powerful device given its low cost and is ideal for building prototypes, one-offs and production devices.

- The RP2040 chip that is at the heart of the Pico is also used in a number of similar devices, all of which can be treated as variations on the basic Pico.

- You need to decide on a development machine to use in conjunction with your Pico. The best and simplest choice is a Pi 4 or a Pi 400. This has GPIO lines which can be connected to the Pico to provide fast program loading and debugging.

- If you want to use a desktop PC, Mac or Linux machine then you need a minimum of two Picos – one to work with, and one to run PicoProbe and act as a debugging connection.

- Although you can get started with the Pico without a debugging connection using drag-and-drop, this isn't a long term solution to developing programs.

- VS Code provides an easy-to-use and efficient development environment, irrespective of the type of development machine you choose.

- To work with electronics, you need a solderless prototyping board, some hookup wires and some components. You also need a multimeter and preferably a logic analyzer. After these basic instruments you can add what you can afford.

- There is an active Pico community forum and if you get stuck it's the place to ask for advice. However, always evaluate any advice proffered and, in general, don't accept it unless you understand it.

Chapter 2
Getting Started

It is natural to program the Pico in C. It is what its system software is written in and it is the only way to get at many of the sophisticated and powerful features it offers. You can get a long way with Python or some other language, but to get all of the way you need C.

You can describe C as a machine-independent assembly language and hence when you learn it you get deeper into the system than with other languages and discover what is really going on. This makes it a good way to improve your understanding of computers and computing in general. If you need to learn C as it is used in IoT programming then see *Fundamental C: Getting Closer To The Machine*, ISBN: 9781871962604.

Sometimes you don't need speed, even in an IoT application. For example, if you just want to flash a few LEDs or read a temperature sensor in a human timescale, then you can write in almost any language. However, if you want to interface directly with other systems and control externally connected hardware at its full speed, C is your best choice. If timing is critical, then C is the only way to go. Put simply, if you can't make your application work fast enough in C, then you probably can't in any language as C, being so "low-level", makes it easy to access the underlying hardware.

Put simply, C is a great language for any interfacing, IoT or embedded program and it leads on to C++ and more sophisticated languages.

So C is worth learning and the Pico provides low-cost hardware to experiment with. How do we get started?

Getting Started In C

The Raspberry Pi Pico website has lots of detailed instructions on how to get started programming it in C. What might surprise you, and perhaps even put you off, is that there are many steps involved. The reason is that you have to install a complete C development system, often called a "toolchain", on the machine that you plan to use to write programs that will run on the Pico. Notice that it isn't sensible to use a Pico to develop code for a Pico – it probably is just powerful enough, but the toolchain generally needs a full operating system which the Pico doesn't have. So you have to use another computer system to develop programs for the Pico and at the moment three types of system are supported – Linux, Windows and Mac OS. The Pico website has a definite preference for using Linux in the form of Pi OS running on a Pi 4 or a Pi 400. This is a very attractive option, but using Windows or a Mac is attractive to any programmer familiar with their operating systems and ways of working.

It isn't useful here to go into the exact steps needed to install the necessary software – the procedures change and they are well-documented on the Pico website. What is useful is to make clear why the steps are necessary and how the parts of the toolchain fit together. This knowledge makes it easier to understand the steps and to troubleshoot should things go wrong.

You also have a choice of exactly how to create programs to run on the Pico – the editor or IDE to use. While the Pico website attempts to be neutral and suggests that you can use almost anything, there are big advantages in opting to use Visual Studio Code, VS Code. It is a free, open source multi-language editor that offers many features that make programming easier, faster and less error-prone. It is advised that you adopt VS Code even though it might take more time to get started if you haven't used it before. It is a general skill that will continue to be useful if and when you move away from programming the Pico in C.

Finally, it is worth saying that is is very worthwhile to use a Pi 4 as your development machine. This is preferable to using another Linux system, Windows or Mac OS. The reason is twofold. First, the Pi4 runs Linux software, which is the basis of the entire toolchain. For example, the toolchain only runs on Windows after some effort to make it feel at home – on Linux it is already at home. Second, the Pi 4 has GPIO lines which are readily available and these can be used to make a debugging connection to the Pico. If you use a Windows or Mac development machine you either have to use a dedicated debugging device or you have to use a second Pico to act as a debugging device. This isn't expensive, but it is more complicated. While you might think that you probably don't need a debug connection – you do. The difficulties of working without one are so great that you have to regard a debugging connection as part of a "standard configuration" and hence how difficult it is to set up is an issue.

Pico On Pi

Using a Pi 4 as the development machine is the recommended option. If you want to make Pico development as easy as possible, this is the way to go.

If you opt to use a Pi 4 or a Pi 400 then there is an installation script that does all of the work for you. All you have to do is download it from the Raspberry Pi site, set it to be executable and execute it:

```
wget https://raw.githubusercontent.com/raspberrypi/pico-setup/
                                        master/pico_setup.sh
chmod +x pico_setup.sh
./pico_setup.sh
```

This works well and doesn't install anything you already have installed. You do have to reboot for it all to take effect, however.

The script does all of the steps that you could do for yourself.

1. Creates a `pico` directory in the user's home directory.
2. Installs the GCC ARM compiler, CMake and a support library:
   ```
   sudo apt install cmake gcc-arm-none-eabi
                              libnewlib-arm-none-eabi
   ```
3. Clones the GitHub SDK repository:
   ```
   git clone -b master https://github.com/raspberrypi/pico-
   sdk.git
   cd pico-sdk
   git submodule update —init~
   cd ..
   ```
4. Clones the examples and playground repositories – these aren't essential:
   ```
   git clone -b master https://github.com/raspberrypi/
                                        pico-examples.git
   ```
5. Sets up paths by defining `PICO_SDK_PATH`, `PICO_EXAMPLES_PATH`, `PICO_EXTRAS_PATH`, and `PICO_PLAYGROUND_PATH` in your `~/.bashrc`
6. Builds the `blink` and `hello_world` examples in `pico-examples/build/blink` and `pico-examples/build/hello_world`
7. Downloads and builds `picotool` and copies it to `/usr/local/bin` - this isn't essential.
8. Downloads and builds `picoprobe` - this is necessary to do easy debugging with another Pico acting as a SWD (Serial Wire Debug) device.
9. Downloads and compiles the debugging tool OpenOCD.
10. Downloads and installs Visual Studio Code.
11. Installs the required Visual Studio Code extensions.
12. Configures the Raspberry Pi UART for use with the Pico.

Notice that the only things you actually need installed to get started are the GCC ARM compiler, CMake and the SDK. The other items will be useful later.

Pico On Windows

There is no question that it is easier to work with a Raspberry Pi or other Linux system as the development machine. As already mentioned, the reason it is harder on Windows is that the software isn't native Windows software. There is also the issue that you have to find a way to make a debug connection to the machine and this is much easier with access to GPIO lines as on the Pi 4 or P400.

There is an installation script for Windows, but it isn't an official installer. You can find it at:

`https://github.com/ndabas/pico-setup-windows`

and it is easy to use and it works.

At the time of writing it automatically installs and configures the following:

1. Creates a `pico` directory in the user's home directory
2. GNU Arm Embedded toolchain
3. CMake
4. Build Tools for Visual Studio 2019
5. Python 3
6. Git for Windows
7. Visual Studio Code
8. Doxygen
9. Graphviz
10. Zadig

At the end of the installation it asks if you want to clone the SDK from the GitHub repo and the usual answer is "Yes". Of the items installed, the only essential ones are GNU Arm Embedded Toolchain, CMake and Build Tools for Visual Studio 2019 and you can install these separately if you don't want to use the script.

Notice that the build tools are for Visual Studio not VS Code. You don't actually use Visual Studio, but this is the easiest way to get NMake which is needed to execute the output of CMake. It is also important to realize that you have to run VS Code from the VS Studio Command Prompt. If you don't then the paths to the various tools aren't correctly set up. If you use the installer then you will find:

`Visual Studio Code for Pico`

in the `pico` directory and you can simply click on this to start VS Code with it correctly configured.

The only manual configuration you need to perform is to set NMake as the build tool to use. If you don't do this then VS Code makes use of Ninja and your build will fail. To do this open the File,Settings dialog and search for cmake generator and enter NMake Makefiles in the field:

Once you have VS Code running the procedure for running the first example `blinky.c` is the same as using a Pi as the development machine.

Blinky Using VS Code

The official documentation takes you through various steps on the way to creating your own project. If you want to do this then it is a good learning experience, but it is much more efficient to move directly to creating your own project using the tools that you are going to use for all the projects you create. So, we will start off using VS Code and our own project created from scratch.

First open VS Code – it is in the Programming section of the menu. If you have installed everything using the installation script, it will be set up and ready to work with a CMake project. That is, the two CMake and debug extensions will already be installed and this is worth checking before moving on:

To create a new project first create a folder called `blinky` within the `pico` directory – it has to be within the `pico` directory to find the SDK. Next open VS Code and use the File,Open Folder command to open the newly created `blinky` folder. Use the File,New command and the editor to create `blinky.c` containing:

```
#include "pico/stdlib.h"

int main() {
    gpio_init(25);
    gpio_set_dir(25, GPIO_OUT);
    while (true) {
        gpio_put(25, 1);
        sleep_ms(500);
        gpio_put(25, 0);
        sleep_ms(500);
    }
}
```

Although we haven't explored how to use the GPIO lines or any aspect of the SDK, you should be able to understand this simple program. It makes use of GPIO pin 25, which is connected to the on-board LED, to flash the LED every half second. You can see that there is a call to initialize the pin, set it to output and after that a loop which sets it to 1 and 0 with a half a second pause.

In a simple system this is all you would need to make the device flash, but programs written for the Pico make use of an extensive library of code. The simplest thing to do would be to link your program to the entire library and just run the program, but this would be hopelessly inefficient. What we actually do is use a build system that only compiles the parts of the library, and our own code, that actually have changed and need to be recompiled. It then only links in the parts of the library that we have used and this creates a more efficient program. The only problem is that we now have the increased complexity that the build system has to manage. The Pico makes use of the CMake build system. This takes a specification for the project and then outputs instructions to a lower-level build utility to actually create the executable program. The instructions that CMake uses are usually stored in a file called `CMakeLists.txt` which is stored in the root of the project directory. In this case we only need a simple set of instructions that describes the project and makes clear that it uses the SDK.

Create a file called `CMakeLists.txt` in the `blinky` folder and enter:

```
cmake_minimum_required(VERSION 3.13)
include(pico_sdk_import.cmake)
project(blinky C CXX ASM)
set(CMAKE_C_STANDARD 11)
set(CMAKE_CXX_STANDARD 17)
pico_sdk_init()
add_executable(blinky
 blinky.c
)
target_link_libraries(blinky pico_stdlib)
pico_add_extra_outputs(blinky)
```

This states that the minimum version of CMake that this works with is 3.13. It then includes the file `pico_sdk_import.cmake` – this is a CMake file that defines how the entire SDK is to be built. You need this in nearly all of the projects you create. The project statement defines the blinky project to be one that uses C, C++ and ARM assembly – your main program might be in C but the rest of the project uses more. After that we indicate the standards in use and then make a call to a routine defined in `pico_sdk_import.cmake` which initializes the SDK part of the project. Finally we define the files in our project that are not in the SDK, set the targets for the build and add a call to a predefined routine which converts the raw output into formats that we can use to load onto the Pico. The options are:

File extension	Description
.bin	Raw binary dump of the program code and data
.elf	The full program output, possibly including debug information
.uf2	The program code and data in a UF2 form that you can drag-and-drop on to the RP2040 board when it is mounted as a USB drive
.dis	A disassembly of the compiled binary
.hex	Hexdump of the compiled binary
.map	A map file to accompany the .elf file describing where the linker has arranged segments in memory

As we "include" `pico_sdk_import.cmake` this has to be copied into the root of the project. You can get it from any existing project, but you can get an up-to-date copy from `pico/pico-sdk/external`.

The final stage is to get VS Code to use the CMake extension to first configure and then build the project. You can do this by closing the project and reopening it, at which point the extension should notice the `CMakeList.txt` file in the root and ask you if you want to configure the project. If this doesn't work and the `CMakeLists.txt` file isn't detected then use the command Palette to issue the command CMake Quick Start, but don't overwrite the `CMakeLists.txt` file you already have. In response to:

you should select Yes and answer any questions that pop up in dialog boxes. The one very important aspect of configuring the system is defining which "Kit" to use. Essentially a kit is a compiler collection that can be used to build the project. As you have installed GCC you should see it in the list – if you don't see it then use the [Scan for kits] option. If you still don't see it check that it is installed and on the path. The GCC version that you need is `GCC for arm-non-eabi` which is at version 7.3.1 at the time of writing:

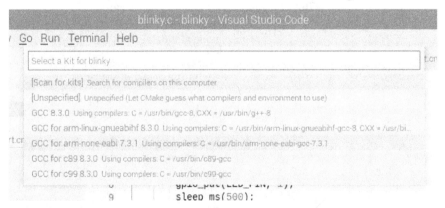

There are many ways to start a build of the project, but all of the commands are available if you select the CMake extension and then click on the three dots menu. The Clean Reconfigure All Projects option executes CMake to create a set of makefiles that can be used to build the project. You need to select this if the current build fails for reasons of configuration.

The Clean Rebuild All Projects option rebuilds everything in the project including the SDK and files that haven't changed since the last build. If you click the Build All Projects icon then only the files that have changed since the last build are recompiled. This is usually much faster and is the option to use unless something doesn't work because files have become out of sync.

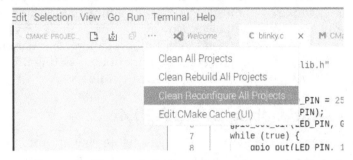

For a first compile you will see a lot of messages about what is being compiled and so on and it will take a few minutes. On a subsequent build only files that have changed are recompiled and so things are quicker. Once the compile is complete you will find the results in the `build` directory. The file that you want in this instance is `blinky.uf2` which can be run by dragging-and-dropping it onto the USB drive that a connected Pico presents to the development machine.

To run the program the simplest thing to do is connect a Pico to the development machine via USB. The USB connection will also power the Pico, and to get the Pico to present a USB drive to the development machine you have to hold down the `BootSel` button which is to the left of the USB connector as the power is applied. If you have done this correctly you will see a new drive added to the development machine and you will have to supply a password to mount it:

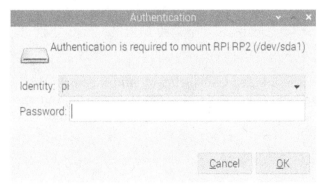

If you don't see this dialog box then you haven't held down the `BootSel` button while the power is being applied. Now you can drag-and-drop the `blinky.uf2` file and you should see the on-board LED start to flash slowly.

While this approach to running programs works for a first program, it isn't a sustainable way to develop programs for the Pico. There are ways to make the job easier, for example by connecting a reset button which restarts the Pico without having to remove the power. However, none of these ways provides the sort of ease of use that you need to test modifications to programs quickly, let alone debug them. So spending a little more time in setting things up to use a dedicated debug connection is very worthwhile.

Download And Debug Using A Pi 4

Although using the USB file system is a reasonable way of running a first program, it really isn't up to the job of developing any non-trivial program. To do this you need to set up an SWD connection. This has the advantage of allowing automatic download of programs and debugging. SWD, Serial Wire Debug, is a standard protocol for downloading programs and for debugging them on devices based on the Cortex M processor – like the Pico.

The Pico has a debug connector at the bottom edge composed of three pins:

This is a three-wire interface consisting of ground, clock and data lines. These have to be connected either to another SWD three-wire interface or to three general purpose GPIO lines that have been programmed to work as an SWD interface.

If you are using a Pi 4 to program the Pico then three GPIO lines is the simpler option. By default the pins used are GND, GPIO24 and GPIO25:

Pi 4	Pi Pico
GND (Pin 20)	SWD GND
GPIO24 (Pin 18)	SWDIO
GPIO25 (Pin 22)	SWCLK

These are best connected using direct jumper wires between the two boards to make sure there is no noise or disturbance. To make this easy, solder three pins onto the side of the board away from the prototyping board pins.

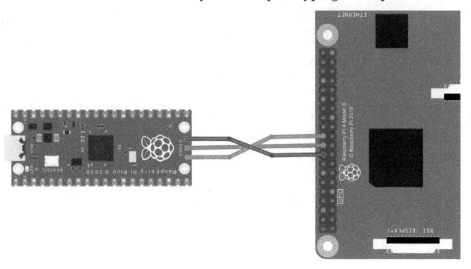

You also need to supply the Pico with a USB power connection, but this USB connection isn't used to download your program. Once you have the Pico connected in this way you can test it using the command line. However, moving directly to using VS Code is also very easy and you might want to skip straight to it:

```
openocd -f interface/raspberrypi-swd.cfg -f target/rp2040.cfg
 -c "program /home/pi/pico/blinky/build/blinky.elf
    verify reset exit"
```

This assumes that you have compiled the blinky program given earlier and you are logged on as user pi. Change the command if this isn't correct. It also assumes that you have OpenOCD installed. Notice that the SWD download makes use of the .elf file and not the .uf2 file.

The most sensible thing to do is to move to VS Code which makes running a program automatic and provides easy debug facilities. All you have to do is create a file called launch.json in the .vscode folder containing:

```json
{
  "version": "0.2.0",
  "configurations": [
    {
      "name": "Cortex Debug",
      "cwd": "${workspaceRoot}",
      "executable": "${command:cmake.launchTargetPath}",
      "request": "launch",
      "type": "cortex-debug",
      "servertype": "openocd",
      "gdbPath": "gdb-multiarch",
      "device": "RP2040",
      "configFiles": [
        "interface/raspberrypi-swd.cfg",
        "target/rp2040.cfg"
        ],
      "svdFile":
      "${env:PICO_SDK_PATH}/src/rp2040/hardware_regs/rp2040.svd",
      "runToMain": true,
      // Give restart the same functionality as runToMain
      "postRestartCommands": [
          "break main",
          "continue"
      ]
    }
  ]
}
```

Next you can select the debug configuration. Select the small green arrow labeled RUN in the Debug toolbar on the left. Select Pico Debug from the drop-down list and your program should be downloaded and run:

Although your program is running you won't see much happening because by default it is paused at the first instruction. You will see the debug toolbar appear and this is what you need to use to debug your program:

```c
#include "pico/stdlib.h"

int main() {
    const uint LED_PIN = 25;
    gpio_init(LED_PIN);
    gpio_set_dir(LED_PIN, GPIO_OU
```

To get the program running, simply click the blue triangle Run icon. You can also use the red square Stop icon to stop the program and the green circular arrow Restart icon to restart the program. If there are breakpoints in the code, click in the left-hand margin, the program will automatically stop and display the current state of variables in the left-hand debug pane. You can also single-step, step into called functions and step out of any called function. All of these also show you the current status of the variables. Notice that you have to stop the program using the Stop icon before you can rebuild it and run it again.

You now have a workable system that allows you to edit, build and debug Pico programs. You will need to modify the CMakeLists.txt file to include specific parts of the library, but this is fairly standard.

Debug Using PicoProbe For Windows

Using the USB file system is a reasonable way of checking that you have VS Code installed correctly, but it isn't suitable as a way to develop programs. You need to install and use an SWD link between the Pico and the Windows system you are using to develop programs and this is made more difficult because PCs generally don't have suitable interfaces to make this possible. One solution is to buy an SWD programmer, but it is easier, and usually cheaper, to use a second Pico to act as one. This is possible with the help of a Pico program called PicoProbe. This converts a Pico into an SWD programmer which can be used under Windows or Linux. It could also be used with a Pi 4, but this seems to offer no advantages over direct connection to GPIO lines.

As described in the section on using SWD with a Pi 4, the Pico has three debug pins:

These are most easy to work with if you solder three pins onto the top side of the board. The connections to the second, or PicoProbe Pico are:

PicoProbe	Pi Pico
GND	SWD GND
GP2	SWDIO
GP3	SWCLK

These are the only connections you need to make to turn the Pico into an SWD programmer.

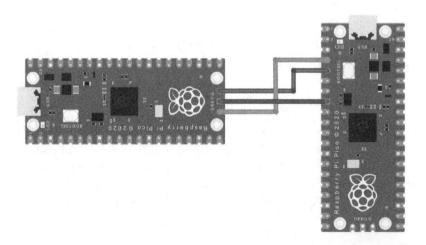

A good way to implement this is to solder three male/female jumper cables known as Dupont wires onto the PicoProbe. You can then use the PicoProbe as if it was a proper SWD programmer. There are also some 3D printed cases that you can download that can be used to turn the Pico into a debugging device, see the Resources section on this book's page on the I/O Press website.

Both Picos need to be powered. The Pico that is running the program can be powered by a USB connection or any method you care to use. The PicoProbe, however, has to have a USB connection to the PC as this is the method used to communicate with it.

To make the Pico act like an SWD programmer you have to download the PicoProbe program. You can find this on the Raspberry Pi Pico Getting Started page or, if you used the installation script, you will find a UF2 file, `picoprobe.uf2`, in `pico/picoprobe/build`. To install it all you have to do is connect power to the Pico while holding down the BootSel button and then drag-and-drop the UF2 file onto the USB driver that is installed on the PC. After this your Pico is a PicoProbe device whenever you turn it on.

The USB connection also needs an additional driver. This can be installed using Zadig which was installed automatically, in `pico/tools`, if you used the install script – if not download and install it. When you run Zadig you need to install Picoprobe(Interface 2) and the `libusb-win32` driver:

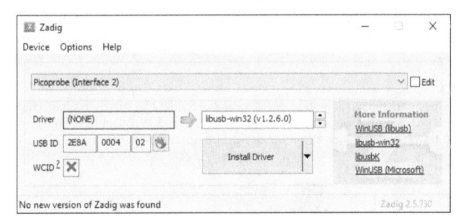

If the two Picos are connected, powered and the PicoProbe is connected via USB to the PC, we can start to use VS Code to run and debug new programs. All you have to do is create a file called `launch.json` in the `.vscode` folder containing:

```
{
    "version": "0.2.0",
    "configurations": [
    {
        "name": "Pico Debug",
        "cwd": "${workspaceRoot}",
        "executable": "${command:cmake.launchTargetPath}",
        "request": "launch",
        "type": "cortex-debug",
        "servertype": "openocd",
        "gdbPath": "arm-none-eabi-gdb",
        "device": "RP2040",
        "configFiles": [
        "interface/picoprobe.cfg",
        "target/rp2040.cfg"
        ],
        "svdFile":
          "${env:PICO_SDK_PATH}/src/rp2040/hardware_regs/rp2040.svd",
        "runToMain": true,
 // Work around for stopping at main on restart
        "postRestartCommands": [
        "break main",
        "continue"
        ]
    }
    ]
}
```

Next you can select the debug configuration. Select the small green arrow labeled RUN in the Debug toolbar on the left. Select Pico Debug from the drop-down list and your program should be downloaded and run:

Although your program is downloaded and running you won't see much happening because by default it is paused at the first instruction. You will see the debug toolbar appear and this is what you need to use to debug your program:

To get the program running simply click the triangle run icon. You can also use the red square stop icon to stop the program and the green circle arrow icon to restart the program. You can set breakpoints in the code by clicking in the left-hand margin. After this the program will automatically stop at the breakpoint and display the current state of variables in the left-hand debug pane. You can also single-step, step into called functions and step out of any called function. All of these also show you the current status of the variables. Notice that you have to stop the program using the stop icon before you can rebuild it and run it again.

You now have a workable system that allows you to edit, build and debug Pico programs. You will need to modify the CMakeLists.txt file to include specific parts of the library, but this is fairly standard.

Automatic Project Creation

You can work by manually modifying and adding to the CMakeLists.txt file. However, there is an automatic project creation tool, written in Python, that will generate a complete project for you. You can then copy the CMakeLists.txt to an existing project or use the folder that has been created with VS Code.

You can install it on the Pi 4 using:

```
git clone https://github.com/raspberrypi/pico-project-generator.git
```

If you used the installation script for Windows it is already installed and you will find the project generator in Pico\pico-project-generator where you can run it from the command line:

```
pico_project.py --gui
```

This starts it in GUI mode:

Enter the new project name and location, select the libraries you want to use and tick the Create VSCode project option and select the debugger, SWD or PicoProbe, that you want to use. After you have clicked OK, the project is created.

At the time of writing, the generator occasionally doesn't create a project that can run in a given environment. For example, under Windows it generates the wrong name for the GDI debugger in VS Code. However, it usually provides a good starting point for the files that you need and it will get better with time.

What Is Missing?

At this point we now have workable development environments using the Pi 4 and a Windows/Linux system. The documentation includes extra features in both of these environments which complicates things. Later you may want to add connections and software to make the UART usable – this is dealt with in Chapter 6. There is also a program called Picotool which will interrogate a Pico to discover what software is installed. This is well described in the documentation where you can find out about it if you think that it might be useful.

Summary

- C is a very good language to learn for any IoT project. It is fast and efficient and close to the machine. There are lots of other languages that are derived from it, so it is worth learning.

- You can write programs in C using just an editor and the command line compilers, but VS Code provides an easy-to-use and productive environment and is used throughout this book.

- A development environment for the Pico requires a lot of different items of software to be installed. You can do this manually, but it is much easier to use the installation scripts provided by the Raspberry Pi Foundation.

- The best way to develop for the Pico is to use a Pi 4 system to host the development software. The advantage is that it provides GPIO lines which can be connected to the Pico to facilitate debugging.

- You can use a Windows or general Linux system, but in this case you either need an SWD programmer or an additional Pico to act as one.

- There are installation scripts for a general Linux/Pi 4 system and for a Windows system and they are the recommended way to install the software.

- Initially you can install software by manually copying UF4 using the Pico as a USB drive, but this very quickly becomes unworkable and you need to move to using an SWD programmer to download and debug programs.

- Using a Pi 4 as the development system you can implement an SWD programmer just by connecting some GPIO lines to the Pico.

- Using a Windows or general Linux system, which lack GPIO lines, you need to use a second Pico as an SWD programmer. A program, PicoProbe, is provided which converts a Pico into an SWD programmer.

- VS Code can easily be configured to use an SWD programmer to automatically download code to the Pico and provide debugging facilities.

Chapter 3

Getting Started With The GPIO

In this chapter we take a look at the basic operations involved in using the Pico's General Purpose Input/Output (GPIO) lines with an emphasis on output. We'll consider questions such as how fast can you change a GPIO line, how do you generate pulses of a given duration and how can you change multiple lines in sync with each other?

Pico Pins

The first thing to make ourselves familiar with is the layout and range of GPIO pins available on a standard Pico – some compatible devices have fewer or differently arranged pins. The RP2040 chip has 30 GPIO lines, GP0 to GP29, of which the Pico makes 26 available for general use on the edge of the board. The other four are used internally. GP23 is used as a power control line, GP24 is used to sense the USB power input, GP25 powers the on-board LED and GP29 is used to measure the system voltage. There are also four additional GPIO lines, but these are dedicated for use as a quad SPI bus to interface to flash memory.

As is the case with most microprocessors, each GPIO line, with the exception of GP22, has multiple uses as you can see in the diagram on the next page.

You can select what mode a pin is used in and in this chapter we concentrate on using pins in the simplest GPIO mode. Even so, which pins you select for general-purpose use should take into account what other uses you might put pins to. For example, using GP26 as a general GPIO line when you need an additional A-to-D converter, which is one of its alternative functions. The only pin that has no alternative function is GP22 and this should be your first choice for any general-purpose duties.

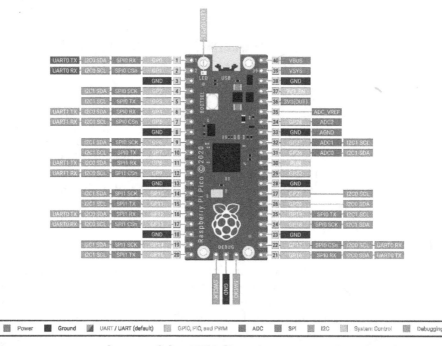

| Power | Ground | UART / UART (default) | GPIO, PIO, and PWM | ADC | SPI | I2C | System Control | Debugging |

In most cases, to make use of the GPIO lines in a prototyping situation you need to solder pins onto the board so that it can be plugged into a prototype board. There is some argument about which side the pins should be soldered to. One side leaves the PCB legend visible, but the on-board LED is obscured, and the other leaves the LED visible, but obscures the legend. Whichever side you decide to use, it is generally a good idea to solder the three debug pins on the other side so that they can also be connected while the device is plugged into a prototyping board.

Basic GPIO Functions

There are a great many GPIO functions provided by the SDK, but the most basic are those that let you work with a single GPIO line. You refer to all GPIO lines by their number – a simple integer. There are four important functions when you are using GPIO lines starting with:

```
void gpio_init (uint gpio)
```

This initializes a single line to work as a simple software controlled GPIO line (GPIO_FUNC_SIO). It is also set to input, which is a safe option from the hardware point of view.

If you want to set a line to any of the many possible modes then you use:

```
void gpio_set_function (uint gpio, enum gpio_function fn)
```

where gpio_function is one of:

GPIO_FUNC_XIP	Special function for QSPI pins
GPIO_FUNC_SPI	SPI bus
GPIO_FUNC_UART	UART
GPIO_FUNC_I2C	I2C bus
GPIO_FUNC_PWM	PWM
GPIO_FUNC_SIO	Software IO control
GPIO_FUNC_PIO0	Programmable IO control
GPIO_FUNC_PIO1	Programmable IO control
GPIO_FUNC_GPCK	GPIO Clock
GPIO_FUNC_USB	USB
GPIO_FUNC_NULL	

Notice that not all GPIO lines can be set to any particular function.

The gpio_init function leaves the line set as an input. To explicitly set a line to input or output you can use:

```
static void gpio_set_dir (uint gpio, bool out)
```

with out set to true for output and false for input.

Once you have the line set to input you can use:

```
static bool gpio_get (uint gpio)
```

to read the line and:

```
gpio_put (uint gpio, bool value)
```

to write to the line.

There are lots of other GPIO functions, but these are the ones you need to do simple I/O with a single GPIO line.

Blinky Revisited

We have already written the customary Blinky program as part of getting started but a real program to flash an LED should use a general I/O line and an external LED. With this in mind let's flash an LED connected to GP22.

Then enter the program:

```
#include "pico/stdlib.h"
int main()
{
    gpio_init(22);
    gpio_set_dir(22, true);
    while (true)
    {
        gpio_put(22, 1);
        sleep_ms(1000);
        gpio_put(22, 0);
        sleep_ms(1000);
    }
}
```

This uses the same CmakeLists.txt file as blinky in the previous chapter and the same launch.json file. The only difference is that now we are using GP22. The program also doesn't use any constants in order to make what is happening clearer. It first initializes GP22, which sets it to an input, then sets it to an output and sets it repeatedly high and low.

If you want to connect an LED to see the "blinking" for real then this is easy enough, but you do need a current-limiting resistor to avoid the LED drawing more current than the Pico GPIO line can supply and possibly damaging the chip. A 200Ω resistor is a good choice, see Chapter 5. A better way to drive an LED is discussed more fully in Chapter 5.

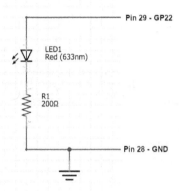

How you build the circuit is up to you. You can use a prototyping board or just a pair of jumper wires. The short pin and/or the flat on the side of the case marks the negative connection on the LED – the one that goes to ground.

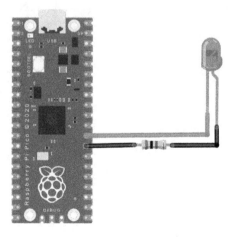

If you can't be bothered to go though the ritual of testing "Blinky" with a real LED, then just connect a logic analyzer to Pin 7 and you will see one-second pulses.

Summary

- The Pico has 34 GPIO lines in total. Four are used to interface to flash memory and of the remainder, GP0 to GP29, the Pico makes 26 available for general use on the edge of the board.

- Some of the GPIO lines have alternative functions and these are best avoided if all you need is a simple GPIO input/output line.

- The only GPIO line that doesn't have another important function is GP22 and this is your best first choice for a general use GPIO line.

- The SDK provides some basic GPIO functions - `gpio_init`, `gpio_set_dir`, `gpio_get` and `gpio_put`.

Chapter 4

Simple Output

A GPIO line is either configured to be an input or an output. The electronics of working with inputs and outputs are discussed in the next chapter. In this chapter we focus on the software side of the task of using GPIO lines in output mode. While it isn't possible to ignore some electronics in this chapter, keep in mind that this is discussed in detail in the next chapter.

It is worth noting at this stage that output is easy. Your program chooses the time to change a line's state and you can use the system timer to work out exactly when things should happen. The real problems only start to become apparent when you are trying to change the state of lines very fast or when they need to be changed synchronously. This raises the question of how fast the Pico can change a GPIO line and this is something we consider at this early stage because it puts constraints on what we can easily do.

Basic GPIO Functions

There are a number of basic functions that let you work with a single GPIO line. Some of these we have already met in the previous chapter.

There are two ways to initialize a GPIO line, specified by gpio, to act as a simple software controlled line:

```
gpio_set_function (uint gpio, GPIO_FUNC_SIO)
```

or:

```
gpio_init (uint gpio)
```

After either we have a GPIO line set to software control and the second initializes it to input.

You can then set the direction of the line using:

```
gpio_set_dir (uint gpio, bool out)
```

The line is set to output if out is true and input if it is false.

You can find out the direction of any line using:

```
static uint   gpio_get_dir (uint gpio)
static bool   gpio_is_dir_out (uint gpio)
```

The `gpio_get_dir` returns 0 or 1 for input and output and `gpio_is_dir_out` returns `true` if the line is set to output.

Once the line direction is set you can use:

```
static bool   gpio_get (uint gpio)
```

to read the state of the line and:

```
gpio_put (uint gpio, bool value)
```

to set the state of the line. Both of these work irrespective of the direction the line is set to.

There is also:

```
gpio_set_input_enabled (uint gpio, bool enabled)
```

which, if `enabled` is false, stops the line responding to input. There is currently no similar function for output, even though the hardware supports it.

Working With Multiple GPIO Lines

So far the functions have allowed us to change one line at at time. If you want to change more than one line then there are a range of mask functions which affect only the lines specified in a binary mask.

The mask is very simple; each of the first 30 bits in the mask represents a GPIO line – bit zero is for GP0, bit one is for GP1 and so on. Of course, the problem is making up the mask.

It is very easy to automatically make up a mask that corresponds to any set of GPIO lines specified by pin number. Suppose you want a mask for pin GP3 then this means you need to set the third bit in the mask. This can be done using 1<<3, i.e. 1 shifted three places to the left. If you want to know about bit manipulation of this sort, see Chapter 12 of *Fundamental C: Getting Closer To The Machine*, ISBN: 9781871962604.

This is the mask you require and it has been found by a general algorithm. If you want a mask for pin n all you have to do is:

```
1<<n
```

Now suppose you want a mask for pin n and pin m. All you have to do is use the bitwise operator, |, to OR the masks for each pin together, so the complete mask is:

```
(1<<n) | (1<<m)
```

Of course, you can use pin enumeration in place of pin numbers. So, to create a mask for pin 3 and pin 5, you would use:

```
uint32_t mask=(1 << 3) | (1 << 5);
```

Once you have the mask you can use it in any of the mask functions.

The gpio_init_mask function will initialize the lines specified in the mask to inputs:

```
gpio_init_mask (uint gpio_mask)
```

Once you have initialized the lines you can set their direction using:

```
gpio_set_dir_out_masked (uint32_t mask)
gpio_set_dir_in_masked (uint32_t mask)
gpio_set_dir_masked (uint32_t mask, uint32_t value)
```

The gpio_set_dir_masked function sets the lines specified in the mask to 0 or 1 corresponding to input or output according to the bits in value.

Once you have set the direction you can set the output state using any of:

```
gpio_set_mask (uint32_t mask)
gpio_clr_mask (uint32_t mask)
gpio_xor_mask (uint32_t mask)
gpio_put_masked (uint32_t mask, uint32_t value)
```

The set and clr functions set the lines high and low respectively. The xor function inverts the current state of the specified lines – i.e. a low line is set high and a high line is set low. The final put_masked function sets each of the specified lines to the state indicated by the corresponding bit in value.

Only the lines specified in the mask are modified – the rest are left in their current state. For example:

```
uint32_t mask=(1 << 3) | (1 << 5);
gpio_set_mask (mask);
```

sets both pin 3 and pin 5 to high in a single operation.

You can use `gpio_put_masked` to change the state of multiple lines to different values. For example:

```
uint32_t mask=(1 << 3) |(1 << 5);
uint32_t value=1<< 5);
gpio_set_dir_masked (mask,value)
```

will set pin 3 to low and pin 5 to high because the `mask` specifies these pins and in `value` the bit corresponding to pin 3 is 0 and the bit corresponding to pin 5 is 1. Notice the state of bits in `value` that do not correspond to bits set to 1 in `mask` have no effect.

The mask functions are very useful when you want coordinated changes across a number of GPIO lines, see later. It is worth saying at this early stage that you can set a group of lines in one operation and you can unset a group of lines in one operation, but if you want to set some lines and unset others this is always two separate operations.

As well as mask functions, there are also three functions that operate on all of the GPIO lines. You can use:

```
static void  gpio_set_dir_all_bits (uint32_t values)
```

to set the directions of all GPIO lines in one go. The function:

```
static uint32_t  gpio_get_all ()
```

returns the current state of all of the lines as a 29-bit value and:

```
static void  gpio_put_all (uint32_t value)
```

sets the state of all 29 lines. These are only occasionally useful.

How Fast?

A fundamental question that you have to answer for any processor intended for use in embedded or IoT projects is, how fast can the GPIO lines work?

Sometimes the answer isn't of too much concern because what you want to do only works relatively slowly. Any application that is happy with response times in the tens of millisecond region will generally work with almost any processor. However, if you want to implement custom protocols or anything that needs microsecond, or even nanosecond, responses the question is much more important.

It is fairly easy to find out how fast a single GPIO line can be used if you have a logic analyzer or oscilloscope. All you have to do is run the program:

```c
#include "pico/stdlib.h"
int main()
{
 gpio_set_function(22, GPIO_FUNC_SIO);
 gpio_set_dir(22, true);
 while (true)
 {
  gpio_put(22, 1);
  gpio_put(22, 0);
 }
}
```

However, to get the best possible result you have to compile the program as a Release build. Click on the CMake item in the status bar and select the build you want from the drop down menu:

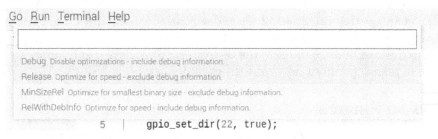

When you run the program you will not see any debug information relating to the C program, only the assembler that it creates.

If you do this the pulses are about 50ns in width – which compares well to the 70ns a similar program creates on a Pi Zero or Pi 4. There are no major irregularities due to interrupts or system software, but the pulses occur in groups of two or three with a long 200ns gap:

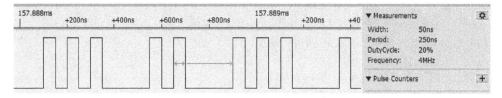

The reason for the difference from a Pi Zero or Pi 4 is probably due to the larger and more variable time it takes to perform the loop. The two instructions:

```
gpio_put(22, 1);
gpio_put(22, 0);
```

occur one after the other in a fairly short and regular time, but the loop back to the start is more complex and takes more time. You can see that this is that case by swapping the order of the instructions:

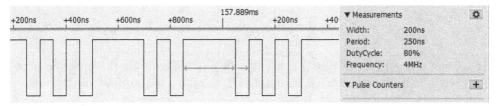

Now you can see that high part of the pulse train is longer and more variable due to the setting back to low having to wait for the loop to repeat. When you are using timings that are close to the fastest that a processor can manage you do have to take account of how long different instructions take.

Including Pauses

To generate pulses of a known duration we need to pause the program between state changes. We have already used sleep_ms to slow things down, but the SDK has a range of different functions for adding pauses to a program. These fall into two groups – the sleep functions and the busy_wait functions. The sleep functions work by putting the processor into a low power state until the time is up when the processor is awakened and the program proceeds. The only problem with the sleep functions is that it takes time to wake up and the pause that they generate is only guaranteed to no shorter than the specified time. The busy_wait functions keep the processor alive and consuming power and as a result they are generally more accurate.

The two sets of functions are very similar:

```
sleep_us (uint64_t us)
busy_wait_us (uint64_t delay_us)
```

Both wait for the specified time in microseconds but the sleep_us saves power and the busy_wait doesn't but is more more accurate. There is also a 32-bit version of the busy_wait which is often more convenient:

```
busy_wait_us_32 (uint32_t delay_us)
```

Any differences between the two approaches only make a practical difference at very short time delays.

If you want a pause as long as a millisecond then you should use:

```
sleep_ms (uint32_t ms)
```

There is no busy_wait equivalent because if you want to pause for milliseconds you might as well save power as the pause is going to be accurate to microseconds.

There are also two functions that let you set a pause until the system time reaches a given value:

```
sleep_until(absolute_time_t target)
busy_wait_until(absolute_time_t t)
```

To compare the two approaches you can try the following program:

```
#include "pico/stdlib.h"
int main()
{
 gpio_set_function(22, GPIO_FUNC_SIO);
 gpio_set_dir(22, true);
 while (true)
    {
        sleep_us(1);
        gpio_put(22, 0);
        sleep_us(1);
        gpio_put(22, 1);
    }
}
```

This attempts to create 1μs pulses, but due to the additional wake-up time what you get are pulses approximately 1.3μs:

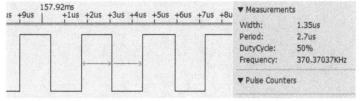

If you replace the instances of sleep_us(1) by busy_wait_us(1) then you get pulses that are very close to 1μs:

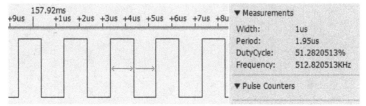

Once the time delay reaches 10μs the difference is negligible.

The traditional way of introducing a busy wait is to simply use a time-wasting for loop. Given that busy_wait_us is accurate at $1\mu s$ there is little reason not to use it for time periods of $1\mu s$ or more. A for loop busy_wait can produce shorter wait times:

```c
#include "pico/stdlib.h"
int main()
{
    gpio_set_function(22, GPIO_FUNC_SIO);
    gpio_set_dir(22, true);
    volatile int i;
    int n = 1;
    while (true)
    {
        for (i = 0; i < n; i++){};
        gpio_put(22, 0);
        for (i = 0; i < n; i++){};
        gpio_put(22, 1);
    }
}
```

which generates pulses according to the setting of n:

n	Time in μs
1	100-150ns
2	200-250ns
3	300-350ns
4	350-400ns
5	450-500ns
6	500-550ns
7	600-650ns
8	700-750ns
9	750-800ns
10	850-900ns
11	900-950ns

Fixed Time Delay

A common problem is making sure that something happens after a fixed time delay when you have a variable amount of work to do during that time interval. Consider the program snippet:

```
gpio_put(22, 1);
for (i = 0; i < n; i++){};
sleep_us (5);
gpio_put(22, 0);
```

where the for loop is intended to stand in for doing some other work. The intention is that the GPIO line should be set high for 5μs, but clearly how long the line is set high depends on how long the loop takes, which depends on n, plus 5μs. What is needed is a pause that takes into account the time that the loop uses up and simply delays the program for the remaining amount of time to make it up to 5μs. This is where the two functions:

```
sleep_until (absolute_time_t target)
busy_wait_until (absolute_time_t t)
```

come in useful. They will pause the program until the system timestamp reaches the specified value. All you need to make use of these is the additional function:

```
uint64_t time_us_64 (void)
```

which returns a 64-bit timestamp in microseconds.

We can now write the program snippet given earlier as:

```
uint64_t t;
gpio_put(22, 1);
t=time_us_64 ()+5;
for (i = 0; i < n; i++){};
sleep_until((absolute_time_t){t});
gpio_put(22, 0);
```

Now we obtain the timestamp after setting the line high and add 5 to it. No matter how long the for loop takes, the sleep_until will provide a delay of 5μs, as long as the loop takes less than this time. Notice that sleep_until needs an absolute_time_t struct and we have to convert the uint64_t to this.

This is a very general technique and one that can often make difficult timing problems very simple.

Phased Pulses

As a simple example of using the output functions, let's try to write a short program that pulses two lines, high and then low, out of phase.

The simplest program to do this job is:

```
#include "pico/stdlib.h"
int main()
{
    gpio_set_function(22, GPIO_FUNC_SIO);
    gpio_set_dir(22, true);
    gpio_set_function(21, GPIO_FUNC_SIO);
    gpio_set_dir(21, true);
    while (true)
    {
        gpio_put(22, 0);
        gpio_put(21, 1);
        gpio_put(22, 1);
        gpio_put(21, 0);
    }
}
```

Notice that there is no delay in the loop so the pulses are produced at the fastest possible speed.

Using a logic analyzer reveals that the result isn't what you might expect:

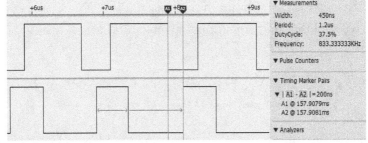

The top train switches on and the bottom train takes about half a pulse before it switches off, although the intent is for both actions to occur at the same time. The point is that it does take quite a long time to access and change the state of an output line.

Of course, if we include a delay to increase the pulse width then the delay caused by accessing the GPIO lines in two separate actions isn't so obvious, but it is still there. There are applications where the switching speed is so low that the delay between switching doesn't matter – flashing LEDs for instance. You could flash a line of 800,000 LEDs before the lag between the first and the last became apparent. On the other hand, if you use out-of-phase pulses to control a motor, then the overlap when both GPIO lines were on would burn out the drivers quite quickly. Of course, any sensible, cautious, engineer wouldn't feed a motor control bridge from two independently generated pulse trains unless they were guaranteed not to switch both sides of the bridge on at the same time.

A better way to generate pulses that are out of phase is to use a masked function. For example, if you change the first program to:

```c
#include "pico/stdlib.h"
int main()
{
    gpio_set_function(22, GPIO_FUNC_SIO);
    gpio_set_dir(22, true);
    gpio_set_function(21, GPIO_FUNC_SIO);
    gpio_set_dir(21, true);

    uint32_t mask = (1 << 22) | (1 << 21);
    uint32_t value1 = 1 << 21;
    uint32_t value2 = 1 << 22;
    while (true)
    {
        gpio_put_masked(mask, value1);
        gpio_put_masked(mask, value2);
    }
}
```

The two GPIO lines are now set to change at the same time and they do it at even at a higher speed:

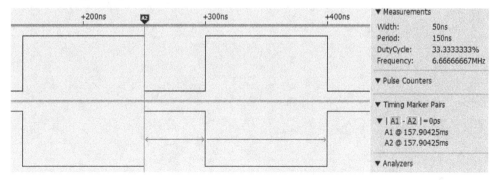

The reason is that the masked operation works by setting a value into a register that changes all of the GPIO lines concerned at once. As a result the action is not only synchronous but faster as it is a single operation to set two GPIO lines as opposed to two operations.

Overrides

There are three functions which change the way that the GPIO lines work. They override the normal operation – hence their names:

```
gpio_set_outover (uint gpio, uint value)
gpio_set_inover (uint gpio, uint value)
gpio_set_oeover (uint gpio, uint value)
```

The first overrides the output behavior, the second the input and the third the enable. The value can be any of:

GPIO_OVERRIDE_NORMAL	where the peripheral signal is selected via gpio_set_function
GPIO_OVERRIDE_INVERT	where the invert peripheral signal is selected via gpio_set_function
GPIO_OVERRIDE_LOW	drive low/disable output
GPIO_OVERRIDE_HIGH	drive high/enable output

So for example:

```
gpio_set_outover (22, GPIO_OVERRIDE_INVERT)
```

sets GP22 to inverted output so that a zero sets the line high and a one sets it low.

Summary

- Output is easy because the program decides when to change the state of a line. Input is hard because you never know when an input line will change state.

- GPIO lines can be set to act as inputs or outputs.

- If a line is set to output it can be set high or low using the put function.

- You can either set or clear a group of GPIO lines in one operation using a mask to indicate which lines to change.

- You can generate pulses as short as 50ns but not reliably.

- A delay can be introduced into a program using the `sleep` or `busy_wait` functions.

- The `sleep_until` and `busy_wait_until` can be used to create a fixed time for a set of instructions no matter how long they take to execute in the given time.

- An alternative is to use a busy wait loop which is simply a loop that keeps the CPU busy for an amount of time. It is easy to obtain an equation that gives the delay per loop repetition.

- If you are going to use a busy wait you should create a function that calibrates the number of loops needed for any given time.

- Producing pulses which are in phase is difficult but can be done using the mask based operations.

- You can override the usual behavior of the GPIO lines using the over function.

Chapter 5

Some Electronics

Now that we have looked at some simple I/O, it is worth spending a little time on the electronics of output and input. We cover the electronics of input before looking at how the software handles input because we need to understand some of the problems that the software has to deal with.

First some basic electronics – how transistors can be used as switches. The approach is very simple, but it is enough for the simple circuits that digital electronics makes use of. It isn't enough to design a high quality audio amplifier or similar analog device, but it might be all you need.

The basis of all electronics is Ohm's law, $V = IR$, and this prerequisite implies an understanding of voltage, current and resistance.

Electrical Drive Characteristics

If you are not familiar with electronics, the important things to know are what voltages are being worked with and how much current can flow. The most important thing to know about the Pico is that it works with two voltage levels – 0V and 3.3V. The RP2040 chip can work at a range of voltages from 1.8V to 3.3V, but the Pico has a power supply that converts whatever you supply it with to 3.3V – as a result the Pico is a 3.3V logic device.

If you have worked with other logic devices you might be more familiar with 0V and 5V as being the low and high levels. The Pico uses a lower output voltage to reduce its power consumption, which is good, but you need to keep in mind that you may have to use some electronics to change the 3.3V to other values. The same is true of inputs, which must not exceed 3.3V or you risk damaging the Pico.

An important question is how much current the GPIO lines can handle without damaging the chip. This isn't an easy question and at the time of writing the documentation isn't clear on the matter. According to the documentation, each GPIO line can be set to "drive" 12mA. However, this doesn't quite mean what you might think. This is not an upper limit on the supplied current, but a configuration that is needed to ensure that the output voltages of the GPIO line are within specification while it is working at 12mA

– see Chapter 18 for more information. What this means is that the designers intended the GPIO line to be used at 12mA, but this is not an upper limit on supply current. The only upper limit quoted is that the total current in the GPIO lines should be less than 50mA. Given that there are 30 GPIO lines this gives an average of 1.6mA per GPIO line. In practice, you are most likely to be safe at around the 12mA maximum for a small number of lines.

In practice, if you are planning to use more than 1.6mA from multiple GPIO lines, consider using a transistor. If your circuits draw more than 50mA from the 3.3V supply rail, consider a separate power supply.

Notice that the 12mA limit means that you cannot safely drive a standard 20mA red LED without restricting the current to below 12mA. A better solution is to use a low-power 2mA LED or use a transistor driver.

Driving An LED

One of the first things you need to know how to do is compute the value of a current-limiting resistor. For example, if you just connect an LED between a GPIO line and ground then no current will flow when the line is low and the LED is off, but when the line is high, at 3.3V, it is highly likely that the current will exceed the safe limit. In most cases nothing terrible will happen as the Pico's GPIO lines are rated very conservatively, but if you keep doing it eventually something will fail. The correct thing to do is to use a current-limiting resistor. Although this is an essential part of using an LED, it is also something you need to keep in mind when connecting any output device. You need to discover the voltage that the device needs and the current it uses and calculate a current-limiting resistor to make sure that is indeed the current it draws from the GPIO line.

An LED is a non-linear electronic component – the voltage across is stays more or less the same irrespective of the current passing through the device. Compare this to a more normal linear, or "ohmic", device where the current and voltage vary together according to Ohm's law, $V = IR$, which means that if the current doubles, so does the voltage and vice versa.

This is not how an LED behaves. It has a fairly constant voltage drop, irrespective of the current. (If you are curious, the relationship between current and voltage for an LED is exponential, meaning that big changes in the current hardly change the voltage across the LED.) When you use an LED you need to look up its forward voltage drop, about 1.7V to 2V for a red LED and about 3V for a blue LED, and the maximum current, usually 20mA for small LEDs. You don't have to use the current specified, this is the maximum current and maximum brightness.

To work out the current-limiting resistor you simply calculate the voltage across the resistor and then use Ohm's law to give you the resistor you need for the current required. The LED determines the voltage and the resistor sets the current.

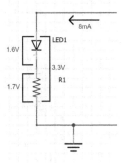

A GPIO line supplies 3.3V and if you assume 1.6V, its forward voltage, across the LED that leaves 1.7V across the current-limiting resistor since voltage distributes itself across components connected in series. If we restrict the current to 8mA, which is very conservative, then the resistor we need is given by:

R = V/I = 1.7/8 = 0.212

The result is in kiloohms, kΩ, because the current is in milliamps, mA. So we need at least a 212Ω resistor. In practice, you can use a range of values as long as the resistor is around 200 ohms – the bigger the resistor the smaller the current, but the dimmer the LED. If you were using multiple GPIO lines then keeping the current down to 1 or 2mA would be better, but that would need a transistor.

You need to do this sort of calculation when driving other types of output device. The steps are always the same. The 3.3V distributes itself across the output device and the resistor in some proportion and we know the maximum current – from these values we can compute the resistor needed to keep the actual current below this value.

LED BJT Drive

Often you need to reduce the current drawn from a GPIO line. The Bipolar Junction Transistor (BJT) may be relatively old technology, but it is a current amplifier, low in cost and easy to use.

A BJT is a three-terminal device - base, emitter and collector - in which the current that flows through the emitter/collector is controlled by the current in the base:

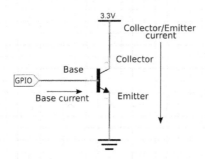

The diagram shows an NPN transistor, which is the most common. This diagram is a simplification in that, in reality, the current in the emitter is slightly larger than that in the collector because you have to add the current flowing in the base.

In most cases you need just two additional facts. Firstly, the voltage on the base is approximately 0.6V, no matter how much current flows since the base is a diode, a non-linear device just like the LED in the previous section. Secondly, the current in the collector/emitter is hfe or ß (beta) times the current in the base. That is, hfe or beta is the current gain of the transistor and you look it up for any transistor you want to use. While you are consulting the datasheets, you also need to check the maximum currents and voltages the device will tolerate. In most cases, the beta is between 100 and 200 and hence you can use a transistor to amplify the GPIO current by at least a factor of 100.

Notice that, for the emitter/collector current to be non-zero, the base has to have a current flowing into it. If the base is connected to ground then the transistor is "cut off", i.e. no current flows. What this means is that when the GPIO line is high the transistor is "on" and current is flowing and when the GPIO line is low the transistor is "off" and no current flows. This high-on/low-off behavior is typical of an NPN transistor.

A PNP transistor works the other way round:

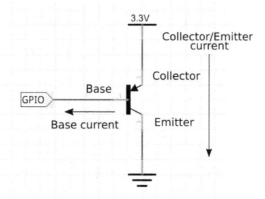

The 0.6V is between the base and the collector and the current flows out of the base. In this case to switch the transistor on you have to connect the base to ground. What this means is that the transistor is off when the GPIO line is high and on when it is low.

This complementary behavior of NPN and PNP BJTs is very useful and means that we can use such transistors in pairs. It is also worth knowing that the diagram given above is usually drawn with 0V at the top of the diagram, i.e. flipped vertically, to make it look the same as the NPN diagram. You always need to make sure you know where the +V line is.

A BJT Example

For a simple example we need to connect a standard LED to a GPIO line with a full 20mA drive. Given that all of the Pi's GPIO lines work at 3.3V and ideally only supply a few milliamps, we need a transistor to drive the LED which typically draws 20mA.

You could use a Field Effect Transistor (FET) of some sort, but for this sort of application an old-fashioned BJT (Bipolar Junction Transistor) works very well and is cheap and available in a thru-hole mount, i.e. it comes with wires. Almost any general purpose NPN transistor will work, but the 2N2222 is very common. From its datasheet you can discover that the max collector current is 800mA and beta is at least 50, which makes it suitable for driving a 20mA LED with a GPIO current of at most 20/50mA = 0.4mA.

The circuit is simple but we need two current-limiting resistors:

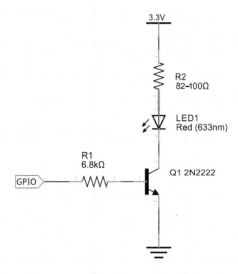

If you connected the base to the GPIO line directly then the current flowing in the base would be unrestricted – it would be similar to connecting the GPIO line to ground. R1 restricts the current to 0.39mA, which is very low and, assuming that the transistor has a minimum gain (hfe) of 50, this provides just short of 20mA to power it.

The calculation is that the GPIO supplies 3.3V and the base has 0.6V across it so the voltage across R1 is 3.3 - 0.6V = 2.7V. To limit the current to 0.4mA would need a resistor of 2.7/0.4kΩ = 6.7kΩ. The closest preferred value is 6.8kΩ, which gives a slightly smaller current.

Without R2 the LED would draw a very large current and burn out. R2 limits the current to 20mA. Assuming a forward voltage drop of 1.6V and a current of 20mA the resistor is given by (3.3-1.6)/20kΩ = 85Ω. In practice, we could use anything in the range 82Ω to 100Ω.

The calculation just given assumes that the voltage between the collector and emitter is zero, but of course in practice it isn't. Ignoring this results in a current less than 20mA, which is erring on the safe side. The datasheet indicates that the collector emitter voltage is less than 200mV.

The point is that you rarely make exact calculations for circuits such as this, you simply arrive at acceptable and safe operating conditions.

You can also use this design to drive something that needs a higher voltage. For example, to drive a 5V dip relay, which needs 10mA to activate it, you would use something like:

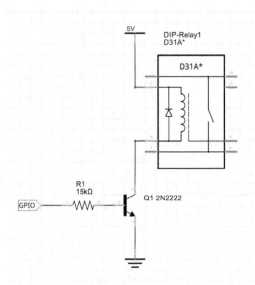

Notice that in this case the transistor isn't needed to increase the drive current – the GPIO line could provide the 10mA directly. Its purpose is to change the voltage from 3.3V to 5V. The same idea works with any larger voltage.

If you are using the 2N2222 then the pinouts are:

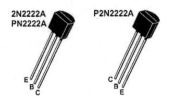

As always, the positive terminal on the LED is the long pin.

MOSFET Driver

There are many who think that the FET (Field Effect Transistor) or more precisely the MOSFET (Metal Oxide Semiconductor FET) is the perfect amplification device and we should ignore BJTs. They are simpler to understand and use, but it can be more difficult to find one with the characteristics you require.

Like the BJT, a MOSFET has three terminals called the gate, drain and source. The current that you want to control flows between the source and drain and it is controlled by the gate. This is analogous to the BJT's base, collector and emitter, but the difference is that it is the voltage on the gate that controls the current between the source and drain.

The gate is essentially a high resistance input and very little current flows in it. This makes it an ideal way to connect a GPIO line to a device that needs more current or a different voltage. When the gate voltage is low the source drain current is very small. When the gate voltage reaches the threshold voltage $V_{GS(th)}$, which is different for different MOSFETs, the source drain current starts to increase exponentially. Basically, when the gate is connected to 0V or below $V_{GS(th)}$ the MOSFET is off and when it is above $V_{GS(th)}$ the MOSFET starts to turn on. Don't think of $V_{GS(th)}$ as the gate voltage that the MOSFET turns on, but as the voltage below which it is turned off.

The problem is that the gate voltage to turn a typical MOSFET fully on is in the region of 10V. Special "logic" MOSFETs need a gate voltage around 5V to fully turn on and this makes the 3.3V at which the Pico's GPIO lines work a problem. The datasheets usually give the fully on resistance and the minimum gate voltage that produces it, usually listed as Drain-Source On-State Resistance. For digital work this is a more important parameter than the gate threshold voltage.

You can deal with this problem in one of two ways – ignore it or find a MOSFET with a very small $V_{GS(th)}$. In practice MOSFETs with thresholds low enough to work at 3.3V are hard to find and when you do find them they are generally only available as surface-mount. Ignoring the problem sometimes works if you can tolerate the MOSFET not being fully on. If the current is kept low then, even though the MOSFET might have a resistance of a few ohms, the power loss and voltage drop may be acceptable.

What MOSFETs are useful for is in connecting higher voltages to a GPIO line used as an input – see later.

Also notice that this discussion has been in terms of an N-channel MOSFET. A P-channel works in the same way, but with all polarities reversed. It is cut off when the gate is at the positive voltage and on when the gate is grounded. This is exactly the same as the NPN versus PNP behavior for the BJT.

MOSFET LED

A BJT is the easiest way to drive an LED, but as an example of using a common MOSFET we can arrange to drive one using a 2N7000, a low-cost, N-channel device available in a standard TO92 form factor suitable for experimentation:

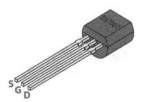

Its datasheet states that it has a $V_{GS(th)}$ typically 2V, but it could be as low as 0.8V or as high as 3V. Given we are trying to work with a gate voltage of 3.3V you can see that in the worst case this is hardly going to work – the device will only just turn on. The best you can do is to buy a batch of 2N7000 and measure their $V_{GS(th)}$ to weed out any that are too high. This said, in practice the circuit given below does generally work.

Assuming a $V_{GS(th)}$ of 2V and a current of 20mA for the LED the datasheet gives a rough value of 6Ω for the on resistance with a gate voltage of 3V. The calculation for the current-limiting resistor is the same as in the BJT case and the final circuit is:

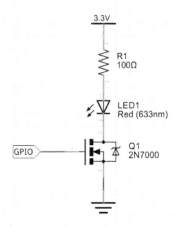

Notice that we don't need a current-limiting resistor for the GPIO line as the gate connection is high impedance and doesn't draw much current. In practice, it is usually a good idea to include a current-limiting resistor in the GPIO line if you plan to switch it on and off rapidly. The problem is that the gate looks like a capacitor and fast changes in voltage can produce high currents. Notice that there are likely to be devices labeled 2N7000 that will not work in this circuit due to the threshold gate voltage being too high, but encountering one is rare.

A logic-level MOSFET like the IRLZ44 has a resistance of 0.028Ω at 5V compared to the 2N2222's of 6Ω. It also has a $V_{GS(th)}$ guaranteed to be between 1V and 2V. It would therefore be a better candidate for this circuit.

Setting Drive Type

The GPIO output can be configured into one of a number of modes, but the most important is pull-up/down. Before we get to the code to do the job it is worth spending a moment explaining the three basic output modes, push-pull, pull-up and pull-down.

Push-Pull Mode

In push-pull mode two transistors of opposite polarity, one PNP and one NPN, are used:

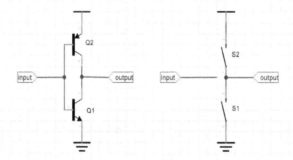

The circuit behaves like the two-switch equivalent shown on the right. Only one of the transistors, or switches, is "closed" at any time. If the input is high then Q1 is saturated and the output is connected to ground - exactly as if S1 was closed. If the input is low then Q2 is saturated and it is as if S2 was closed and the output is connected to 3.3V. You can see that this pushes the output line high with the same "force" as it pulls it low. This is the standard configuration for a GPIO output.

Pull-Up Mode

In pull-up mode one of the transistors is replaced by a resistor:

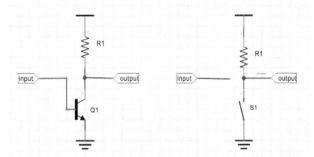

In this case the circuit is equivalent to having a single switch. When the switch is closed, the output line is connected to ground and hence driven low. When the switch is open, the output line is pulled high by the resistor.

You can see that in this case the degree of pull-down is greater than the pull-up, where the current is limited by the resistor. The advantage of this mode is that it can be used in an AND configuration. If multiple GPIO or other lines are connected to the output, then any one of them being low will pull the output line low. Only when all of them are off does the resistor succeed in pulling the line high. This is used, for example, in a serial bus configuration like the I2C bus.

Pull-Down Mode

Finally the pull-down mode, which is the best mode for driving general loads, motors, LEDs, etc, is exactly the same as the pull-up only now the resistor is used to pull the output line low.

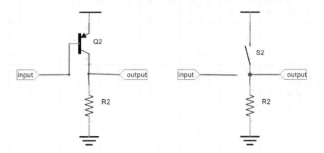

The line is held high by the transistor and pulled low by the resistor only when all the switches are open. Putting this the other way round, the line is high if any one switch is closed. This is the OR version of the shared bus idea.

Setting Output Mode

To set the mode for a GPIO line there are three functions:

```
gpio_pull_down (uint gpio)
gpio_pull_up (uint gpio)
```

and:

```
gpio_set_pulls (uint gpio, bool up, bool down)
```

By default the line is configured as input with a pull-down between 50kΩ and 80kΩ enabled. The pull-up resistance is also between 50kΩ and 80kΩ. Notice that the set_pulls function allows you to set up and down to true with the result that both pull-up and pull-down resistors are enabled.

If you want a pure push-pull mode you can turn off the resistors using:

```
gpio_disable_pulls (uint gpio)
```

Finally, you can test to see if a GPIO line is in pull-up or pull-down mode:

```
static bool  gpio_is_pulled_up (uint gpio)
static bool  gpio_is_pulled_down (uint gpio)
```

Basic Input Circuit - The Switch

Now it is time to turn our attention to the electrical characteristics of GPIO lines as inputs. One of the most common input circuits is the switch or button.

Many beginners make the mistake of wiring a GPIO line to a switch something like:

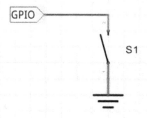

The problem with this is that, if the switch is pressed, the GPIO line is connected to ground and will read as zero. The question is, what does it read when the switch is open? A GPIO line configured as an input without pull up or pull down enabled has a very high resistance. It isn't connected to any

74

particular voltage and the voltage on it varies due to the static it picks up. The jargon is that the unconnected line is "floating". When the switch is open the line is floating and if you read it the result, zero or one, depends on whatever noise it has picked up.

The correct way to do the job is to tie the input line either high or low when the switch is open using a resistor. A pull-up arrangement would be something like:

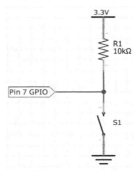

The value of the resistor used isn't critical. It simply pulls the GPIO line high when the switch isn't pressed. When it is pressed a current of a little more than 0.3mA flows in the resistor. If this is too much, increase the resistance to 100kΩ or even more - but notice that the higher the resistor value the noisier the input to the GPIO and the more it is susceptible to RF interference. Notice that this gives a zero when the switch is pressed.

If you want a switch that pulls the line high instead of low, reverse the logic by swapping the positions of the resistor and the switch in the diagram to create a pull-down:

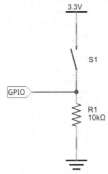

Notice that this gives a one when the switch is pressed.

The good news is that the Pico defaults to an input configuration with a pull-down resistor of around 50kΩ which means you can connect a switch directly to a default GPIO line and it will give a one when the switch is pressed.

Debounce

Although the switch is the simplest input device, it is very difficult to get right. When a user clicks a switch of any sort, the action isn't clean - the switch bounces. What this means is that the logic level on the GPIO line goes high then low and high again and bounces between the two until it settles down. There are electronic ways of debouncing switches, but software does the job much better. All you have to do is insert a delay of a millisecond or so after detecting a switch press and read the line again - if it is still low then record a switch press. Similarly, when the switch is released, read the state twice with a delay. You can vary the delay to modify the perceived characteristics of the switch.

A more sophisticated algorithm is based on the idea of integration to debounce a switch. All you have to do is read the state multiple times, every few milliseconds say, and keep a running sum of values. If you sum say ten values each time then a total of between 6 and 10 can be taken as an indication that the switch is high. A total less than this indicates that the switch is low. You can think of this as a majority vote in the time period for the switch being high or low.

The Potential Divider

If you have an input that is outside of the range of 0V to 3.3V then you can reduce it using a simple potential divider. In the diagram V is the input from the external logic and Vout is the connection to the GPIO input line:

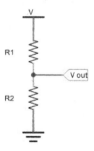

Vout = V R2/(R1+R2)

You can spend a lot of time on working out good values of R1 and R2. For loads that take a lot of current you need R1+R2 to be small and divided in the same ratio as the voltages.

For example, for a 5V device R1=18KΩ or 20KΩ and R2=33KΩ work well to drop the voltage to 3.3V.

A simpler approach that works for a 5V signal is to notice that the ratio R1:R2 has to be the same as (5-3.3):3.3, i.e. the voltage divides itself across the resistors in proportion to their value, which is roughly 1:2. What this means is that you can take any resistor and use it for R1 and use two of the same value in series for R2 and the Vout will be 3.3V.

The problem with a resistive divider is that it can round off fast pulses due to the small capacitive effects. This usually isn't a problem, but if it is then the solution is to use a FET or a BJT as an active buffer:

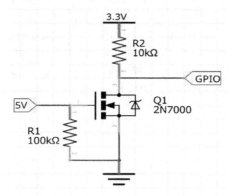

Notice that this is an inverting buffer, the output is low when the input is high, but you can usually ignore this and simply correct it in software, i.e. read a 1 as a low state and a 0 as a high state. The role of R1 is to make sure the FET is off when the 5V signal is absent and R2 limits the current in the FET to about 0.3mA. In most cases you should try the simple voltage divider and only move to an active buffer if it doesn't work.

This very basic look at electronics isn't all that you need to know, but it is enough for you to see some of the problems and find some answers. In general, this sort of electronics is all about making sure that voltages and currents are within limits. As switching speeds increase you have additional problems, which are mainly concerned with making sure that your circuits aren't slowing things down. This is where things get more subtle.

Summary

- You can get a long way with only a small understanding of electronics, but you do need to know enough to protect the Pico and things you connect to it.

- The maximum current from any GPIO line should be less than 12mA and the total current should be less than 30mA.

- All of the GPIO lines work at 3.3V and you should avoid directly connecting any other voltage.

- You can drive an LED directly from a GPIO line, but only at 16mA rather than the nominal 20mA needed for full brightness.

- Calculating a current-limiting resistor always follows the same steps – find out the current in the device, find out the voltage across the device and work out the resistor that supplies that current when the remainder of the voltage is applied to it.

- For any load you connect to a GPIO output, you generally need a current-limiting resistor.

- In many cases you need a transistor, a BJT, to increase the current supplied by the GPIO line.

- To use a BJT you need a current-limiting resistor in the base and generally one in the collector.

- MOSFETs are popular alternatives to BJTs, but it is difficult to find a MOSFET that works reliably at 3.3V.

- GPIO output lines can be set to active push-pull mode, where a transistor is used to pull the line high or low, or passive pull-up or pull-down mode, where one transistor is used and a resistor pulls the line high or low when the transistor is inactive.

- GPIO lines have built-in pull-up and pull-down resistors which can be selected or disabled under software control.

- When used as inputs, GPIO lines have a very high resistance and in most cases you need pull-up or pull-down resistors to stop the line floating.

- The built-in pull-up or pull-down resistors can be used in input mode.

- Mechanical input devices have to be debounced to stop spurious input.

- If you need to connect an input to something bigger than 3.3V then you need a potential divider to reduce the voltage back to 3.3V. You can also use a transistor.

Chapter 6

There is no doubt that input is more difficult than output. When you need to drive a line high or low you are in command of when it happens, but input is in the hands of the outside world. If your program isn't ready to read the input, or if it reads it at the wrong time, then things just don't work. What is worse, you have no idea what your program is doing relative to the event you are trying to capture. Welcome to the world of input.

In this chapter we look at the simplest approach to input – the polling loop. This may be simple, but it is a good way to approach many tasks. In Chapter 8 we look at more sophisticated alternatives – events and interrupts.

GPIO Input

GPIO input is a much more difficult problem than output from the point of view of measurement and verification. For output at least you can see the change in the signal on a logic analyzer and know the exact time that it occurred. This makes it possible to track down timing problems and fine tune things with good accuracy.

Input on the other hand is "silent" and unobservable. When did you read in the status of the line? Usually the timing of the read is with respect to some other action that the device has taken. For example, you read the input line $20\mu s$ after setting the output line high. But how do you know when the input line changed state during that 20 microseconds? The simple answer is in most cases you don't.

In some applications the times are long and/or unimportant but in some they are critical and so we need some strategies for monitoring and controlling read events. The usual rule of thumb is to assume that it takes as long to read a GPIO line as it does to set it. This means we can use the delay mechanisms that we looked at with regard to output for input as well.

One common and very useful trick when you are trying to get the timing of input correct is to substitute an output command to a spare GPIO line and monitor it with a logic analyzer. Place the output instruction just before the input instruction and where you see the line change on the logic analyzer should be close to the time that the input would be read in the unmodified program. You can use this to debug and fine tune and then remove the output statement.

Basic Input Functions

We have already met the functions that sets a GPIO line to input or output:

```
gpio_set_function (uint gpio, GPIO_FUNC_SIO)
```

or:

```
gpio_init (uint gpio)
```

After both we have a GPIO line set to software control and initialized to input.

You can also set the direction using:

```
gpio_set_dir (uint gpio, bool out)
```

The line is set to output if out is true and input if it is false.

Once set to input, the GPIO line is high impedance, it won't take very much current, no matter what you connect it to. However, notice that the Pico uses 3.3V logic and you should not exceed this value on an input line – for a full discussion of how to work with input see the previous chapter.

You can read its input state using:

```
static bool  gpio_get (uint gpio)
```

This is all there is to using a GPIO line as an input, apart from the details of the electronics and the small matter of interrupts. Notice that the function works even if the GPIO line is set to output – it reads the current level of the line as high or low.

There is also:

```
static uint32_t gpio_get_all ()
```

which will read the state of all of the GPIO lines in a single operation.

As introduced in the previous chapter you can also set the internal pull-up or pull-down resistors using one of:

```
gpio_pull_down (uint gpio)
gpio_pull_up (uint gpio)
gpio_set_pulls (uint gpio, bool up, bool down)
```

The pull-up/down resistors are between 50 and 80kΩ.

If you want a pure push-pull mode you can turn off the resistors using:

```
gpio_disable_pulls (uint gpio)
```

The Simple Button

One of the most common input circuits is the switch or button. If you want another external button you can use any GPIO line and the circuit explained in the previous chapter. That is, the switch has to have either a pull-up or pull-down resistor either provided by you or a built-in one enabled using software.

The simplest switch input program using an internal pull-up is:

```
#include "pico/stdlib.h"
int main()
{
    gpio_set_function(21, GPIO_FUNC_SIO);
    gpio_set_dir(21,false);
    gpio_pull_up(21);

    gpio_set_function(22, GPIO_FUNC_SIO);
    gpio_set_dir(22, true);

    while (true)
    {
        if (gpio_get(21))
        {
            gpio_put(22, 0);
        }
        else
        {
            gpio_put(22, 1);
        }
    }
}
```

As the internal pull-down resistor is used, the switch can be connected to the line and ground without any external resistors:

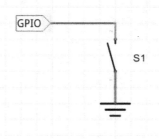

The program simply tests for the line to be pulled low by the switch being closed and then sets GP21 high. If you connect GP21 to an LED or a logic analyzer you will see the effect of the button being closed – the LED will light up while it is pressed. Notice GP22 goes low to indicate that the switch is pressed.

If you change gpio_pull_up(21) to gpio_pull_down(21), the way the switch is connected becomes:

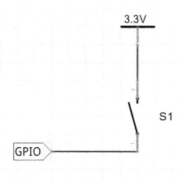

The program still works, but now GP21 is high when the switch is pressed and hence the LED is on when the switch is not pressed.

Should you use an internal or external resistor? The answer is that it mostly doesn't matter as long as there is a resistor. The only problem with using an internal resistor is the possibility that the software fails to set the pull-up/down mode and leaves the input floating.

Also notice that this switch input is not debounced. The simplest way to do this is include a time delay in the loop before the line is sampled again.

If you want to respond to a button press, that is a press and a release event, then you have to test for a double transition:

```
#include "pico/stdlib.h"
int main()
{
    gpio_set_function(21, GPIO_FUNC_SIO);
    gpio_set_dir(21, false);
    gpio_pull_down(21);

    gpio_set_function(22, GPIO_FUNC_SIO);
    gpio_set_dir(22, true);
    gpio_put(22, 0);
    while (true)
    {
        while (gpio_get(21)==0)
        {
        };
        while (gpio_get(21) == 1)
        {
        };
        gpio_put(22, 1);
        sleep_ms(1000);
        gpio_put(22, 0);
    }
}
```

In this case you really do need the debounce delays if you want to avoid responding twice to what the user perceives as a single press.

A 1-millisecond delay is probably the smallest delay that produces a button that feels as if it works. In practice, you would have to tune the delay to suit the button mechanism in use and the number of times you can allow the button to be pressed in one second.

Press Or Hold

You can carry on elaborating on how to respond to a button. For example, most users have grown accustomed to the idea that holding a button down for a longer time than a press makes something different happen. To distinguish between a press and a hold all you need to do is time the difference between line down and line up:

```c
#include "pico/stdlib.h"
int main()
{
    gpio_set_function(21, GPIO_FUNC_SIO);
    gpio_set_dir(21, false);
    gpio_pull_down(21);

    gpio_set_function(22, GPIO_FUNC_SIO);
    gpio_set_dir(22, true);
    gpio_put(22, 0);

    uint64_t t;

    while (true)
    {
        while (gpio_get(21) == 0){};
        t = time_us_64();
        sleep_ms(1);
        while (gpio_get(21) == 1){};
        t = (uint64_t)(time_us_64() - t);
        if (t < 2000*1000)
        {
            gpio_put(22, 1);
            sleep_ms(1000);
            gpio_put(22, 0);
        }
        else
        {
            for (int i = 0; i < 10; i++)
            {
                gpio_put(22, 1);
                sleep_ms(100);
                gpio_put(22, 0);
                sleep_ms(100);
            }
        }
    }
}
```

In this case holding the button for 2s registers a "held" – the LED flashes 10 times and anything less is a "push" – the LED flashes just once. Notice the 1ms debounce pause between the test for no-press and press.

One of the problems with all of these sample programs is that they wait for the button to be pressed or held and this makes it difficult for them to do anything else. You have to include whatever else your program needs to do within the loop that waits for the button – the polling loop. You can do this in an ad hoc way, but the best approach is to implement a finite state machine, see later.

Serial Data

In the next program we need to gather some data and the simplest way of doing this is to use a serial connection between the Pico and the host machine. This topic is covered in detail in Chapter 16. If you have any problems making this work, read the section on setting up the UART. This is the short version and it should "just work".

The Pico has a default UART connected to pins 1 GP0 TX and pin 2 GP1 RX. You simply need to connect the RX/TX pins to the corresponding TX/RX pins on the host machine. In the case of a machine that doesn't have a serial port that can work at 3.3V you need an adapter – usually a USB to serial adapter. If you are using a Raspberry Pi 4 as the development system you can simply connect the Pico's GPIO lines to the Pi's:

Raspberry Pi	Raspberry Pi Pico
GND (Pin 14)	GND (Pin 3)
GPIO15 (UART_RX0, Pin 10)	GP0 (UART0_TX, Pin 1)
GPIO14 (UART_TX0, Pin 8)	GP1 (UART0_RX, Pin 2)

If you have already connected the Pico and the Pi together via the SWD interface you don't need to connect the GND. If you are only interested in transmitting data from the Pico you only need to connect Pin 1 and Pin 10.

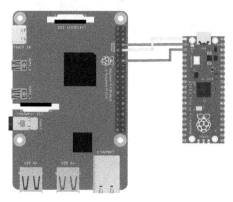

The hardware setup is simple but you also need to use the:

```
sudo raspi-config
```

to set up the serial port on the Pi. Select Interfaces and then disable the Linux shell and enable the serial port. The system will reboot. After this you can use serial0 to communicate with devices connected to the serial port.

To make the connection use:

```
sudo minicom -b 115200  -D /dev/serial0
```

Notice that you can do this in a terminal window in VS Code which is the best way to work.

How Fast Can We Measure?

Buttons are one form of input, but often we want to read data from a GPIO line driven by an electronic device and decode the data. This usually means measuring the width of the pulses and this raises the question of how fast can we accept input?

The simplest way to find out how quickly we can take a measurement is to perform a pulse width measurement. Applying a square wave to GP22 we can measure the time that the pulse is high using:

```
#include <stdio.h>
#include "pico/stdlib.h"

int main()
{
 stdio_init_all();
 gpio_set_function(22, GPIO_FUNC_SIO);
 gpio_set_dir(22, false);
 uint64_t t;

 while (true) {
  while (gpio_get(22) == 1) {};
  while (gpio_get(22) == 0) {};
  t = time_us_64();
  while (gpio_get(22) == 1) {};
  t = (uint64_t)(time_us_64() - t);
  printf("%llu\n", t);
  sleep_ms(1000);
 }
}
```

This might look a little strange at first. The inner while loops are responsible for getting us to the right point in the waveform. First we loop until the line goes low, then we loop until it goes high again and finally measure how long before it goes low. You might think that we simply have to wait for it to go high and then measure how long till it goes low, but this misses the possibility that the signal might be part way through a high period when we first measure it. This can be measured down to around 1 microsecond with an accuracy of $0.5\mu s$ with the accuracy poor at the low end of the range.

Notice that in either case if you try measuring pulse widths much shorter than the lower limit that works, you will get results that look like longer pulses are being applied. The reason is simply that the Pico will miss the first transition to zero but will detect a second or third or later transition. This is the digital equivalent of the aliasing effect found in the Fourier Transform or general signal processing.

The Finite State Machine

If you are working with an application that requires that you deal with a complex set of input and output lines then you need an organizing principle to save you from the complexity. When you first start writing IoT programs that respond to the outside world you quickly discover that all of your programs take a similar form:

```
for(;;){
  wait for some input lines
  process the input data
  write some output lines
  wait for some input lines
  read some more input lines
  write some output lines
}
```

For most programmers this is a slightly disturbing discovery because programs are not supposed to consist of infinite loops, but IoT programs nearly always, in principle if not in practice, take the form of an apparently infinite polling loop. A second, and more important, aspect is that the way in which reading and writing GPIO lines is related can be so complex that it can be difficult to see exactly when any particular line is read and when it is written.

It is natural to try to find implementations that make this simpler. In most cases, programmers discover or invent the idea of the event or, better, the interrupt. In this case when something happens in the outside world a function is automatically called to deal with it and the relation between the external state and the system's response is seemingly well-defined. Of course, in practice it isn't, as you have to deal with what happens when multiple events or interrupts occur at the same, or very nearly the same, time.

Often more sophisticated approaches are used to try and handle more external changes of state in a given time. Somehow the infinite polling loop is seen as wasteful. What is the CPU doing if it spends all its time looping round waiting for something to happen? Of course, if it has nothing better to do then it isn't a waste. In fact IoT devices are often dedicated to just getting one job done so the "polling is wasteful" meme, so prevalent in the rest of computing, is completely unjustified.

What is more, the polling loop is usually the way to get the greatest throughput. If a processor can handle X external state changes per second and respond to these with Y external state changes per second, then moving to an event- or interrupt-based implementation reduces both X and Y. In short, if a processor cannot do the job using a polling loop then it cannot do the job. This is not to say that there aren't advantages to events and interrupts – there are, but they don't increase throughput.

So how should you organize a polling loop so that what it does is self-evident by looking at the code?

There are many answers to this according to the system being implemented and there are no "pure" theoretical answers that solve all problems, but the finite state machine, or FSM, is a model every IoT programmer should know.

A finite state machine is very simple. At any given time the machine/program has a record of the current state S. At a regular interval the external world provides an input I which changes the state from S to S' and produces an output O. That's all there is to a finite state machine. There are variations on the definition of the FSM but this one, a Mealy machine because its outputs depend on both its state and the input, is most suitable for IoT programming.

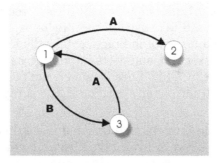

You can design an FSM with the help of a diagram. In the FSM shown we have three states 1, 2 and 3 and if you are in state 1 an input of A moves the system to state 2 and an input of B moves it into state 3.

Your program simply needs to take the form of a polling loop that implements a finite state machine. It reads the input lines as I and uses this and the current state S to determine the new state S' and the output O. There is some overhead in using this organization, but it is usually worth it. Notice that this organization implies that you read input once, make changes once and set outputs once in the loop. If you fix the time that the polling loop takes then you know the characteristic time for any changes to the system.

FSM Button

As an example, let's implement the simple button given earlier in the chapter. The first version used multiple loops to wait for changes in the state of the input line. The finite state version uses only a single polling loop:

```
#include <stdio.h>
#include "pico/stdlib.h"

int main()
{
    stdio_init_all();
    gpio_set_function(22, GPIO_FUNC_SIO);
    gpio_set_dir(22, false);
    uint64_t t;
    int s = 0;
    int i;
    int count=0;
    while (true)
    {
        i = gpio_get(22);
        t = time_us_64() + 100;
        switch (s){
        case 0: //button not pushed
            if (i){
                s = 1;
                count++;
                printf("Button Push %d \n\r",count);
            }
            break;
        case 1: //Button pushed
            if (!i){
                s = 0;
            }
            break;
        default:
            s = 0;
        }
        sleep_until((absolute_time_t){t});
    }
}
```

This looks more complicated than the original, and there are more lines of code, but it is much easier to extend to more complex situations. In this case we have only two states – s = 0 for button not pushed and s = 1 for button pushed. Ideally the states that we use shouldn't refer to inputs or outputs, but to the overall state of the system. For example, if you were using a Pico to control a nuclear reactor you might use a state "CoreMeltdown" in preference to "TempSensorOverLimit". States should be about the consequence of the inputs and the outputs should be the consequence of the current state. In the example above the inputs and output are too simple to give rise to an abstract concept of "state". Even if you were to change the state labels to "LEDOn" or "LEDOff" they are directly related to the state of a single output line.

The key idea, however, is that the states indicate the state of the system at the time of the input. That is, s = 0 (button not pushed) is the state when the system reads in a low on the GPIO line (recall the line is pulled low so pushing the button makes it go high). You can see at the start of the polling loop we read the input line and store its value in the variable i. Next, a case statement is used to process the input depending on the current state. You can see that if s = 0, i.e. button not pushed, then the state moves to s = 1, i.e. button pushed, and a message is printed giving the number of times the button has been pressed as a simple action. In general, the action could be setting a GPIO line high or doing anything that is appropriate for the new state. Notice that actions occur on state changes.

If the state is in s = 1, i.e. button pushed, then the input has to be 0 for anything to happen. In this case the state changes to s = 0 and any actions that are needed to take the system from state 1 to state 0 are performed – none in this case. Finally, if the state is anything other than 0 or 1, we set it to 0 as something is wrong.

Notice that the polling loop is set up so that the whole thing repeats every 100ms. The time is taken at the start of the loop and after everything has been processed we wait for 100ms to be up. What this means is that, no matter how long the processing in the loop takes, as long as it takes less than 100ms the loop will repeat every 100ms.

This is a very simple finite state machine polling loop. In practice, there is usually a switch statement that deals with each current state, but there is often another switch statement within each state case to deal with what happens according to different inputs. An alternative way of designing a finite state machine loop is to use a lookup table, indexed by state and input, which gives you the new state and the actions.

FSM Hold Button

As a slightly more complicated example of using the FSM approach, let's implement the button with hold. You might think that button with hold has three states – button not pushed, button pushed and button held. You can implement it in this way, but there is an argument that there are still only two states – not pushed and pushed. The held state is better implemented as extra input data to the state, i.e. the time the button has been in the pressed state. Remember, the output of a FSM depends on the state and the input and in this case the input is the line level and the time pressed:

```c
#include <stdio.h>
#include "pico/stdlib.h"
int main()
{
    stdio_init_all();
    gpio_set_function(22, GPIO_FUNC_SIO);
    gpio_set_dir(22, false);
    uint64_t t;
    uint64_t tpush, twait;
    int s = 0,i;
    int count = 0;
    while (true){
        i = gpio_get(22);
        t = time_us_64();
        switch (s){
        case 0: //button not pushed
            if (i){
                s = 1;
                tpush = t;
            }
            break;
        case 1: //Button pushed
            if (!i){
                s = 0;
                if ((t - tpush) > 2000000){
                    printf("Button held \n\r");
                }else{
                    printf("Button pushed \n\r");
                }
                fflush(stdout);
            }
            break;
        default:
            s = 0;
        }
        sleep_until((absolute_time_t){t + 1000});
    }
}
```

It is clear that you can't know the time the button has been pressed until it is released so the actions are now all in the button pushed state. While the button is in the pushed state it can be released and we can compute the time it has been pressed and modify the action accordingly.

FSM Ring Counter

Another very common input configuration is the ring counter. A ring counter moves on to a new output each time it receives an input and repeats when it reaches the last output of the set. For example, if you have three output lines connected to three LEDs then initially LED 0 is on, when the user presses the button LED 1 is on and the rest off, the next user press moves on to LED 2 on and another press turns LED 0 on. You can see that as the user keeps pressing the button the LEDs go on and off in a repeating sequence.

A common implementation of a ring counter has a state for each button press and release for each LED being on. For three LEDs this means six states and this has a number of disadvantages. A better idea is to have just two states, button pressed and button released and use a press counter as an additional input value. This means that what happens when you enter the button pressed state depends on the value in the counter.

We also change from using the measurement of the button as pressed or released and move to considering an "edge" signal. Generally we need inputs that indicate an event localized in time. Button "pressed" and button "released" are events that are extended in time but "press" and "release" are localized to small time intervals that can be thought of as single time measurements. In general we prefer "edge" signals because these indicate when something has changed.

Implementing this is fairly easy:

```
#include <stdio.h>
#include "pico/stdlib.h"

int main()
{
    stdio_init_all();
    gpio_set_function(22, GPIO_FUNC_SIO);
    gpio_set_dir(22, false);
    gpio_set_function(21, GPIO_FUNC_SIO);
    gpio_set_dir(21, true);
    gpio_set_function(20, GPIO_FUNC_SIO);
    gpio_set_dir(20, true);
    gpio_set_function(19, GPIO_FUNC_SIO);
    gpio_set_dir(19, true);
```

```
gpio_put(19, 1);
gpio_put(20, 0);
gpio_put(21, 0);

uint64_t t, tpush,twait;
int s = 0;
int buttonState = gpio_get(22);
int edge;
int buttonNow;

while (true)
{
    t = time_us_64();
    buttonNow = gpio_get(22);
    edge = buttonState - buttonNow;
    buttonState = buttonNow;
    switch (s){
    case 0:
        if (edge==1){
            s = 1;
            gpio_put(19, 0);
            gpio_put(20, 1);
            gpio_put(21, 0);
        }
        break;
    case 1:
        if (edge==1){
            s = 2;
            gpio_put(19, 0);
            gpio_put(20, 0);
            gpio_put(21, 1);
        }
        break;
    case 2:
        if (edge==1){
            s = 0;
            gpio_put(19, 1);
            gpio_put(20, 0);
            gpio_put(21, 0);
        }
        break;

    default:
        s = 0;
    }
    sleep_until((absolute_time_t){t + 1000});
}
}
```

First we set up the GPIO lines for input and output and set the outputs so that LED 0 is on, i.e. s = 0. Next we start the polling loop. Inside the loop there is a `switch` statement that manages three states. At the start of the loop the difference between the current button value and its previous value are used to calculate `edge` which is 1 only when the button has changed from pressed, 1, to released, 0. That is, edge=1 only on a down-going edge. If the button has just been pressed then the state is moved on to the next state, 0→1, 1→2 and 2→0, and the LEDs are set to the appropriate values.

You might wonder why all three LEDs are set and not just the two that are changing? There are a number of reasons including it's easier to see what is happening from the code and it makes sure that all of the LEDs are in the state you intend. Notice that polling loop is set up to repeat every 1000μs so providing debouncing and a predictable service time. If you try this out you will find that the LEDs light up sequentially on each button press.

Like many more advanced methods the FSM approach can make things seem more complicated in simple examples, but it repays the effort as soon as things get more complicated. A polling loop with tens of states and lots of input and outline lines to manage becomes impossible to maintain without some organizing principle.

Summary

- Input is hard because things happen at any time, irrespective of what your program might be doing.

- You can call `gpio_get` at any time to discover the state of a GPIO line – the problem is when and how often to call it.

- You can chose between external or internal pull-up/pull-down resistors.

- Mechanical input devices such as buttons have to be debounced.

- The power of software is that it can enhance a simple device. A simple button is either pushed or released, but you can use this to generate a third "held" state.

- Using a polling loop you can handle inputs as short as a few tens of microseconds.

- Most IoT programs are best written as a polling loop.

- The Finite State Machine (FSM) is one way of organizing a complex polling loop so that inputs are tested and outputs are set once for each time through the loop.

- Ideally the states of a FSM should not be simple statements of the inputs of outputs that determine the state, but for simple systems this can be difficult to achieve.

- It can be difficult to work out what constitutes the events of a FSM. Ideally they should be localized in time so that they indicate the moment that something happens.

Chapter 7

Advanced Input – Events and Interrupts

When you start to work with multiple inputs that mean a range of different things, input really becomes a challenge. You can control much of the complexity using finite state machines and similar organizational principles, but sooner or later you are going to have to deal with the problem of input when your program isn't ready for it. There are two general and closely related ways to deal with this problem – events and interrupts. The Pico SDK doesn't really support events, preferring interrupts, but its hardware certainly is event-capable and it isn't difficult to add some software to make it work. In this chapter we look first at events and then at interrupts.

Events

An event is like a latch or a memory that something happened. Imagine that there is a flag that will be automatically set when an input line changes state. The flag is set without the involvement of software, or at least any software that you have control over. It is useful to imagine an entirely hardware-based setting of the flag, even if this is not always the case. With the help of an event you can avoid missing an input because the polling loop was busy doing something else. Now the polling loop reads the flag rather than the actual state of the input line and hence it can detect if the line has changed since it last polled. The polling loop resets the event flag and processes the event. Of course, it can't always know exactly when the event happened, but at least it hasn't missed it altogether.

A simple event can avoid the loss of a single input, but what if there is more than one input while the polling loop is unavailable? The most common solution is to create an event queue – that is, a FIFO (first in, first out) queue of events as they occur. The polling loop now reads the event at the front of the queue, processes it and reads the next. It continues like this until the queue is empty, when it simply waits for an event. As long as the queue is big enough, an event queue means you don't miss any input, but input events are not necessarily processed close to the time that they occurred. They should be processed in order, but unless the events are timestamped the program has no idea when they happened.

An event queue is a common architecture, but to work or have any advantages, it needs either multiple cores so that events can always be added to the queue before another occurs or it needs the help of hardware, usually in the form of interrupts. Notice that an event, or an event queue, cannot increase the program's throughput or its latency – the time to react to an input. In fact, an event queue decreases throughput and increases latency due to overheads of implementation. All an event system does is to ensure that you do not miss any input and that all input gets processed eventually.

Interrupts Considered Harmful?

Interrupts are often confused with events, but they are very different. An interrupt is a hardware mechanism that stops the computer doing whatever it is currently doing and makes it transfer its attention to running an interrupt handler. You can think of an interrupt as an event flag that, when set, interrupts the current program to run the assigned interrupt handler.

Using interrupts means the outside world decides when the computer should pay attention to input and there is no need for a polling loop. Most hardware people think that interrupts are the solution to everything and polling is inelegant and only to be used when you can't use an interrupt. This is far from the reality. There is a general feeling that real-time programming and interrupts go together and if you are not using an interrupt you are probably doing something wrong. In fact, the truth is that if you are using an interrupt you are probably doing something wrong. So much so that some organizations are convinced that interrupts are so dangerous that they are banned from being used at all.

Interrupts are only really useful when you have a low-frequency condition that needs to be dealt with on a high-priority basis. Interrupts can simplify the logic of your program, but rarely does using an interrupt speed things up because the overhead involved in interrupt handling is usually quite high.

If you have a polling loop that takes 100ms to poll all inputs and there is an input that demands attention in under 60ms then clearly the polling loop is not going to be good enough. Using an interrupt allows the high-priority event to interrupt the polling loop and be processed in less than 100ms. However, if this happens very often the polling loop will cease to work as intended. An alternative is to simply make the polling loop check the input twice per loop.

For a more real world example, suppose you want to react to a doorbell push button. You could write a polling loop that simply checks the button status repeatedly and forever or you could write an interrupt service routine (ISR) to respond to the doorbell. The processor would be free to get on with other things until the doorbell was pushed when it would stop what it was doing and transfer its attention to the ISR.

How good a design this is depends on how much the doorbell has to interact with the rest of the program and how many doorbell pushes you are expecting. It takes time to respond to the doorbell push and then the ISR has to run to completion - what is going to happen if another doorbell push happens while the first push is still being processed? Some processors have provision for forming a queue of interrupts, but that doesn't help with the fact that the process can only handle one interrupt at a time. Of course, the same is true of a polling loop, but if you can't handle the throughput of events with a polling loop, you can't handle it using an interrupt either, because interrupts add the time to transfer to the ISR and back again.

Finally, before you dismiss the idea of having a processor do nothing but ask repeatedly "is the doorbell pressed", consider what else it has to do. If the answer is "not much" then a polling loop might well be your simplest option. Also, if the processor has multiple cores, then the fastest way of dealing with any external event is to use one of the cores in a fast polling loop. This can be considered to be a software emulation of a hardware interrupt – not to be confused with a software interrupt or trap, which is a hardware interrupt triggered by software.

If you are going to use interrupts to service input then a good design is to use the interrupt handler to feed an event queue. This at least lowers the chance that input will be missed.

Despite their attraction, interrupts are usually a poor choice for anything other than low-frequency events that need to be dealt with quickly.

Hardware Events

The Pico SDK doesn't support events, but the hardware does as part of its implementation of GPIO interrupts. Each GPIO line records four events:

```
GPIO_IRQ_LEVEL_LOW
GPIO_IRQ_LEVEL_HIGH
GPIO_IRQ_EDGE_FALL
GPIO_IRQ_EDGE_RISE
```

The level events are not latched and simply reflect the current state of the GPIO line. The edge events are latched and stay set until you clear them. In practice, the edge events are far more useful.

Each of these events can also be set to cause an interrupt and this is something we look at later in this chapter. For the moment, all we are concerned with is using these events as "memories" that something happened.

Currently the SDK doesn't have any functions that support events, but it is fairly easy to add a pair of functions that do the job:

```
uint32_t gpio_get_events(uint gpio)
{
 int32_t mask = 0xF << 4 * (gpio % 8);
 return (iobank0_hw->intr[gpio / 8] & mask) >> 4 * ( gpio % 8);
}
void gpio_clear_events(uint gpio, uint32_t events) {
 gpio_acknowledge_irq(gpio,  events);
}
```

How these work is explained in Chapter 18, for the moment all you really need to know is that gpio_get_events will return four bits that reflect the status of the events corresponding to gpio. Similarly, gpio_clear_events is used to clear the latched events on gpio. The latched events correspond to the constants:

```
GPIO_IRQ_EDGE_FALL
GPIO_IRQ_EDGE_RISE
```

For example:

```
 int32_t event = gpio_get_events(22);
 if (event & GPIO_IRQ_EDGE_RISE)
```

tests to see if a rising edge event has occurred on GP22.

Putting all this together, the steps in using events are:

1. Set the line to be an input:

    ```
    gpio_set_function(22, GPIO_FUNC_SIO);
    gpio_set_dir(22, false);
    ```

2. Clear the event:

    ```
    gpio_clear_events(22, GPIO_IRQ_EDGE_RISE);
    ```

3. After this you can do something else and eventually read the status bit to see if the event occurred in the intervening time, clearing the event to allow it to record another:

    ```
    int32_t event = gpio_get_events(22);
    gpio_clear_events(22, GPIO_IRQ_EDGE_RISE);
    ```

An Edgy Button

To make the difference between reading the line to detect a change of state and using the events, let's consider another version of our button program given earlier. In this case the GPIO line is set up for input and a message to press the button is printed. Then the program waits for 20 seconds and finally tests the state of the line. Even if the user has pressed the button lots of times during the pause, all that matters is the final state of the line as read when the `sleep_ms(20000)` ends:

```c
#include <stdio.h>
#include "pico/stdlib.h"

int main()
{
    stdio_init_all();
    gpio_set_function(22, GPIO_FUNC_SIO);
    gpio_set_dir(22, false);
    gpio_pull_down(22);

    printf("Press Button\n");
    sleep_ms(20000);
    if (gpio_get(22))
    {
        printf("Button Pressed\n");
    }
    else
    {
        printf("Button Not Pressed\n");
    }
}
```

In other words, this program misses any button presses during the 20-second pause. This is a silly program, but now compare it to a version using edge events:

```c
#include <stdio.h>
#include "pico/stdlib.h"
#include "hardware/structs/iobank0.h"

uint32_t gpio_get_events(uint gpio)
{
    int32_t mask = 0xF << 4 * (gpio % 8);
    return (iobank0_hw->intr[gpio / 8] & mask) >> 4 * ( gpio % 8);
}
void gpio_clear_events(uint gpio, uint32_t events)
{
    gpio_acknowledge_irq(gpio, events);
}
```

```c
int main()
{
    stdio_init_all();
    gpio_set_function(22, GPIO_FUNC_SIO);
    gpio_set_dir(22, false);
    gpio_pull_down(22);

    printf("Press Button\n");
    gpio_clear_events(22, GPIO_IRQ_EDGE_RISE);
    sleep_ms(20000);
    int32_t event = gpio_get_events(22);
    gpio_clear_events(22, GPIO_IRQ_EDGE_RISE);
    if (event & GPIO_IRQ_EDGE_RISE)
    {
        printf("Button Pressed\n");
    }
    else
    {
        printf("Button Not Pressed\n");
    }
}
```

In this case the GPIO line is set up as an input with a pull-down and we test for a rising edge event rather than the line state. The difference is that if the user presses the button at any time during the 20-second sleep, the flag is set and the program registers the button press. The flag is set no matter what the program is doing, so instead of sleeping it could be getting on with some work, confident that it won't miss a button press. However, it cannot know exactly when the button was pressed and it cannot know how many times the button was pressed.

Events allow you to avoid missing a single input while polling, but cannot handle multiple inputs – if the user presses the button multiple times you still only detect a single press. You could implement a full queue-based event handling system, but this probably isn't worth the effort. A more reasonable alternative is to use the interrupt abilities of the GPIO lines – see later.

Measuring Pulses With Events

Now we have all of the functions we need to implement a pulse measurement program using events. In this case we can measure the width of any pulse as the distance between a rising and a falling edge or a falling and a rising edge. The main difference between this and the previous program that measured the width of a pulse is that now we are using the hardware to detect the state transitions, i.e. the "edges" of the signal.

To do this we need to detect the rising and falling edge for the pin.

The complete program is:

```c
#include <stdio.h>
#include "pico/stdlib.h"
#include "hardware/structs/iobank0.h"

uint32_t gpio_get_events(uint gpio)
{
 int32_t mask = 0xF << 4 * ( gpio % 8);
 return (iobank0_hw->intr[gpio / 8] & mask) >> 4 * (gpio % 8);
}
void gpio_clear_events(uint gpio, uint32_t events)
{
 gpio_acknowledge_irq(gpio, events);
}

int main()
{
 uint64_t t;
 stdio_init_all();
 gpio_set_function(22, GPIO_FUNC_SIO);
 gpio_set_dir(22, false);
 gpio_pull_down(22);

 while(true){
  gpio_clear_events(22, GPIO_IRQ_EDGE_RISE | GPIO_IRQ_EDGE_FALL);
  while (!(gpio_get_events(22) & GPIO_IRQ_EDGE_RISE)){ };
  t = time_us_64();
  gpio_clear_events(22, GPIO_IRQ_EDGE_RISE | GPIO_IRQ_EDGE_FALL);
  while (!(gpio_get_events(22) & GPIO_IRQ_EDGE_FALL)) { };
  t = (uint64_t)(time_us_64() - t);
  printf("%llu\n", t);
  sleep_ms(1000);
 }
}
```

After clearing both events we wait for a rising edge, clear it and then wait for a falling edge and take the time difference between the two.

This program produces very similar results to those of the previous program that simply read the inputs on the GPIO line. In this case there is no real advantage in using the events approach to polling as we are reading data as fast as we can anyway. However, if you had multiple GPIO lines, and perhaps multiple conditions to test you could set all the events you were interested in and then check to see if any of them had happened.

Interrupts

The Pico supports 32 distinct interrupts, but only 26 are actually used. All of the user GPIO lines act together to create a single IO interrupt. A subtle point is that each of the Pico's two processors can respond at the same time to an IO interrupt caused by a different GPIO line – that is, the IO interrupts are not shared between cores. In all other cases interrupts can only be enabled on one core at a time.

The fact that there is only a single interrupt for all of the GPIO lines means it is up to the interrupt handler to work out which line caused the interrupt and to reset it after dealing with it. Which GPIO line can generate an interrupt is specified by the same bits in the same register that we have been using as event indicators in the earlier sections. If an interrupt is enabled for a given line and a given event then the interrupt will occur if that bit is set to one.

The events that you can use are the same as before:
```
GPIO_IRQ_LEVEL_LOW
GPIO_IRQ_LEVEL_HIGH
GPIO_IRQ_EDGE_FALL
GPIO_IRQ_EDGE_RISE
```
The SDK provides three basic functions for working with GPIO interrupts. The most important is:
```
gpio_set_irq_enabled_with_callback (uint gpio, uint32_t events,
                    bool enabled, gpio_irq_callback_t callback)
```
This enables or disables the interrupt associated with the specified GPIO line and event. The callback is the function that is executed when the interrupt occurs, i.e. it is the interrupt handler. Although it looks as if you can associate a different callback with each GPIO line, at the time of writing this isn't the case. While comments in the SDK code indicate that perhaps this is a feature that might be added in the future, there is currently only one GPIO interrupt handler for all of the GPIO lines, despite appearances to the contrary. If you do try to set different callbacks for each GPIO line, only the last one you set is actually used. Notice that all this means that it is up to your interrupt handler to respond to which GPIO line and which event caused the interrupt. This is made easier by the two parameters passed to the event handler:
```
void gpio_callback(uint gpio, uint32_t events)
```
The first parameter gives the line which caused the interrupt and *events* gives the event that caused it.

Once you have set a callback you can enable the interrupt:
```
gpio_set_irq_enabled (uint gpio, uint32_t events, bool enabled)
```
This enables or disables the ability of the specified GPIO line to cause an interrupt when the specified event occurs.

Edge interrupts are the most commonly used and, as these are latched, you do need to clear the event bit using:

```
void   gpio_acknowledge_irq (uint gpio, uint32_t events)
```

This is also the function `gpio_clear_events` that you call to clear an event on a given GPIO line.

This is all there is to using GPIO to generate an interrupt and handling it. In practice, things are more difficult to get right than you might expect. There is the question of what happens if an interrupt occurs while you are in the interrupt handler and what about accessing shared resources while in the interrupt handler?

First a simple example:

```
#include <stdio.h>
#include "pico/stdlib.h"

static uint64_t t;
void MyIRQHandler(uint gpio, uint32_t events)
{
    t = time_us_64() - t;
    printf("GPIO %d %X %d \n", gpio, events, t);
}

int main()
{
    stdio_init_all();
    gpio_set_function(22, GPIO_FUNC_SIO);
    gpio_set_dir(22, false);
    gpio_pull_down(22);

    gpio_set_irq_enabled_with_callback(22, GPIO_IRQ_EDGE_RISE |
                        GPIO_IRQ_EDGE_FALL, true, &MyIRQHandler);
    while (1){};
    return 0;
}
```

This sets up an interrupt handler which prints the GPIO line, event and time since the last event. If the events occur slowly enough then you should just see one event as the cause of the interrupt, but if they occur more quickly than the print takes to complete you will see both edge events as having occurred. Only one of the events will have initiated the interrupt, the other will simply have been recorded while the interrupt handler was being called.

If you experiment with this program you will discover that the interrupts are being cleared so that you don't get an immediate call of the interrupt handler on its return. You also don't get an interrupt during the interrupt handler. Part of the reason for this is that the SDK doesn't deliver the interrupt mechanism directly. It sets up its own IRQ handler, which does the housekeeping and then calls your IRQ handler:

```
static void gpio_irq_handler(void) {
    io_irq_ctrl_hw_t *irq_ctrl_base = get_core_num() ?
        iobank0_hw->proc1_irq_ctrl : &iobank0_hw→proc0_irq_ctrl;

    for (uint gpio = 0; gpio < NUM_BANK0_GPIOS; gpio++) {
        io_rw_32 *status_reg = &irq_ctrl_base->ints[gpio / 8];
        uint events = (*status_reg >> 4 * (gpio % 8)) & 0xf;

        if (events) {
        // TODO: If both cores care about this event then
        //the second core won't get the irq?
         gpio_acknowledge_irq(gpio, events);
         gpio_irq_callback_t callback = _callbacks[get_core_num()];

         if (callback) {
             callback(gpio, events);
         }
        }
    }
}
```

The most interesting part of this function is the for loop which tests each GPIO line's IRQ status register to discover if it caused an interrupt. For each GPIO line it detects as causing an interrupt, it first resets the interrupt and then calls the IRQ handler with the number of that GPIO line and the event. This means that you don't have to reset the IRQ in your own routine, but notice that the loop takes time to scan through the GPIO registers and your IRQ handler will be called for each GPIO line that caused an interrupt. This may change in the future.

How Fast Is An Interrupt?

Let's find out how much overhead is inherent in an interrupt by repeating the pulse width measurement. This time, we can't simply print the results as this would stop the interrupt-handling. As a compromise, we save 20 readings in an array and then print them. It is also important to keep the interrupt-handling routines short as how long they take to complete governs how fast the next interrupt can be handled.

The new interrupt handler is:

```
uint64_t t[20];
int count=0;
void myHandler(int fd) {
    struct gpioevent_data edata;
    read(fd, &edata, sizeof edata);
    t[count++]=edata.timestamp;
    if(count>19){
        for(int i=1;i<19;i++){
            printf("%llu \n\r", t[i]-t[i-1]);
            fflush(stdout);
        }
        count=0;
    }
}
```

It records reasonably accurate times for pulses longer than $6\mu s$. It is less capable than the polling loop, which works better down to $1\mu s$, but the difference isn't that great. What this means is that even with the overhead of the SDK, interrupts are very usable. However, a lot depends on the time that the interrupt handler takes to relinquish control.

Race Conditions and Starvation

One of the big problems of using interrupts on a small processor like the Pico is that there is no operating system to make sure that different tasks get a fair share of the processor. It is entirely possible for an interrupt routine to be called so often that the main program, or some other function, doesn't get a chance to execute.

For example, if you try a program that prints a message in the main program and responds to interrupts then you can see the starvation of the main program's code very easily:

```c
#include <stdio.h>
#include "pico/stdlib.h"

 uint64_t t;

void MyIRQHandler(uint gpio, uint32_t events)
{
    t = time_us_64() ;
    printf("GPIO %d %X %d \n", gpio, events, t);
}

int main()
{
    stdio_init_all();
    gpio_set_function(22, GPIO_FUNC_SIO);
    gpio_set_dir(22, false);
    gpio_pull_down(22);

    gpio_set_irq_enabled_with_callback(22, GPIO_IRQ_EDGE_RISE |
                           GPIO_IRQ_EDGE_FALL, true, &MyIRQHandler);

    while (1)
    {
        printf("doing something\n\r");
    };

    return 0;
}
```

If you apply a square wave input to GP22 then you will see both the "doing something" and the interrupt message, as long as the frequency is 200Hz or less. Above this frequency the interrupt routine is called almost at once after it returns to the main program. As a result the main program makes little or no progress – it is starved of CPU time. The reason for the very low interrupt rate that causes starvation is due to the time the interrupt routine takes to run as printing is slow. A faster routine would work at a higher frequency before starvation set in, but it is a constant problem with interrupt-driven systems.

If you also look closely at the output of the program when the main program is getting a chance to run, you will see the second problem with simple interrupt systems – race conditions.

The output isn't clean, instead it is all jumbled together:

```
doiGPIO 22 8 536873856
ng someGPIO 22 4 536873856
thing
GPIO 22 8 536873856
doingGPIO 22 4 536873856
somethGPIO 22 8 536873856
ing
dGPIO 22 4 536873856
oing soGPIO 22 8 536873856
methingGPIO 22 4 536
```

The reason for this is simply that the interrupt can occur while the program is in the middle of a call to printf. That is, the call to printf is not "atomic" and can be split by the action of the interrupt. The key takeaway is that interrupts can occur anywhere within your program, even within actions that you think of as atomic, i.e. which cannot be interrupted.

What is even more confusing is that often attempts to remove the problem of race conditions can lead to starvation. For example, you might think that the solution is to disable interrupts while printing:

```
while (1)
{
    gpio_set_irq_enabled(22, GPIO_IRQ_EDGE_RISE |
                         GPIO_IRQ_EDGE_FALL, false);
    printf("doing something\n\r");
    gpio_set_irq_enabled(22, GPIO_IRQ_EDGE_RISE |
                         GPIO_IRQ_EDGE_FALL, true);
};
```

If you try this out you will discover that you don't ever see the interrupt routine print its message. The reason is that the time that the interrupt is enabled for is very, very small and only if an interrupt occurs in this interval will the interrupt routine get to run. Now it is the interrupt routine that is starved of CPU attention. If you add:

```
sleep_us(1000);
```

at the end of the loop you will see both messages and they won't be interwoven.

In this case the problem is made worse by the gpio_set_irq_enabled function always clearing any pending interrupts. If an interrupt occurs during the printf it won't be remembered because it is reset when the IRQ is enabled.

If you want to disable interrupts while remembering any that occur while disabled then you need to add:

```
#include "hardware/structs/iobank0.h"
#include "hardware/sync.h"
void gpio_set_irq_active(uint gpio, uint32_t events, bool enabled) {
    io_irq_ctrl_hw_t *irq_ctrl_base = get_core_num() ?
        &iobank0_hw->proc1_irq_ctrl : &iobank0_hw->proc0_irq_ctrl;
    io_rw_32 *en_reg = &irq_ctrl_base->inte[gpio / 8];
    events <<= 4 * (gpio % 8);
    if (enabled)
        hw_set_bits(en_reg, events);
    else
        hw_clear_bits(en_reg, events);
}
```

You also need change the main program while loop to:

```
while (1)
{
    gpio_set_irq_active(22, GPIO_IRQ_EDGE_RISE |
                            GPIO_IRQ_EDGE_FALL, false);
    printf("doing something\n\r");
    gpio_set_irq_active(22, GPIO_IRQ_EDGE_RISE |
                            GPIO_IRQ_EDGE_FALL, true);
};
```

Now you will see both messages without a pause. The solution isn't perfect as some interrupts will still be missed, but in many cases this is a better way to work.

If you have encountered this sort of problem before you might be thinking of traditional solutions such as mutex, semaphore and critical sections. These are all available within the SDK, but without threads they are only really necessary when you start to use the second core. In nearly all cases you can control access by simply pausing interrupts.

Responding To Input

This look at methods of dealing with the problems of input isn't exhaustive – there are always new ways of doing things, but it does cover the most general ways of implementing input. As already mentioned, the problem with input is that you don't know when it is going to happen. What generally matters is speed of response.

For low-frequency inputs, interrupts are worthwhile. They can leave your program free to get on with other tasks and simplify its overall structure. For high-frequency inputs that need to be serviced regularly, a polling loop is still the best option for maximum throughput. How quickly you can respond to an input depends on how long the polling loop is and how many times you test for it per loop.

Summary

- Events are a stored indication that something happened.

- Interrupts are events that cause something to happen.

- You can use an event with a polling loop to protect against missing input because the program is busy doing something else.

- If an event occurs before the current event has been cleared then it might be missed. To avoid missing events, you can use an event queue which stores events in the order they happened until they are processed.

- The Pico SDK doesn't support events but it is easy to add a function to make use of them. You can enable a bit to be set if a GPIO line goes high, low or is high or low. Edge-triggered events are the easiest to work with.

- Using events in a polling loop hardly slows things down at all.

- You can use events to generate an interrupt and call an interrupt handler.

- Pico interrupts are fast and hence usable for many tasks but they are best for low frequency events that need rapid attention.

Chapter 8

Pulse Width Modulation

One way around the problem of getting a fast response from a microcontroller is to move the problem away from the processor. In the case of the Pico there are some built-in devices that can use GPIO lines to implement protocols without the CPU being involved. In this chapter we take a close look at Pulse Width Modulation (PWM) including generating sound, driving LEDs and servos.

When performing their most basic function, i.e. output, the GPIO lines can be set high or low by the processor. How fast they can be set high or low depends on the speed of the processor.

Using the GPIO line in its Pulse Width Modulation (PWM) mode you can generate pulse trains up to 60MHz. The reason for the increase in speed is that the GPIO is connected to a pulse generator and, once set to generate pulses of a specific type, the pulse generator just gets on with it without needing any intervention from the GPIO line or the processor. In fact, the pulse output will continue after your program has ended.

Of course, even though the PWM line can generate pulses very fast pulses, usually what you want to do is change the nature of the pulses and this is a slower process involving the processor.

Some Basic Pico PWM Facts

There are some facts worth getting clear right from the start, although some of their significance will only become clear as we progress.

First, what is PWM? The simple answer is that a Pulse Width Modulated signal has pulses that repeat at a fixed rate - say one pulse every millisecond, but the width of the pulse can be changed.

There are two basic things to specify about the pulse train that is generated, its repetition rate and the width of each pulse. Usually the repetition rate is set as a simple repeat period and the width of each pulse is specified as a percentage of the repeat period, referred to as the duty cycle.

So, for example, a 1ms repeat and a 50% duty cycle specifies a 1ms period, which is high for 50% of the time, i.e. a pulse width of 0.5ms. The two extremes are 100% duty cycle, i.e. the line is always high, and 0% duty cycle, i.e. the line is always low.

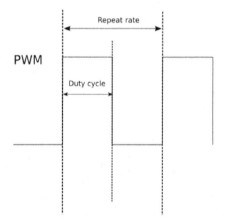

Notice it is the duty cycle that carries the information in PWM and not the frequency. What this means is that generally you select a repeat rate and stick to it and what you change as the program runs is the duty cycle.

In many cases PWM is implemented using special PWM-generator hardware that is built either into the processor chip or provided by an external chip. The processor simply sets the repeat rate by writing to a register and then changing the duty cycle by writing to another register. This generally provides the best sort of PWM with no load on the processor and, generally, glitch-free operation. You can even buy add-on boards that will provide additional channels of PWM without adding to the load on the processor.

The alternative to dedicated PWM hardware is to implement it in software. You can quite easily work out how to do this. All you need is to set a timing loop to set the line high at the repetition rate and then set it low again according to the duty cycle. You can implement this either using interrupts or a polling loop and in more advanced ways, such as using a DMA (Direct Memory Access) channel.

Pico PWM Initialization

In the case of the Pico, the PWM lines are implemented using special PWM hardware. It has eight PWM generators, each capable of two PWM outputs. Any of the GPIO lines can be used as PWM lines and this means you can have up to 16 PWM lines in operation at any given time. Things are a little more complicated in that each pair of outputs has the same frequency which means you have eight, independently set, pairs of outputs. In addition, one of the outputs can be used as an input and this reduces the number of outputs available.

The PWM generators are assigned to GPIO pins in a fixed order:

GPIO	0	1	2	3	4	5	6	7	8	9	10	11	12	13	14	15
PWM Channel	0A	0B	1A	1B	2A	2B	3A	3B	4A	4B	5A	5B	6A	6B	7A	7B

GPIO	16	17	18	19	20	21	22	23	24	25	26	27	28	29		
PWMChannel	0A	0B	1A	1B	2A	2B	3A	3B	4A	4B	5A	5B	6A	6B		

To make use of the PWM hardware you need to change the libraries statement in CMakeLists.txt to:

```
target_link_libraries(myprogram  pico_stdlib
                              hardware_gpio hardware_pwm)
```

that is you you need to add `hardware_pwm` to the libraries. You also need to add:

```
#include "hardware/pwm.h"
```

to the start of your program.

Many of the programs that follow are variations on the main program and hence only the main program is presented. If you want a listing of the full program then visit this book's web page at www.iopress.info.

When you enable PWM functions on a GPIO line:

```
gpio_set_function(gpio, GPIO_FUNC_PWM);
```

the PWM generator "slice" that you get is as shown in the table. Which slice and channel you are working with is important because you have to specify this to configure the hardware. You could just look at the table and work out that when you use a particular GPIO line you have to use a particular slice. For example, if you use GP22 then you are working with 3A, which is the A output of the third slice. That is, the slice number is 3 and the channel number is 0.

Alternatively you can use the functions:

```
static uint   pwm_gpio_to_slice_num (uint gpio)
static uint   pwm_gpio_to_channel (uint gpio)
```

to return the slice and channel number for the PWM hardware connected to the specified pin. For example:

```
gpio_set_function(22, GPIO_FUNC_PWM);
slice=pwm_gpio_to_slice_num (22);
channel=pwm_gpio_to_channel (22);
```

returns slice 3 and channel 0.

Once you have set the pin function and set up the PWM you can start and stop it generating a signal using:

```
pwm_set_enabled (uint slice_num, bool enabled)
```

There are times when you need to turn multiple PWM signals on or off and for this you can use:

```
pwm_set_mask_enabled (uint32_t mask)
```

The mask represents the eight PWM slices as the first eight bits.

You also need to modify the `target_link_libraries` instruction in the `CMakeLists.txt` file to read:

```
target_link_libraries(blinky pico_stdlib hardware_pwm)
```

PWM Configuration

You can see a simplified model of the PWM generator below. This isn't the full story, but it is how best to think of things when you are just getting started or when you are generating simple PWM signals:

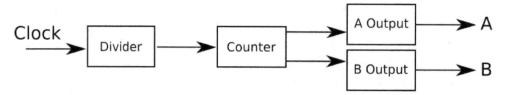

The way that the 16-bit counter works is the key to understanding PWM generation. The default clock is 125MHz and the divider is initialized to 1, which means the counter is stepped on every 8ns. You can modify the counter's behavior by setting a wrap value:

```
pwm_set_wrap (uint slice_num, uint16_t wrap)
```

116

This is the highest value the counter will count up to before either rolling over to zero or starting to count down to zero. These two different behaviors are controlled by enabling or disabling the "phase-correct" mode, the reason for the name will be explained later:

```
pwm_set_phase_correct (uint slice_num, bool phase_correct)
```

Phase correction disabled results in the counter counting up to the wrap value and then resetting to zero. Phase correction enabled makes the counter count up to the wrap value and then down to zero.

The PWM signal is generated from the counter value by setting the channel's level:

```
pwm_set_chan_level (uint slice_num, uint chan, uint16_t level)
```

or for both channels at the same time:

```
pwm_set_both_levels (uint slice_num, uint16_t level_a, uint16_t level_b)
```

There is also the helper function:

```
pwm_set_gpio_level (uint gpio, uint16_t level)
```

which will set the level of the specified GPIO line without being told the slice or channel.

Each time the counter exceeds the level, the state of the output line changes. The line is set high when the count starts and is set low when the level is exceeded. The count continues and the line is set high again when it restarts. You can see this in action in non-phase-correct mode in the diagram below (taken from the documentation):

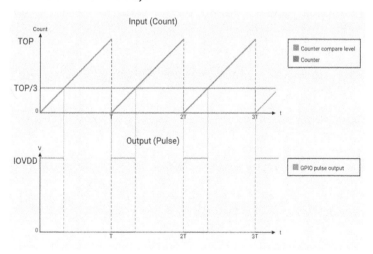

In phase-correct mode we have a similar diagram:

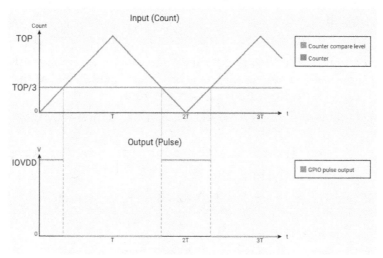

You can see that the counter wrap value sets the frequency and the level sets the duty cycle. It is also obvious that the frequency is halved in phase-correct mode. You can now also see the reason it is called phase-correct mode. In the non-phase-correct mode, as you change the duty cycle the start of the pulse stays fixed, but the center of the pulse moves. In phase-correct mode the start and end of the pulse move, but the center of the pulse stays fixed – its phase is unchanged. There are applications where this difference matters, but for most PWM situations you can ignore the difference.

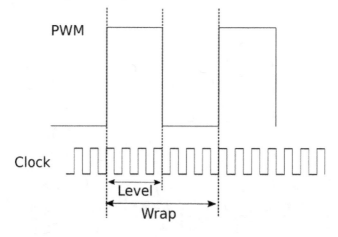

Another subtle point is that you can change the level at any time but the change only takes effect when the counter resets, so you can't accidentally get two pulses during one count cycle.

As already stated, the wrap value determines the frequency. It doesn't take too much algebra to work out that in non-phase-correct mode:

$$f = \frac{f_c}{wrap+1}$$

where f_c is the frequency of the clock after any division has been taken into account. More usefully you can work out the wrap needed to give any PWM frequency:

$$wrap = \frac{f_c}{f} - 1$$

Similarly, the level sets the duty cycle:

$$level = wrap \times duty$$

where *duty* is the duty cycle as a fraction.

For example, with a clock frequency of 125MHz in non-phase-correct mode you can generate a PWM signal of 10kHz using a wrap of 12,500 and a 25% duty cycle implies a level of 3,125.

In phase-correct mode the formulas have to be adjusted to take into account counting both up and down, which halves the frequency:

$$f = \frac{f_c}{2(wrap+1)}$$

$$wrap = \frac{f_c}{2f} - 1$$

$$level = wrap \times duty$$

Clock Division

The PWM counter is 16 bits and this means that once you reach a wrap of 65,534 you cannot decrease the frequency. Given a clock input of 125MHz this puts the lowest PWM frequency at 1.9kHz. This isn't much good if you need a 50Hz signal to drive a servo, see later. The solution is to use the clock divider to reduce the 125MHz clock to something lower.

The clock divider is a 16-bit fractional divider with eight bits for the integer part and four bits for the fraction. You can set the clock using:

```
pwm_set_clkdiv_int_frac (uint slice_num, uint8_t integer,
                                         uint8_t fract)
```

and if you want to specify the divider as a floating point value you can use:

```
pwm_set_clkdiv (uint slice_num, float divider)
```

The divider is decomposed into an 8-bit integer and a 4-bit fractional part, which specifies the fraction as `fract/16`. This means that the largest divisor is `256 15/16` which which gives the lowest clock frequency as:

`520,833 1/3`

You can use the formulas listed above to work out the wrap and level as long as f_c is the resulting clock after division. For example, if you set a clock divider of 2 with a clock frequency of 125MHz in non-phase-correct mode you can generate a PWM signal of 5kHz using a wrap of 12,500 and a 50% duty cycle implies a level of 6,250.

This is simple enough, but notice that you now usually have more than one way to generate any particular PWM frequency – how should you choose a clock divider? The answer is to do with the resolution of the duty cycle you can set. For example, suppose you select a divider that means that to get the frequency you want you have to use a wrap of 2. Then the only duty cycles you can set are 0, 1/3, 2/3 or 100%, corresponding to levels of 0, 1, 2 and 3. If you want to set more duty cycles then clearly you need to keep wrap as big as possible. In fact, it is easy to see that the resolution in bits of the duty cycle is given by $\log_2$ wrap and, as the maximum value of wrap is 65,535, obviously the maximum resolution is 16 bits, i.e. the size of the counter.

Putting all this together you can see that you should always choose a divider that lets you use the largest value of wrap to generate the frequency you are looking for.

In other words, the divider should be chosen to be bigger than the frequency you need, but as close as possible. In other words:

$$divider = \frac{Ceil\left(\dfrac{f_c}{f_{pwm} \times 65536} \times 16\right)}{16} = \frac{Ceil\left(\dfrac{f_c}{f_{pwm} \times 4,096}\right)}{16}$$

Where f_c is the clock frequency, f_{pwm} is the required frequency and Ceil is the ceiling function which returns the integer just bigger than its argument.

For example, if we want a PWM signal at 50Hz the calculation is:

$$divider = \frac{Ceil\left(\dfrac{125000000}{50 \times 4096}\right)}{16}$$

$$divider = \frac{Ceil(610.35)}{16} = \frac{611}{16} = 38.1875$$

If you are setting the divider using the integer and 4-bit fractional part then it is the 611 value that is useful as its bottom four bits 0011 gives the fractional part. So the clock divider is set using:

```
pwm_set_clkdiv_int_frac (slice_num,   38,3);
```

Using this divisor gives the effective clock frequency of:

$$\frac{125000000 \times 16}{611} = 3,273,322.42$$

Using this we can now compute the wrap needed:

$$wrap = \frac{f_c}{f} - 1 = \frac{3,273,322.42}{50} - 1 = 65,465.45$$

If you try this out you will discover that:

```
pwm_set_clkdiv_int_frac (slice_num,   38,3);
pwm_set_wrap(slice_num,65465);
pwm_set_chan_level(slice_num, PWM_CHAN_A, 65465/2);
```

produces a PWM wave form with a frequency of 50Hz:

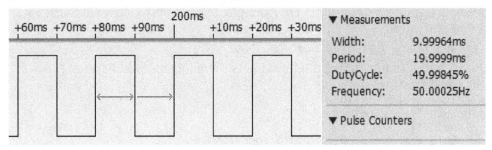

A Frequency and Duty Cycle Function

In most cases you simply want to set a PWM frequency and duty cycle – you don't want to have to calculate the best clock, wrap and level for the task, but sometimes this is necessary. In most cases you can do the job automatically with a function which makes use of the formulas listed above:

```
uint32_t pwm_set_freq_duty(uint slice_num,uint chan,
                                        uint32_t f, int d)
{
 uint32_t clock = 125000000;
 uint32_t divider16 = clock / f / 4096 + (clock % (f * 4096) != 0);
 if (divider16 / 16 == 0)
 divider16 = 16;
 uint32_t wrap = clock * 16 / divider16 / f - 1;
 pwm_set_clkdiv_int_frac(slice_num, divider16/16, divider16 & 0xF);
 pwm_set_wrap(slice_num, wrap);
 pwm_set_chan_level(slice_num, chan, wrap * d / 100);
 return wrap;
}
```

This works by first working out the divider before division by 16, i.e. divider16. Notice that:
```
+ (clock % (f * 4096) != 0)
```
is a standard way of rounding up positive values as it adds one if there is a remainder. The if statement checks to see if the divider is less than one and if it is we set divide16 to its minimum value. Next, we compute the wrap needed to achieve the specified frequency using that divider. Finally, we use the pwm functions to set the clock divider, wrap and level. The value of wrap is returned so that the calling program can check that the duty cycle is being set with sufficient resolution. For example, to set a PWM signal at 50Hz with a 75% duty cycle:

```
pwm_set_freq_duty(slice_num,chan, 50, 75);
```

A full main program using the function is (remember to add hardware_pwm to the CMakeLists.txt file):

```
#include "pico/stdlib.h"
#include "hardware/pwm.h"
int main(){
    gpio_set_function(22, GPIO_FUNC_PWM);
    uint slice_num = pwm_gpio_to_slice_num(22);
    uint chan = pwm_gpio_to_channel(22);
    pwm_set_freq_duty(slice_num,chan, 50, 75);
    pwm_set_enabled(slice_num, true);
    return 0;
}
```

Using PWM Lines Together

Each of the PWM slices can be set to a single divider and wrap, but each of the channels can be set to a different level. What this means is that the A and B channels of each PWM slice are set to the same PWM frequency, but can generate different duty cycles. This may sound restrictive, but it is usually what you need in most applications. For example, if you are driving a pair of servo motors, one from A and one from B, then the frequency of both has to be set to 50Hz and you can vary the duty cycle of each independently.

This, however, does raise a small problem in that setting the duty cycle depends on knowing the wrap value and that could have been set at some other time. One solution is to read the wrap register, but the SDK doesn't currently have a function to do this job. Fortunately it is very easy to create one:

```
uint32_t pwm_get_wrap(uint slice_num){
    valid_params_if(PWM, slice_num >= 0 &&
                           slice_num < NUM_PWM_SLICES);
    return pwm_hw->slice[slice_num].top;
}
```

Using this you can set a duty cycle without setting the wrap or the clock divider, for example:

```
int d=25;
pwm_set_chan_level(slice_num, chan,
                    pwm_get_wrap(slice_num) * d / 100);
```

and you can easily create a function to set the duty cycle:

```
void pwm_set_duty(uint slice_num, uint chan, int d)
{
  pwm_set_chan_level(slice_num,chan,pwm_get_wrap(slice_num)*d/100);
}
```

Using this is very easy, for example:

```
pwm_set_duty(slice_num, chan, 50);
```

sets 50% duty cycle without changing the frequency or explicitly stating the wrap in use.

Just to demonstrate that two PWM lines can be used independently of one another, here is a program that sets each one of the two possible lines to a different duty cycle (remember to add `hardware_pwm` to the CMakeLists.txt file):

```c
#include "pico/stdlib.h"
#include "hardware/pwm.h"
int main()
{
 gpio_set_function(20, GPIO_FUNC_PWM);
 gpio_set_function(21, GPIO_FUNC_PWM);
 uint slice_num = pwm_gpio_to_slice_num(20);
 uint chan20 = pwm_gpio_to_channel(20);
 uint chan21 = pwm_gpio_to_channel(21);
 uint wrap = pwm_set_freq_duty(slice_num, chan20, 50, 75);
 pwm_set_duty(slice_num, chan21, 25);

 pwm_set_enabled(slice_num, true);

 return 0;
}
```

This uses the `pwm_set_freq_duty` and `pwm_set_duty` functions given earlier. Notice that we have used GP20 and GP21 because they use channels A and B of slice 2 respectively. Also notice that we only set the frequency on the slice and the duty cycle on the channels.

You can see the result in this logic analyzer display:

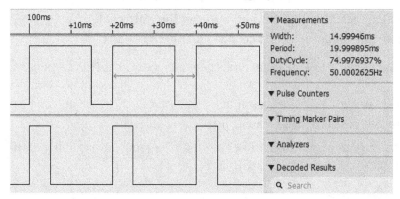

You can clearly see on the logic analyzer plot that the PWM pulses start together and end at different times.

Compare this to what you get if you set phase-correct mode by adding:

```
pwm_set_phase_correct (slice_num, true)
```

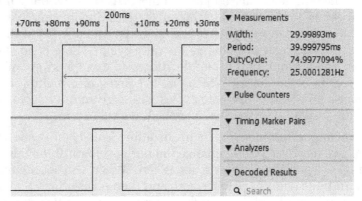

Now you can see that the pulses don't start at the same time, but they are centered around the same time.

As well as being able to set the level for each channel, you can also set the polarity using:

```
pwm_set_output_polarity (uint slice_num, bool a, bool b)
```

Using this you can create pulses from channel A and B which are in anti-phase. For example, if you add:

```
pwm_set_output_polarity(slice_num, false, true);
```

the pattern of pulses changes to:

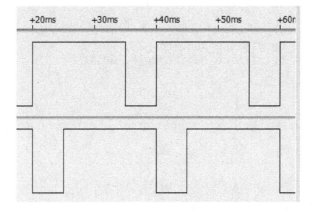

and you can see that the output of channel B is inverted.

Changing The Duty Cycle

For reasons that will be discussed later, in most cases the whole point is to vary the duty cycle or the period of the pulse train. This means that the next question is, how fast can you change the characteristic of a PWM line? In other words, how fast can you change the duty cycle? There is no easy way to give an exact answer and, in most applications, an exact answer isn't of much value. The reason is that for a PWM signal to convey information it generally has to deliver a number of complete cycles with a given duty cycle. This is because of the way pulses are often averaged in applications.

We also have another problem – synchronization. This is more subtle than it first seems. The hardware won't change the duty cycle until the current pulse is complete, i.e. when the counter reaches zero. When you set the duty cycle it is stored until the counter reaches zero and then takes effect. So you might think that the following program works to switch between two duty cycles on a per pulse basis (remember to add hardware_pwm to the CMakeLists.txt file):

```
#include "pico/stdlib.h"
#include "hardware/pwm.h"
int main()
{
    gpio_set_function(20, GPIO_FUNC_PWM);

    uint slice_num = pwm_gpio_to_slice_num(20);
    uint chan20 = pwm_gpio_to_channel(20);

    uint wrap = pwm_set_freq_duty(slice_num, chan20, 50, 50);

    pwm_set_enabled(slice_num, true);
    while (true)
    {
        pwm_set_duty(slice_num, chan20, 25);
        pwm_set_duty(slice_num, chan20, 50);
    }
    return 0;
}
```

If you try this out the result isn't what you might expect on a first analysis:

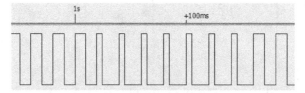

You don't get one 25% and one 50% pulse but a set of each of varying number. The reason is, of course, that the duty cycle is being set asynchronously to the counter wrap. This means that the effective duty cycle depends on the last update. To make this work you need to detect when the counter reaches zero and only update once per zero detected. To do this we need some counter functions.

Working With The Counter

It is clear that to change the duty cycle synchronously we need access to the current state of the counter. The SDK provides the following functions:

```
static uint16_t pwm_get_counter (uint slice_num)
pwm_set_counter (uint slice_num, uint16_t c)
pwm_advance_count (uint slice_num)
pwm_retard_count (uint slice_num)
```

The most generally useful is pwm_get_counter, which returns the counter's current value. You can use this to test where in the PWM period the slice is.

Less generally useful are the pwm_set_counter, pwm_advance_count and pwm_retard_count functions. These can be used to modify the counter by setting it to a new value or adding or subtracting one from its current value. Why would you want to do this? By setting the counter to a new value you can modify the instantaneous frequency of the PWM signal, which is something you would want to do if you were using PWM for signaling or generating musical tones. You also need to know that the advance and retard functions work by blocking clock pulses, not modifying the counter register, and for the advance to work you have to be using a clock divider greater than one.

Returning to the example in the previous section we can make use of the pwm_get_counter function to test when it is time to update the duty cycle (remember to add hardware_pwm to the CMakeLists.txt file):

```
int main()
{
    gpio_set_function(20, GPIO_FUNC_PWM);
    uint slice_num = pwm_gpio_to_slice_num(20);
    uint chan20 = pwm_gpio_to_channel(20);
    uint wrap = pwm_set_freq_duty(slice_num, chan20, 50, 50);
    pwm_set_enabled(slice_num, true);
    while (true) {
        pwm_set_duty(slice_num, chan20, 25);
        while (pwm_get_counter(slice_num)){ };
        pwm_set_duty(slice_num, chan20, 50);
        while (pwm_get_counter(slice_num)){ };
    }
    return 0;
}
```

Notice that as the duty cycle is set after the counter reaches zero, it is the pulse after the next pulse that has its duty cycle changed.

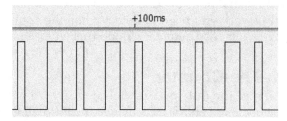

If you want to change the next pulse you need to set the duty cycle at a count of one.

What is the fastest PWM signal you can generate using this method so that the duty cycle changes at every pulse? The answer is surprisingly low, around 300Hz. This could be improved on by optimizing the program, but overall this is not a fast way to modify the PWM slice. A better way is to use interrupts.

Using PWM Interrupts

Changing the duty cycle is one time when interrupts are faster than polling. The reason is that testing the value of the counter is slow but it firing an interrupt on wrap is fast. We could make the polling loop faster than the interrupt by testing on events rather than the counter's value, but the SDK supports PWM interrupts and not events.

There are a number of PWM interrupt functions:

```
pwm_set_irq_enabled (uint slice_num, bool enabled)
pwm_set_irq_mask_enabled (uint32_t slice_mask, bool enabled)
pwm_clear_irq (uint slice_num)
static uint32_t pwm_get_irq_status_mask (void)
pwm_force_irq (uint slice_num)
```

The two important functions are pwm_set_irq_enabled and pwm_clear_irq. The first enables the interrupt on the specified slice and the second clears the interrupt. In general, you need to clear the interrupt before enabling it and clear it when you enter the IRQ handler. You can enable multiple slices using the pwm_set_irq_mask_enabled function. The mask simply has one bit per slice starting with bit 0 and slice 0 and so on. The pwm_get_irq_status_mask function gets the status of which slices are enabled using the same mask format. Finally pwm_force_irq triggers an interrupt under software control.

At this point, you might be wondering where the function that defines the interrupt handler is. The GPIO lines have such a function for their IRQ handler, but the PWM slices make use of the more general Pico interrupt handling. The function:

irq_set_exclusive_handler (uint num, irq_handler_t handler)

sets an interrupt handler for one of the Pico's interrupts. The PWM slices all use IRQ 4 or PWM_IRQ_WRAP. That is, any slice that causes an interrupt generates an IRQ 4 and calls the IRQ 4 handler. There is a mechanism to allow multiple handlers to be attached to a given IRQ number, but the simplest way of doing things is to use irq_set_exclusive_handler to set a single IRQ handler for the interrupt number. In the case of the PWM hardware you can do this using:

irq_set_exclusive_handler(PWM_IRQ_WRAP, MyIRQHandler);

Now we have a handler set we also have to enable the IRQ using:

irq_set_enabled (uint num, bool enabled)

which for the PWM interrupt gives:

irq_set_enabled(PWM_IRQ_WRAP, true);

Notice that you have to enable two things to make PWM IRQs work. First you need to enable the interrupt itself and then the slices that can generate that interrupt. It isn't enough just to enable the slice.

We can now put all this together and write a program that changes the duty cycle of each pulse using an interrupt (remember to add hardware_pwm to the CMakeLists.txt file):

```
#include "pico/stdlib.h"
#include "hardware/pwm.h"
#include "hardware/irq.h"

uint slice_num;
uint chan20;
uint state = 0;
void MyIRQHandler(){
 pwm_clear_irq(slice_num);
 if (state)
 {
        pwm_set_duty(slice_num, chan20, 25);
    }
    else
    {
        pwm_set_duty(slice_num, chan20, 50);
    }
    state = ~state;
}
```

```
int main()
{
    gpio_set_function(20, GPIO_FUNC_PWM);

    slice_num = pwm_gpio_to_slice_num(20);
    chan20 = pwm_gpio_to_channel(20);

    pwm_clear_irq(slice_num);
    pwm_set_irq_enabled(slice_num, true);
    irq_set_exclusive_handler(PWM_IRQ_WRAP, MyIRQHandler);
    irq_set_enabled(PWM_IRQ_WRAP, true);

    uint wrap = pwm_set_freq_duty(slice_num, chan20, 100000, 25);
    pwm_set_enabled(slice_num, true);
    while (true)
    {
    }
    return 0;
}
```

You also need the functions defined in previous sections and:

```
#include "hardware/irq.h"
```

You can see that the IRQ handlers simply change the duty cycle by keeping an odd/even state variable. Also notice that we have to clear any pending IRQs – if you don't the program will simply hang.

If you try this out you will discover that it works up to around 100kHz, which is a considerable improvement on the 300Hz of the polling method that tests the counter value.

Uses Of PWM – Digital To Analog

What sorts of things do you use PWM for? There are lots of very clever uses for PWM. However, there are two use cases which account for most PWM applications - voltage or power modulation and signaling to servos.

The amount of power delivered to a device by a pulse train is proportional to the duty cycle. A pulse train that has a 50% duty cycle is delivering current to the load only 50% of the time and this is irrespective of the pulse repetition rate. So the duty cycle controls the power, but the period still matters in many situations because you want to avoid any flashing or other effects. A higher frequency smooths out the power flow at any duty cycle.

If you add a low-pass filter to the output of a PWM signal then what you get is a voltage that is proportional to the duty cycle. This can be looked at in many different ways, but again it is the result of the amount of power delivered by a

PWM signal. You can also think of it as using the filter to remove the high-frequency components of the signal, leaving only the slower components due to the modulation of the duty cycle.

How fast you can work depends on the duty cycle resolution. If you work with 8-bit resolution your D-to-A conversion will have 256 steps, which at 3.3V gives a potential resolution of 3.3/256 or about 13mV. This is often good enough. With a wrap of 255 and a clock divider of 1 this gives a sampling frequency of approximately 488kHz. The PWM output in this configuration mimics the workings of an 8-bit A-to-D converter. You set the duty cycle using a value of 0 to 256 for level and you get a voltage output that is 3.3*level/256V. The theoretical (Nyquist) rate gives the maximum frequency that can be represented as 488/2=244kHz, but for simple reproduction systems the upper limit is smaller. A typical rule of thumb is that the sampling frequency should be at least seven times higher than the highest frequency you hope to generate, i.e. around 70KHz.

If you use 16-bit resolution, which is what CD quality audio uses, then the sampling rate drops to 1.9kHz, which is well below the 44kHz generally used.

To demonstrate the sort of approach that you can take to D-to-A conversion, the following program creates a sine wave. To do this we need to compute the duty cycle for 256 points in a complete cycle. We could do this each time a value is needed, but to make the program fast enough we have to compute the entire 256 points and store them in an array. While there are fixed point arithmetic ways of computing the sine or the cos of an angle, it is simpler to use the Pico's built-in floating-point software. Notice that the Pico doesn't have floating-point arithmetic implemented in hardware and it is best to avoid it if possible. As we only want to update the duty cycle once for each sample point, the simplest solution is to use an interrupt handler to do the job. The program is:

```
#include "pico/stdlib.h"
#include "hardware/pwm.h"
#include "hardware/irq.h"
#include "math.h"

uint32_t pwm_get_wrap(uint slice_num)
{
 valid_params_if(PWM, slice_num >= 0 && slice_num < NUM_PWM_SLICES);
 return pwm_hw->slice[slice_num].top;
}

void pwm_set_duty(uint slice_num, uint chan, int d)
{
 pwm_set_chan_level(slice_num, chan, pwm_get_wrap(slice_num)*d/100);
}
```

```c
uint slice_num;
uint chan20;
uint state = 0;
uint8_t wave[256];

void MyIRQHandler()
{
 pwm_clear_irq(slice_num);
 pwm_set_duty(slice_num, chan20, wave[state]);
 state = (state + 1) % 256;
}

int main()
{
 for (int i = 0; i < 256; i++)
 {
 wave[i] = (uint8_t)((128.0 + sinf((float)i * 2.0 * 3.14159 / 256.0)
                                       * 128.0) * 100.0 / 256.0);
 }

    gpio_set_function(22, GPIO_FUNC_PWM);

    slice_num = pwm_gpio_to_slice_num(22);
    uint chan22 = pwm_gpio_to_channel(22);

    pwm_clear_irq(slice_num);
    pwm_set_irq_enabled(slice_num, true);
    irq_set_exclusive_handler(PWM_IRQ_WRAP, MyIRQHandler);
    irq_set_enabled(PWM_IRQ_WRAP, true);

    pwm_set_clkdiv_int_frac(slice_num, 1, 0);
    pwm_set_wrap(slice_num, 255);

    pwm_set_enabled(slice_num, true);
    while (true)
    {
    }
    return 0;
}
```

The duty cycle values needed are computed and stored in the wave array.
Then the PWM is set up to use a divider of 1 and a wrap of 255 and the
interrupt is enabled. The interrupt handler simply sets the level to each value
in the wave array in turn. The waveform repeats after around $526\mu s$, which
makes the frequency around 1.9KHz.

To see the analog waveform, we need to put the digital output into a low-pass filter. A simple resistor and capacitor work reasonably well:

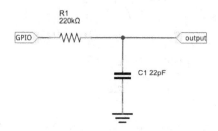

The filter's cutoff is around 33kHz and might be a little on the high side for this low-frequency, 2kHz, output, but it produces a reasonable waveform:

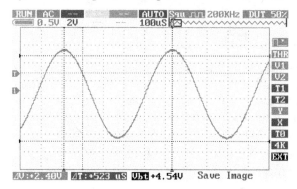

You can create a sine wave, or any other waveform you need, using the same techniques, but for high quality audio you need a higher sampling rate.

Frequency Modulation

Using PWM to create musical tones, and sound effects in general, is a well-explored area which is too big to cover in this book. In most cases we choose to vary the duty cycle at a fixed sample rate, but an alternative is to leave the duty cycle fixed at, say, 50% and modulate the frequency. You can use this approach to create simple musical tones and scales.

As the frequency of middle C is 281.6Hz, to generate middle C you could use:

```
int main()
{
    gpio_set_function(22, GPIO_FUNC_PWM);
    uint slice_num = pwm_gpio_to_slice_num(22);

    uint chan22 = pwm_gpio_to_channel(22);
    pwm_set_freq_duty(slice_num, chan22, 281, 50);

    pwm_set_enabled(slice_num, true);
}
```

The resulting output is a square wave with a measured frequency of 281Hz which isn't particularly nice to listen to. You can improve it by feeding it through a simple low-pass filter like the one used above for waveform synthesis. You can look up the frequencies for other notes and use a table to generate them.

Controlling An LED

You can also use PWM to generate physical quantities such as the brightness of an LED or the rotation rate of a DC motor. The only differences required by these applications are to do with the voltage and current you need and the way the duty cycle relates to whatever the physical effect is. In other words, if you want to change some effect by 50%, how much do you need to change the duty cycle? For example, how do we "dim" an LED?

The simplest example is to drive the onboard LED using a PWM signal:

```
#include "pico/stdlib.h"
#include "hardware/pwm.h"
int main()
{
    gpio_set_function(25, GPIO_FUNC_PWM);
    uint slice_num = pwm_gpio_to_slice_num(25);
    uint chan = pwm_gpio_to_channel(25);
    pwm_set_freq_duty(slice_num, chan, 2000, 0);
    pwm_set_enabled(slice_num, true);

    while (true)
    {
        for (int d = 0; d <= 100; d++)
        {
            pwm_set_duty(slice_num, chan, d);
            sleep_ms(50);
        }
    }
}
```

If you try this out you will see the LED slowly increase in brightness, but there seems to be a longer time that it is at maximum brightness than any other value. This is a consequence of the non-linear relationship between duty cycle and perceived brightness.

By changing the duty cycle of the PWM pulse train you can set the amount of power delivered to an LED, or any other device, and hence change its brightness. If you use a 50% duty cycle, the LED is on 50% of the time and it has been determined that this makes it look as if it is half as bright. However, this is not the end of the story as humans don't respond to physical brightness in a linear way. The Weber-Fechner law gives the general relationship between perceived intensity and physical stimulus as logarithmic.

In the case of an LED, the connection between duty cycle and brightness is a complicated matter, but the simplest approach uses the fact that the perceived brightness is roughly proportional to the cube root of the physical brightness. The exact equations, published as CIE 1931, are:

$L = 903.3 \cdot (Y / Y_n)$ $\qquad (Y/ Y_n) \leq 0.008856$

$L = 116 \cdot (Y / Y_n)^{1/3} - 16$ $\qquad (Y/ Y_n) > 0.008856$

where L is the perceived brightness and Y / Y_n is a measure of physical brightness.

The exact relationship is complicated, but in most cases a roughly cubic law, obtained by inverting the CIE relationship, can be used:

$d = kb^3$

where b is the perceived brightness and d is the duty cycle. The constant k depends on the LED. The graph below shows the general characteristic of the relationship for a duty cycle of 0 to 100% on the y-axis and arbitrary, 0 to 100, perceived brightness units on the x-axis.

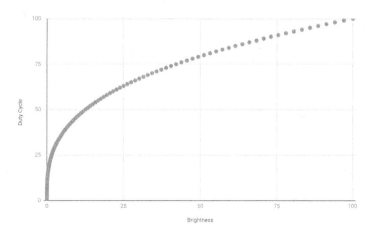

Notice that, as the LED when powered by a PWM signal is either full on or full off, there is no effect in the change in LED light output with current - the LED is always run at the same current.

What all of this means is that if you want an LED to fade in a linear fashion you need to change the duty cycle in a non-linear fashion. Intuitively it means that changes when the duty cycle is small produce bigger changes in brightness than when the duty cycle is large.

A program to implement cubic dimming is:

```
#include "pico/stdlib.h"
#include "hardware/pwm.h"
int main()
{
    gpio_set_function(25, GPIO_FUNC_PWM);
    uint slice_num = pwm_gpio_to_slice_num(25);
    uint chan = pwm_gpio_to_channel(25);

    pwm_set_freq_duty(slice_num, chan, 2000, 0);

    pwm_set_enabled(slice_num, true);
    int d = 0;
    while (true)
    {
        for (int b = 0; b <= 100; b++)
        {
            d = (b * b * b) / 10000;
            pwm_set_duty(slice_num, chan, d);
            sleep_ms(50);
        }
    }
}
```

If you try this out you should notice that the LED changes brightness more evenly across its range. The only problem is that now 100 steps isn't enough to mask the steps in brightness at the lower level. The solution is to work with a more precise specification of duty cycle.

In most cases it is irrelevant exactly how linear the response of the LED is - a rough approximation looks as smooth to the human eye. You can even get away with using a square law to dim the LED. The only exception is when you are trying to drive LEDs to create a gray-level or color display when color calibration is another level of accuracy.

There is also the question of what frequency we should use. Clearly it has to be fast enough not to be seen as flickering and this generally means it has to be greater than 80Hz, the upper limit for human flicker fusion, but because of the strobe effect flickering becomes more visible in connection with moving objects. The faster the LED switches on and off the less flicker should be visible, but before you select frequencies in the high kHz range it is worth knowing that an LED has a minimum time to turn on and so frequencies at low kHz work best.

If you want to dim something other than the onboard LED, you will, in many cases, need a driver to increase the brightness. For a simple example, we can connect a standard LED to the PWM line and can use the BJT driver circuit introduced in Chapter 5.

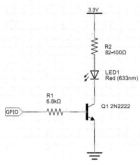

PWM Input

The B Channel of each slice can also be used as an input. In this mode the block diagram of the slice is:

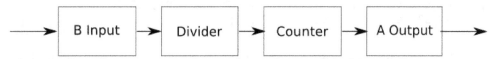

The signal on the B input can be configured to modify the way the counting works:

- Count when B is high – in this mode the input starts and stops the count
- Increment count when B has a rising edge
- Increment count when B has a falling edge

To set the mode you need to use `pwm_set_clkdiv_mode`:

`pwm_set_clkdiv_mode (uint slice_num, enum pwm_clkdiv_mode mode)`

with `pwm_clkdiv_mode` enumeration:

```
PWM_DIV_FREE_RUNNING,
PWM_DIV_B_HIGH
PWM_DIV_B_RISING
PWM_DIV_B_FALLING
```

The first option is the usual configuration where the clock simply increments the counter.

What can you use input mode for? At its simplest you can use it as an alternative clock input for the PWM generator. In PWM_DIV_B_RISING or PWM_DIV_B_FALLING mode the counter is incremented just once for each specified edge. The important fact to take into account is that the clock divider is still operational and the edge signal is divided by the specified value.

For example, consider a configuration in which a 1kHz pulse is fed into the B channel. If the clock divider is set to 1 and the counter is set up with a wrap of 127 and a level of 63 and the mode is set to PWM_DIV_B_RISING then the output is 1000/128 = 7.8 Hz at 50% duty cycle. If we set the clock divider to 2 then the output frequency is 1000/(2*128) = 3.9 Hz and so on:

```
#include "pico/stdlib.h"
#include "hardware/pwm.h"
int main()
{
    gpio_set_function(20, GPIO_FUNC_PWM);
    gpio_set_function(21, GPIO_FUNC_PWM);
    uint slice_num = pwm_gpio_to_slice_num(20);

    uint chanA = pwm_gpio_to_channel(20);
    uint chanB = pwm_gpio_to_channel(21);
    pwm_set_clkdiv_int_frac(slice_num, 2, 0);
    pwm_set_wrap(slice_num, 127);
    pwm_set_chan_level(slice_num, chanA,63);
    pwm_set_clkdiv_mode (slice_num,PWM_DIV_B_RISING );
    pwm_set_enabled(slice_num, true);
}
```

Notice that the output frequency now depends on the signal input to the B input and you can use this to generate a varying frequency PWM signal. To be clear, the output frequency depends on the signal applied to B, the clock divider and the wrap. The duty cycle depends on the level as usual.

By allowing the count to proceed for a known amount of time using PWM_DIV_B_HIGH, you can, in theory, use the PWM slice to measure the duty cycle or frequency of the input wave form. There is an example of this included in the Pico documentation, but it doesn't emphasize the conditions required to make it work. The PWM_DIV_B_HIGH mode is different from the edge modes in that it doesn't act as a clock, but as a gate for the internal clock. That is, the clock is provided in the usual way via the system clock and the divider to the counter. The counter only advances, however, when the B input is high. This means that, in this mode, the slice is configured to count the time that the B input is high. So for example, if we enable the slice with a clock of approximately 488kHz, wait 10ms, disable the slice and read the counter – what does it tell us? Suppose the count is 100, this means that the B input was high for 100 clock pulses or $100 \times 0.2 \mu s = 20 \mu s$. You cannot infer the frequency from this measurement, it simply gives you the time that the signal was high in a 10ms period. However, you can work out that it has a 50% duty cycle as at any frequency this would allow the count to proceed for half of the measurement period. In general the duty cycle is:

```
d = time high/measurement time %
```

Of course, this is just the average duty cycle over the measurement time. To get an estimate that is close to the instantaneous duty cycle, the measurement time has to be small, but this reduces accuracy because of the possibility of including fractional pulses at the start and end of the period. The clock frequency should also be selected so that for a 100% duty cycle we get a maximum count, i.e.:

```
max count = clock frequency*measurement time
```

or assuming we want the max count to be 65535:

```
clock frequency = 65535/measurement time
```

which gives the frequency in kiloHertz if the measurement time is in milliseconds.

For example with a measurement time of 10ms, we need a clock of:

```
65535/10 = 6553.5kHz.
```

A more useful quantity is the divider needed to get the clock rate:

```
divider = 125000*measurement time/65535
```

For example, a measurement time of 10ms gives a clock divider of:

```
divider = 125000*10/65535 =19.074
```

Selecting the next largest integer divider gives you a clock rate that doesn't quite get to the maximum count. If you select the lower integer then you will get a complete wrap and the start of another cycle which will return a low count at the end of the period. You don't want the counter to wrap during the measurement period. If we use 20 as the divider then the maximum count is:

```
max count=125000000*1000/(20*10)
        = 62500
```

Putting all of this together gives a duty cycle measurement program:

```
int main()
{
 stdio_init_all();
 gpio_set_function(20, GPIO_FUNC_PWM);
 gpio_set_function(21, GPIO_FUNC_PWM);
 uint slice_num = pwm_gpio_to_slice_num(20);

    uint chanA = pwm_gpio_to_channel(20);
    uint chanB = pwm_gpio_to_channel(21);

    pwm_set_clkdiv_int_frac(slice_num, 20, 0);
    int maxcount=125000000*10/20/1000;

    pwm_set_wrap(slice_num, 65535);
    pwm_set_chan_level(slice_num, chanA, 100);
    pwm_set_clkdiv_mode(slice_num, PWM_DIV_B_HIGH);

 while (true)
 {
      pwm_set_enabled(slice_num, true);
      sleep_ms(10);
      pwm_set_enabled(slice_num, false);
      uint16_t count =pwm_get_counter(slice_num);
      pwm_set_counter(slice_num, 0);
      printf("count= %u  duty cycle=%d %%\n",
             count, (int)count*100/maxcount);
      sleep_ms(1000);
    }
}
```

This program will work and give a reasonably accurate result as long as the frequency of the signal being measured presents a reasonable number of cycles in a 10ms period – about 200Hz in practice.

A Configuration Struct

The SDK provides an alternative way of configuring a PWM slice. Instead of making separate calls to configuration functions, you can set values in a struct:

```
typedef struct {
    uint32_t csr;
    uint32_t div;
    uint32_t top;
} pwm_config;
```

and then use functions to set some of the values:

```
pwm_config_set_phase_correct (pwm_config *c, bool phase_correct)
pwm_config_set_clkdiv (pwm_config *c, float div)
pwm_config_set_clkdiv_int (pwm_config *c, uint div)
pwm_config_set_clkdiv_mode (pwm_config *c,
                                        enum pwm_clkdiv_mode mode)
pwm_config_set_output_polarity (pwm_config *c, bool a, bool b)
pwm_config_set_wrap (pwm_config *c, uint16_t wrap)
```

You can initialize the struct to default values using:

```
pwm_get_default_config (void)
```

and apply the configuration using:

```
pwm_init (uint slice_num, pwm_config *c, bool start)
```

The advantage is that once you have set the config struct you can reuse it. For example:

```
pwm_config cfg = pwm_get_default_config();
pwm_config_set_wrap(&cfg, wrap);
pwm_init(slice_num, &cfg, true);
```

Use whichever method to initialize the slice seems natural.

What Else Can You Use PWM For?

PWM lines are incredibly versatile and it is always worth asking the question "could I use PWM?" when you are considering almost any problem. The LED example shows how you can use PWM as a power controller. You can extend this idea to a computer-controlled switch-mode power supply. All you need is a capacitor to smooth out the voltage and perhaps a transformer to change the voltage. You can also use PWM to control the speed of a DC motor and, if you add a simple bridge circuit, you can control its direction and speed. Finally, you can use a PWM signal as a modulated carrier for data communications. For example, most infrared controllers make use of a 38kHz carrier, which is roughly a $26\mu s$ pulse. This is switched on and off for 1ms and this is well within the range that the PWM can manage. So all you have to do is replace the red LED in the previous circuit with an infrared LED and you have the start of a remote control, or data transmission, link.

One big area of use is in controlling motors and servo motors in particular and this is the subject of the next chapter.

Summary

- PWM, Pulse Width Modulation, has a fixed repetition rate but a variable duty cycle, i.e. the amount of time the signal is high or low changes.

- PWM can be generated by software simply by changing the state of a GPIO line correctly, but it can also be generated in hardware so relieving the processor of some work.

- As well as being a way of signaling, PWM can also be used to vary the amount of power or voltage transferred. The higher the duty cycle, the more power/voltage.

- The Pico has eight hardware PWM generators and these are capable of a range of operational modes.

- The PWM lines are controlled by a counter and two values wrap which gives the frequency and level which gives the duty cycle.

- You can generate phase correct PWM or allow the phase to vary with the duty cycle.

- The higher the wrap value the higher the resolution of the duty cycle. It is possible to work out the best value for the clock frequency for any PWM frequency to maximize the duty cycle resolution.

- Changing the duty cycle is slow using polling but fast using interrupts.

- PWM can be used to implement a DAC simply by varying the duty cycle.

- In the same way, by varying the duty cycle, you can dim an LED.

- You can use the PWM hardware in input mode to count the number of cycles that the line is high and so estimate the duty cycle.

Chapter 9

Controlling Motors And Servos

Controlling motors is an obvious use for the low cost Pico, but it is important to understand the different types of motor that you can use and exactly how to control them using PWM. In addition to PWM control, we also look at the very useful stepper motor which doesn't make use of PWM.

The simplest division among types of motor is AC and DC. AC motors are generally large and powerful and run from mains voltage. As they are more difficult to work with, and they work at mains voltages, these aren't used much in IoT applications. DC motors generally work on lower voltage and are much more suitable for the IoT. In this chapter we will only look at DC motors and how they work thanks to pulse width modulation. The parts used are listed in the Resources section of the book's webpage at www.iopress.info.

DC Motor

There are two big classes of DC motor – brushed and brushless. All motors work by using a set of fixed magnets, the stator, and a set of rotating magnets, the rotor. The important idea is that a motor generates a "push" that rotates the shaft by the forces between the magnet that makes up the stator and the magnet that makes up the rotor. The stronger these magnets are, the stronger the push and the more torque (turning force) the motor can produce. To keep the motor turning, one of the two magnetic fields has to change to keep the rotor being attracted to a new position.

DC motors differ in how they create the magnetism in each component, either using a permanent magnet or an electromagnet. This means there are four possible arrangements:

	1	2	3	4
Stator	Permanent	Permanent	Electromagnet	Electromagnet
Rotor	Permanent	Electromagnet	Permanent	Electromagnet
Type	Can't work	Brushed DC	Brushless DC	Series or shunt

Arrangement 1 can't produce a motor because there is no easy way of changing the magnetic field. Arrangement 4 produces the biggest and most powerful DC motors used in trains, cars and so on. Arrangement 2, Brushed DC, is the most commonly encountered form of "small" DC motor. However, arrangement 3, brushless DC, is becoming increasingly popular.

Different arrangements produce motors which have different torque characteristics, i.e. how hard they are to stop at any given speed. Some types of motor are typically low torque at any speed, i.e. they spin fast but are easy to stop.

Low torque motors are often used with gearboxes, which reduce the speed and increase the torque. The big problem with gearboxes, apart from extra cost, is backlash. The gears don't mesh perfectly and this looseness means that you can turn the input shaft and at first the output shaft won't move. Only when the slack in the gears has been taken up will the output shaft move. This makes a geared motor less useful for precise positioning, although there are ways to improve on this using feedback and clever programming.

Brushed Motors

To energize the electromagnets, a brushed motor supplies current to the armature via a split ring or commutator and brushes. As the rotor rotates, the current in the coil is reversed and it is always attracted to the other pole of the magnet.

The only problem with this arrangement is that, as the brushes rub on the slip ring as the armature rotates, they wear out and cause sparks and hence RF interference. The quality of a brushed motor depends very much on the design of the brushes and the commutator.

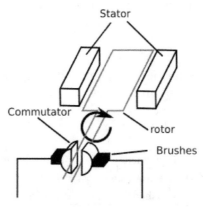

Very small, cheap, brushed DC motors, of the sort in the picture below, tend to not have brushes that can be changed and when they wear out the motor has to be replaced. They also tend to have very low torque and high speed. This usually means that they have to be used with a gearbox. If you overload a brushed motor then the tendency is to demagnetize the stator magnets. The cheapest devices are basically toys.

Higher quality brushed motors are available and they also come in a variety of form factors. For example, the 775 motor is 66.7 by 42mm with a 5mm shaft:

Even these motors tend not to have user-serviceable brushes, but they tend to last a long time due to better construction.

Unidirectional Brushed Motor

A brushed motor can be powered by simply connecting it to a DC supply. Reversing the DC supply reverses the direction of the motor. The speed is simply proportional to the applied voltage. If all you want is a unidirectional control then all you need is a PWM driver that can supply the necessary current and voltage.

A single transistor solution is workable as long as you include a diode to allow the energy stored in the windings to discharge when the motor is rotating, but not under power:

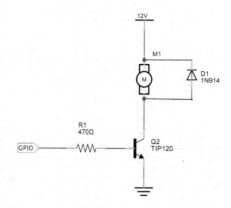

This circuit is simple and will work with motor voltages up to 40V and motor currents up to 5A continuous, 8A peak. The only small point to note is that the TIP120 is a Darlington pair, i.e. it is two transistors in the same case, and as such the base voltage drop is twice the usual 0.6V, i.e. 1.2V, and this has to be taken into account when calculating the current-limiting resistor.

It is sometimes said that the TIP120 and similar are inefficient power controllers because, comprising two transistors, they have twice the emitter-collector voltage you would expect, which means they dissipate more power than necessary.

If you are running a motor from a battery you might want to use a MOSFET, but, as described earlier, 3.3V is low to switch a MOSFET on and off. One solution is to use a BJT to increase the voltage applied to the gate:

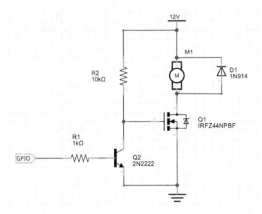

The BJT connects the gate to 12V. As the IRFZ44NPBF has a threshold voltage between 2V and 4V, devices should work at 5V and sometimes at 3.3V without the help of the BJT, but providing 12V ensures that the MOSFET is fully on. One problem with the circuit is that the use of the BJT inverts the signal. When the GPIO line is high the BJT is on and the MOSFET is off and vice versa. In other words, GPIO line high switches the motor off and low switches it on. This MOSFET can work with voltages up to 50V and currents of 40A. The 2N2222 can only work at 30V, or 40V in the case of the 2N2222A.

A third approach to controlling a unidirectional motor is to use half an H-bridge. Why this is so-called, and why you might want to do it, will become apparent in the next section on bidirectional motors. Half an H-bridge makes use of two complementary devices, either an NPN and a PNP BJT or an N- and P-type MOSFET.

For example:

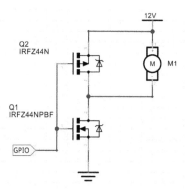

If the GPIO line is high then Q1 is on and Q2 off and the motor runs. If the GPIO line is low then Q1 is off and Q2 is on and the motor is braked – it has a resistance to rotating because of the back electromotive force (EMF) generated when the rotor turns. You probably need a BJT to feed the MOSFETs as selected.

Unidirectional PWM Motor Controller

A function to control the speed of a unidirectional motor is very simple. The speed is set by the duty cycle – the only parameter you have to choose in addition is the frequency. If you want an optimal controller then setting the frequency is a difficult task. Higher speeds make the motor run faster and quieter – but too high a frequency and the motor loses power and the driving transistor or MOSFET becomes hot and less efficient. The determining factor is the inductance of the motor's coil and any other components connected to it such as capacitors. In practice, PWM frequencies from 100Hz to 20kHz are commonly used, but in most cases 1kHz to 2kHz is a good choice.

How should we implement code to make motor control easy?

A good pattern, which has many of the advantages of object-oriented programming, is to create a struct which has fields that represent the state of the entity.

For example, to implement a unidirectional motor we can create a `Motor` struct:

```
typedef struct
{
    uint gpio;
    uint slice;
    uint chan;
    uint speed;
    uint freq;
    uint resolution;
    bool on;
} Motor;
```

You can see that this has all of the information needed to define the current state of a motor. All we need now are some functions to modify the fields and implement the changes to the state. The first is an initialization function:

```
void motorInit(Motor *m, uint gpio, uint freq)
{
    gpio_set_function(gpio, GPIO_FUNC_PWM);
    m->gpio = gpio;
    m->slice = pwm_gpio_to_slice_num(gpio);
    m->chan = pwm_gpio_to_channel(gpio);
    m->freq = freq;
    m->speed = 0;
    m->resolution = pwm_set_freq_duty(m->slice, m->chan,
                                      m->freq, m->speed);
    m->on=false;
}
```

Next, we need a function to set the speed:

```
void motorspeed(Motor *m, int s)
{
    pwm_set_duty(m->slice, m->chan, s);
    m->speed = s;
}
```

and finally, two functions, one to turn the motor on and one to turn it off:

```
void motorOn(Motor *m){
    pwm_set_enabled(m->slice, true);
    m->on=true;
}

void motorOff(Motor *m){
    pwm_set_enabled(m->slice, false);
    m->on=false;
}
```

With this struct and its associated functions. plus the functions from the previous chapter, we can create and use a motor very easily (remember to add `hardware_pwm` to the CMakeLists.txt file):

```
#include "pico/stdlib.h"
#include "hardware/pwm.h"
int main()
{
    Motor mot1;
    motorInit(&mot1, 21, 2000);
    motorspeed(&mot1, 50);
    motorOn(&mot1);
    return 0;
}
```

This sets up a motor connected to GP21, using 2kHz for the frequency, then sets it to 50% speed and turns it on. You can see that the functions can be used to control multiple motors connected to different GPIO lines – simply create a `Motor` struct for each one.

Bidirectional Brushed Motor

If you want bidirectional control then you need to use an H-bridge:

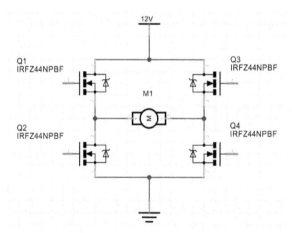

It is easy to see how this works. If Q1 and Q4 are the only MOSFETs on the motor, + is connected to 12V and – to ground. The motor runs in the forward direction. If Q2 and Q3 are the only MOSFETs on the motor, + is connected to ground and – is connected to 12V. The motor runs in the reverse direction. Of course, if none or any single one is on the motor is off. If Q1 and Q3, or Q2 and Q4, are on then the motor is braked as its windings are shorted out and the back EMF acts as a brake.

You can arrange to drive the four MOSFETs using four GPIO lines - just make sure that they switch on and off in the correct order. To make the bridge easier to drive, you can add a NOT gate to each pair so that you switch Q1/Q2 and Q3/ Q4 to opposite states.

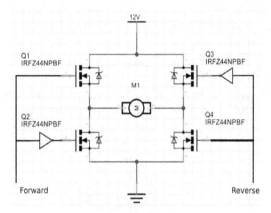

An alternative design is to use complementary MOSFETs:

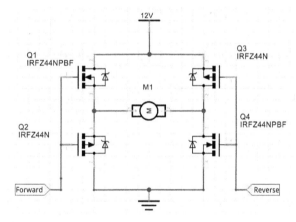

In this configuration, the first GPIO line drives the motor forward and the second drives it in reverse. The effect of setting the two lines is:

Forward	Reverse	Motor
Low	Low	Off
Low	High	Reverse
High	Low	Forward
High	High	Braked

You can also drive the GPIO lines for Forward/Reverse with a PWM signal and control the motor's speed as well as direction. If you use the MOSFETs shown in the diagram then you would also need a BJT to increase the drive voltage to each MOSFET, as in the unidirectional case. You also need to include diodes to deal with potential reverse voltage on each of the MOSFETs. The most important thing about an H-bridge is that Q1/Q2 and Q3/Q4 should never be on together – this would short circuit the power supply.

If working with four power BJTs or MOSFETs is more than you want to tackle, the good news is that there are chips that implement two H-bridges per device. You can also buy low-cost ready-made modules with one or more H-bridges. One of the most used devices is the L298 Dual H-bridge which works up to 46V and total DC current of 4A.

The block diagram of one of the two H-bridges shows exactly how it works:

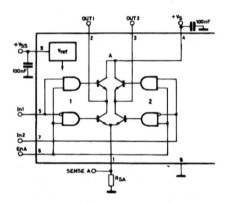

You can see that the bridge is made up of four BJTs and there are logic gates to allow IN1 and IN2 to select the appropriate pairs of devices. The only extras are AND gates and that the ENA (enable) line is used to switch all of the transistors off. The line shown as SENSE A can be used to detect the speed or load of the motor, but is rarely used.

A typical module based on the L298 can be seen below.

It is easier to describe how to use this sort of module with a single motor. The motor is connected to OUT1 and OUT2. Three GPIO lines are connected to ENA, IN1 and IN2. ENA is an enable line, which has to be high for the motor to run at all. IN1 and IN2 play the role of direction control lines – which one is forward and which is reverse depends on which way round you connect the motor. Putting a PWM signal onto ENA controls the speed of the motor and this allows IN1 and IN2 to be simple digital outputs.

Notice that the power connector shows 5V and 12V supplies, but most of these modules have a voltage regulator which will reduce the 12V to 5V. In this case you don't have to supply a 5V connection. If you want to use more than 12V then the regulator has to be disconnected and you need to arrange for a separate 5V supply – check with the module's documentation. Notice that the transistors in the H-bridge have around a 2V drop, so using 12V results in just 10V being applied to the motor.

Another very popular H-bridge device is the SN754410 driver. This is suitable for smaller, lower-powered, motors and has two complete H-bridges. It can supply up to 1A per driver and work from 4.5 to 36V. It has the same set of control lines as the L298, i.e. each motor has a forward/reverse control line and an enable line. You don't have use the enable line - it can be connected to +5V to allow PWM to be applied on the forward/reverse lines.

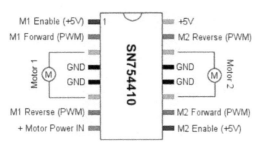

Bidirectional Motor Software

We can easily extend the Motor struct and its functions to work with a bidirectional motor. The only real difference is that now we have to use two GPIO lines and these are most easily used if they are the A and B channels of the same slice – note for simplicity the code doesn't check this condition. For forward we activate the first GPIO line and for reverse we activate the second (remember to add hardware_pwm to the CMakeLists.txt file and the functions from the previous chapter):

```
typedef struct
{
 uint gpioForward;
 uint gpioBackward;
 uint slice;
 uint Fchan;
 uint Bchan;
 bool forward;
 uint speed;
 uint freq;
 uint resolution;
 bool on;
} BiMotor;

void BiMotorInit(BiMotor *m, uint gpioForward,
                             uint gpioBackward, uint freq)
{
 gpio_set_function(gpioForward, GPIO_FUNC_PWM);
 m->gpioForward = gpioForward;
 m->slice = pwm_gpio_to_slice_num(gpioForward);
 m->Fchan = pwm_gpio_to_channel(gpioForward);

 gpio_set_function(gpioBackward, GPIO_FUNC_PWM);
 m->gpioBackward = gpioBackward;
    m->Bchan = pwm_gpio_to_channel(gpioBackward);

    m->freq = freq;
    m->speed = 0;
    m->forward = true;
    m->resolution = pwm_set_freq_duty(m->slice, m->Fchan,
                                             m->freq, 0);
    pwm_set_duty(m->slice, m->Bchan, 0);
    m->on = false;
}
```

```c
void BiMotorspeed(BiMotor *m, int s, bool forward)
{
    if (forward)
    {
        pwm_set_duty(m->slice, m->Bchan, 0);
        pwm_set_duty(m->slice, m->Fchan, s);
        m->forward = true;
    }
    else
    {
        pwm_set_duty(m->slice, m->Fchan, 0);
        pwm_set_duty(m->slice, m->Bchan, s);
        m->forward = true;
    }
    m->speed = s;
}

void BiMotorOn(BiMotor *m)
{
    pwm_set_enabled(m->slice, true);
    m->on = true;
}

void BiMotorOff(BiMotor *m)
{
    pwm_set_enabled(m->slice, false);
    m->on = false;
}

int main()
{
    BiMotor mot1;
    BiMotorInit(&mot1, 20, 21, 2000);

    BiMotorOn(&mot1);
    while (true)
    {
        BiMotorspeed(&mot1, 50, true);
        sleep_ms(2000);
        BiMotorspeed(&mot1, 25, false);
        sleep_ms(2000);
    }

    return 0;
}
```

This is a very basic set of functions, you can add others to improve motor control according to how sophisticated you want it to be. For example, a brake function would set both lines high for brake mode or you could introduce limits on how fast the speed can be changed.

There are H-bridges that use two lines to control Phase and Enable. These map to the usual Forward, Reverse and Enable as shown below:

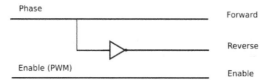

The disadvantage of this arrangement is that you cannot set Forward and Reverse to one to put the motor into brake mode. If you do have this sort of controller, anything based on the MAX14870/2 for example, then you can modify the functions to use a single PWM line and one standard GPIO line for speed and direction.

Using A Single Full H-Bridge As Two Half H-Bridges

It is easy to think of an H-bridge as being only for bidirectional control, but each full bridge is composed of two half bridges and this means a typical dual full H-bridge can control four unidirectional motors:

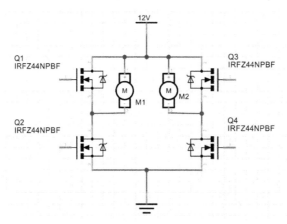

In this case Forward is now MotorM1 speed control and Reverse is now MotorM2 speed control. Any enable line has to be set high to allow the two motors to be controlled. You can make use of this arrangement with the unidirectional software given earlier.

Controlling a Servo

Hobby servos, of the sort used in radio control models, are very cheap and easy to use and they connect via a standard PWM protocol. Servos are not drive motors, but positioning motors. That is, they don't rotate at a set speed, they move to a specified angle or position.

A servo is a motor, usually a brushed DC motor, with a feedback sensor for position, usually a simple variable resistor (potentiometer) connected to the shaft. The output is usually via a set of gears which reduces the rotation rate and increases the torque. The motor turns the gears, and hence the shaft, until the potentiometer reaches the desired setting and hence the shaft has the required angle/position.

A basic servo has just three connections, ground, a power line and a signal line. The colors used vary, but the power line is usually red, ground is usually black or brown and the signal line is white, yellow or orange. If a standard J-connector is fitted then the wire nearest the notch, pin 3, is Signal, the middle wire, pin 2, is 5V and outer wire, pin 1, is Ground.

The power wire has to be connected to a 5V supply capable of providing enough current to run the motor - anything up to 500mA or more depending on the servo. The good news is that the servo's signal line generally needs very little current, although it does, in theory, need to be switched between 0 and 5V using a PWM signal.

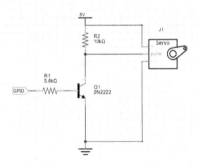

You can assume that the signal line needs to be driven as a voltage load and so the appropriate way to drive the servo is:

- ◆ The servo's + line needs to be connected to an external 5V power supply.
- ◆ The 10K resistor R1 can be a lot larger for most servos - 47K often works. The 5.6K resistor limits the base current to slightly less than 0.5mA.

Notice, however, that if you are using a single BJT driver, like the one shown above, the input is inverted.

This is the correct way to drive a servo, but in nearly all cases you can drive the servo signal line directly from the 3.3V GPIO line with a 1K resistor to limit the current if anything goes wrong with the servo. Some servos will even work with their motor connected to 3.3V, but at much reduced torque.

Now all we have to do is set the PWM line to produce 20ms pulses with pulse widths ranging from 0.5ms to 2.5ms – i.e. a duty cycle of 2.5 to 12.5%.

Once again, it is easier to use a struct to represent the current state of a servo and create functions to change the state:

```
typedef struct
{
    uint gpio;
    uint slice;
    uint chan;
    uint speed;
    uint resolution;
    bool on;
    bool invert;
} Servo;
```

This struct includes a field to specify an inversion of the output. Initialization is easy:

```
void ServoInit(Servo *s, uint gpio, bool invert)
{
    gpio_set_function(gpio, GPIO_FUNC_PWM);
    s->gpio = gpio;
    s->slice = pwm_gpio_to_slice_num(gpio);
    s->chan = pwm_gpio_to_channel(gpio);

    pwm_set_enabled(s->slice, false);
    s->on = false;
    s->speed = 0;
    s->resolution = pwm_set_freq_duty(s->slice, s->chan, 50, 0);
    pwm_set_dutyH(s->slice, s->chan, 250);
```

```
if (s->chan)
    {
        pwm_set_output_polarity(s->slice, false, invert);
    }
    else
    {
        pwm_set_output_polarity(s->slice, invert, false);
    }
    s->invert = invert;
}
```

Notice that we set the frequency to 50Hz. If you want to work with a non-standard servo you can change this or make it settable. We also need a higher accuracy version of the function to set the duty cycle. The function given earlier works with percentages, but as the percentage range for a servo is just 2.5% to 12.5% we need to specify two decimal places and so we need to work with percent*100:

```
void pwm_set_dutyH(uint slice_num, uint chan, int d)
{
    pwm_set_chan_level(slice_num, chan, pwm_get_wrap(slice_num) *
d / 10000);
}
```

With this in place we can write on/off and positioning functions:

```
void ServoOn(Servo *s)
{
    pwm_set_enabled(s->slice, true);
    s->on = true;
}

void ServoOff(Servo *s)
{
    pwm_set_enabled(s->slice, false);
    s->on = false;
}
void ServoPosition(Servo *s,uint p)
{
    pwm_set_dutyH(s->slice, s->chan, p*10+250);
}
```

The ServoPosition function sets the position in terms of percentages. That is ServoPosition(&s,50) sets the servo to the middle of its range. This assumes that the servo has a standard positioning range and most don't. In practice, to get the best out of a servo you need to calibrate each servo and discover what range of movement is supported.

The simplest servo program you can write is something like:

```
int main()
{
    Servo s1;
    ServoInit(&s1, 20, false);
    ServoOn(&s1);
    while (true)
    {
        ServoPosition(&s1, 0);
        sleep_ms(500);
        ServoPosition(&s1, 100);
        sleep_ms(500);
    }

    return 0;
}
```

This moves the servo to two positions, the minimum and the maximum, pausing between each.

If you run the program using the circuit given earlier, you will discover that the servo does nothing at all, apart perhaps from vibrating. The reason is that the transistor voltage driver is an inverter. When the PWM line is high the transistor is fully on and the servo's pulse line is effectively grounded. When the PWM line is low the transistor is fully off and the servo's pulse line is pulled high by the resistor. The solution is to use an inverted output from the GPIO line using:

```
ServoInit(&s1, 20, true);
```

It is worth mentioning that servos make good low-cost DC motors, complete with gearboxes. All you have to do is open the servo, unsolder the motor from the control circuits and solder two wires to the motor. If you want to use the forward/reverse electronics you can remove the end stops on the gearbox, usually on the large gearwheel, and replace the potentiometer with a pair of equal value resistors, 2.2kΩ, say.

Brushless DC Motors

Brushless DC motors are more expensive than brushed DC motors, but they are superior in many ways. They don't fail because of commutator or brush wear and need no maintenance. They provide maximum rotational torque at all points of the rotation and generally provide more power for the same size and weight. They can also be controlled more precisely. The only negative points are higher cost and slightly more complex operation. In practice, it is usually better to use a brushed DC motor unless you really need something extra.

A brushless DC motor is basically a brushed motor turned inside out – the stator is a set of electromagnets and the rotor is a set of permanent magnets. In some designs the permanent magnets are inside the stator in the manner of a brushed motor, an inrunner, and sometimes the magnets are outside of the stator, an outrunner.

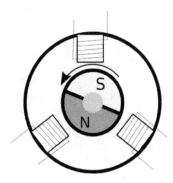

An inrunner – the permanent magnets form the rotor and the coils are switched to attract.

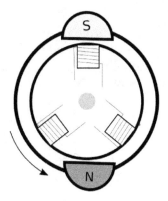

An outrunner – the permanent magnets are on the outside of the stator and the whole cover rotates.

A brushless motor works in exactly the same way as a brushed motor. As the coils are stationary there is no need for a mechanical commutator, but there is still need for commutation – the coils have to be switched on in sequence to create a rotating magnetic field which pulls the rotor around with it. This means that you have to implement an electronic commutator, which is another name for a brushless DC motor.

An electronic commutator has to sense the position of the rotor and change the magnetic field generated by the stator to keep the rotor moving. Brushless motors differ in the number of magnets they have and the number of phases. The most common is a three-phase motor as these are used in radio control modeling. Essentially you need at least a driver for each of the phases and a GPIO line to generate the signal. In practice, you need two drivers for each phase and they have to be driven from a dual supply so that the magnetic field can be positive, zero or negative.

This would be possible to do with software, but it isn't easy and a more reasonable alternative is to buy a ready-built controller. There are two types of brushless motor – with Hall sensors and without. The former are more expensive, but easier to control because the electronics always knows where the rotor is and can apply the correct drive. The ones without sensors are controlled by measuring the back EMF from the motor and this is much harder. Most of the lower-cost speed controllers need motors with Hall sensors.

The radio control community has taken to using three-phase brushless motors and this has resulted in a range of motors and controllers at reasonable prices intended as high-power, high-speed, unidirectional motors for use in quadcopters and model planes.

If you can live with their limitations they provide a good way to couple a Pico to a brushless motor. In this case all you need is a three-phase brushless motor of the sort used in RC modeling and an ESC (Electronic Speed Controller) of the sort shown below:

The three leads on the left go to the three phases of the motor and the red and black leads on the right go to a power supply – often a LiPo battery. The small three-wire connector in the middle is a standard servo connector and you can use it exactly as if the brushless motor was a servo, with a few exceptions. The first is that pin 2 supplies 5V rather than accepts it. Don't connect this to anything unless you want a 5V supply. The second problem is that ESCs are intelligent. When you first apply power they beep and can be programmed into different modes by changing the PWM signal from Max to Min. Also, to use an ESC you have to arm it. This is to avoid radio control modelers from being injured by motors that start unexpectedly when the power is applied. The most common arming sequence is for the ESC to beep when power is applied. You then have to set the PWM to Min, when the ESC will beep again. After a few moments you will have control of the motor.

The need for an arming procedure should alert you to the fact that these model motors are very powerful. Don't try working with one loose on the bench as it will move fast if switched on and at the very least make a twisted mess of your wires. Most importantly of all, don't run a motor with anything attached to it until you have everything under control.

Stepper Motors

There is one sort of brushless motor that is easy to use and low cost – the stepper motor. This differs from a standard brushless motor in that it isn't designed for continuous high-speed rotation. A stepper motor has an arrangement of magnets and coils such that powering some of the coils holds the rotor in a particular position. Changing which coils are activated makes the rotor turn until it is aligned with the coils and stops moving. Thus the stepper motor moves the rotor in discrete steps. This makes driving it much simpler, but note it doesn't use PWM for speed control. Stepper motors have no brushes and so don't wear out as fast as brushed motors. They also have roughly the same torque at any speed and can be used at low speeds without a gearbox. They can remain in a fixed position for a long time without burning out, as DC motors would. Unlike a servo, however, if a stepper motor is mechanically forced to a new position, it will not return to its original position when released.

The only disadvantage of a stepper motor is that the continuous rotation produced by repeated stepping can make the motor vibrate. Stepper motors vary in the size of step they use – typically 1.8 degrees giving 200 steps per rotation, although gearing can be used to reduce the step size. Another big difference is that the rotor is made up either of permanent magnets or soft iron. The first type is called a Permanent Magnet or PM stepper and the second is called a Variable Reluctance or VR and they differ in how you drive them with PM steppers being easier to understand. There are also hybrid steppers which share the good characteristics of both PM and VR stepper motors. These are more expensive and are generally only used where accuracy of positioning is important. They also differ in the number of phases, i.e. independent banks of coils, they have.

The diagram below shows a two-phase PM motor with Phase 1 activated:

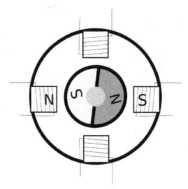

If Phase two is activated, the rotor turns through 90 degrees:

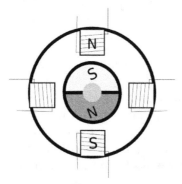

This is the simplest stepper motor you can make. A typical stepper motor will have many more coils than four, but they are usually connected into two or three phases.

Another big difference is bipolar versus unipolar. A bipolar motor is like the one shown in the diagram. To generate a north pole the current has to flow in the opposite direction to when you want to create a south pole. This means you have to drive each bank of coils with a bidirectional driver, e.g. an H-bridge. A unipolar motor has two windings, one in each direction, and both windings can be driven by a unidirectional driver – one giving a north pole and the other a south pole. Notice that a unipolar motor has twice the number of coils to drive and the switching sequence is slightly different.

A two-phase bipolar motor with Phases A and B would switch on in the sequence:

A → B → A- → B- → A etc

where the minus sign means the current flows the other way.

A two-phase unipolar motor has two coils per phase, A1, A2 and B1, B2 with the 1 and 2 windings creating opposite magnetic fields for the same current flow. Now the sequence is:

A1 → B1 → A2 → B2 → A1 etc

and all driven in the same direction.

Switching single phases fully on and off in sequence makes the motor make repeated steps. You can also switch on more than one phase at a time to generate micro-steps. For example, in our two-phase example, switching on two phases makes the rotor settle between the two, so producing a half micro-step:

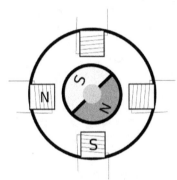

The driving sequence for a two-phase bipolar motor is:

A → AB → B → BA- → A- → A- B- → B- → AB- → A

with minus indicating that the coil is energized in the opposite direction, giving a total of eight, rather than four, steps.

You can even vary the current through the coils and move the rotor to intermediate positions. At the extreme limit you can vary the current sinusoidally and produce a smooth rotation. Micro-stepping is smoother and can eliminate buzzing. For high accuracy positioning, micro-stepping is a poor performer under load.

Stepper Motor Driver

How best to drive a stepper motor using a Pico? There are some specialized chips that work with unipolar and bipolar stepper motors. However, you can easily control a bipolar stepper motor using one the H-bridges described in the section on directional motor control.

For example, using complementary MOSFETS:

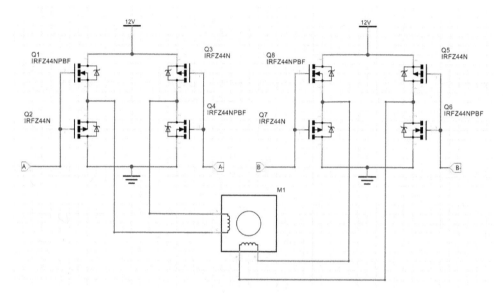

You can use a dual H-bridge module in the same way if you don't want to build it from scratch. The motor has to be a bipolar two-phase motor, often called a four-wire stepper motor. You can see that for this arrangement you need four GPIO lines, A, A-, B and B-.

What about driving the dual H-bridge using software? You need four GPIO lines and you need to pulse them in a specific phase to make the motor rotate. This could be done using the PIO, see Chapter 13, but it is easier to start with software-controlled GPIO lines. The first question to answer is how to specify the four GPIO lines to be used. As we will see, there is a big advantage and simplification in using a block of four consecutive lines. The reason is that we can easily set the bits corresponding to these lines in a mask and so set them in a single operation. In this case we simply record the number of the numerically lowest GPIO line.

As before, we use a struct to record the current state of the motor:

```
typedef struct
{
    uint gpio;
    uint speed;
    bool forward;
    uint32_t gpiomask;
    uint phase;
} StepperBi;
```

We also need an array that specifies the states of the four lines at each position of the motor. It is more efficient to create an array of masks needed to set the lines correctly:

```
uint32_t stepTable[8] =
        (uint32_t[8]){0x8, 0xC, 0x4, 0x6, 0x2, 0x3, 0x1, 0x9};


/*
    {1, 0, 0, 0},
    {1, 1, 0, 0},
    {0, 1, 0, 0},
    {0, 1, 1, 0},
    {0, 0, 1, 0},
    {0, 0, 1, 1},
    {0, 0, 0, 1},
    {1, 0, 0, 1}
*/
```

You can see that the array is just the hex value corresponding to the binary representation of which line is high and which is low in each state. The bits correspond to the GPIO lines such that the low order bits control the lowest numbered GPIO line. So for example, if we use GP28 as the first GPIO line the four lines are GP18, GP19, GP20 and GP21 and the first element of stepTable sets just GP21 to high.   You can see that if GP21 is A, GP20 is B, GP19 is A- and GP18 is B- and stepping through the stepTable gives the sequence given earlier:

A → AB → B → BA- → A- → A-B- → B- → AB- → A

We need a function to initialize the GPIO lines and the struct:

```
void StepperBiInit(StepperBi *s, uint gpio)
{
 s->gpio = gpio;

 for (int i = 0; i < 4; i++)
 {
 gpio_set_function((s->gpio) + i, GPIO_FUNC_SIO);
 gpio_set_dir((s->gpio) + i, true);
 }
 s->gpiomask = 0x0F << gpio;
 gpio_put_masked(s->gpiomask, stepTable[0] << gpio);
 s->phase = 0;
 s->speed = 0;
 s->forward = true;
}
```

This sets up the four GPIO lines to output and creates the mask needed to select them. It also places the stepper into state zero and initializes phase, speed and direction.

Now all we need are some methods to set and work with the phase:

```
void setPhase(StepperBi *s, uint p)
{
    uint32_t mask = stepTable[p] << (s->gpio);
    gpio_put_masked(s->gpiomask, mask);
}

void stepForward(StepperBi *s)
{
    s->phase = (s->phase + 1) % 8;
    setPhase(s, s->phase);
}

void stepReverse(StepperBi *s)
{
    s->phase = (s->phase - 1) % 8;
    setPhase(s, s->phase);
}
```

The setPhase function uses the gpio_put_masked function to change only the GPIO lines we are using to the bit pattern in the stepTable for the specified phase. The stepForward and stepReverse simply move down or up in the phase table, making sure to go back to the start when the end is reached. This is what the modulus operator, %, does for us and phase follows the sequence 0,1,2,3,4,5,6,7,0,1 and so on.

You can use a full step table if you want to as long as you remember to work in mod 4 rather than 8:

```
uint32_t stepTable[4] = (uint32_t[8]){0x8,0x4,0x2, 0x1};
/* [
            [1, 0, 0, 0],
            [0, 1, 0, 0],
            [0, 0, 1, 0],
            [0, 0, 0, 1],
        ]
*/
```

Of course, these are identical to the even elements of the half step table so we can achieve the same result by using that table but increasing the increment by 2 instead of 1:

```
void stepForward(StepperBi *s)
{
    s->phase = (s->phase + 2) % 8;
    setPhase(s, s->phase);
}

void stepReverse(StepperBi *s)
{
    s->phase = (s->phase - 2) % 8;
    setPhase(s, s->phase);
}
```

Putting all this together, we can write a program that rotates the stepper at a constant speed:

```
#include <stdio.h>
#include "pico/stdlib.h"

typedef struct
{
    uint gpio;
    uint speed;
    bool forward;
    uint32_t gpiomask;
    uint phase;
} StepperBi;
```

```c
uint32_t stepTable[8] =
            (uint32_t[8]){0x8, 0xC, 0x4, 0x6, 0x2, 0x3, 0x1, 0x9};
/*
    {1, 0, 0, 0},
    {1, 1, 0, 0},
    {0, 1, 0, 0},
    {0, 1, 1, 0},
    {0, 0, 1, 0},
    {0, 0, 1, 1},
    {0, 0, 0, 1},
    {1, 0, 0, 1}
*/
void StepperBiInit(StepperBi *s, uint gpio)
{
    s->gpio = gpio;
    for (int i = 0; i < 4; i++){
        gpio_set_function((s->gpio) + i, GPIO_FUNC_SIO);
        gpio_set_dir((s->gpio) + i, true);
    }
    s->gpiomask = 0x0F << gpio;
    volatile uint32_t mask = stepTable[0] << gpio;
    gpio_put_masked(s->gpiomask, mask);
    s->phase = 0;
    s->speed = 0;
    s->forward = true;
}

void setPhase(StepperBi *s, uint p)
{
    uint32_t mask = stepTable[p] << (s->gpio);
    gpio_put_masked(s->gpiomask, mask);
}
void stepForward(StepperBi *s)
{
    s->phase = (s->phase + 1) % 8;
    setPhase(s, s->phase);
}
void stepReverse(StepperBi *s)
{
    s->phase = (s->phase - 1) % 8;
    setPhase(s, s->phase);
}
void rotate(StepperBi *s, bool dir, int speed)
{
    s->forward = dir;
    s->speed = speed;
}
```

```
int main()
{
    stdio_init_all();
    StepperBi s1;
    StepperBiInit(&s1, 18);
    while (true)
    {
        stepForward(&s1);
        sleep_ms(1);
    }
    return 0;
}
```

In this case, H-bridge GP21 is A, GP20 is B, GP19 is A- and GP18 is B-. The stepping speed is such that a 200-step motor, i.e. 400 half steps, will rotate in 400*1 ms= 0.4 s, i.e. 2.5rpm, which is a good starting speed. Decrease the sleep time for a higher speed.

If you are using one of the many dual H-bridge modules then the wiring is as shown below:

Notice that you have to connect the ground of the power supply and the Pico's ground together. It is also a good idea to use a power supply with a current trip when first trying things out.

The logic analyzer reveals that the switching times are accurate and there is no measurable overlap between pulses:

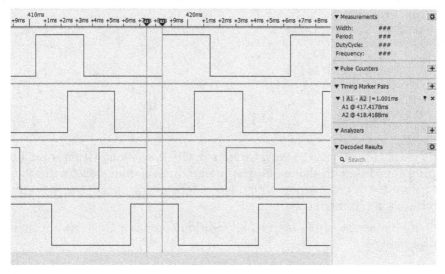

Stepper Motor Rotation – Using Timers

Most of the time you use a stepper motor to move to a given position by executing an exact number of steps. If you do want to make a stepper motor rotate then you need to arrange to step at a regular rate. The simplest way to do this with a Pico is to use a timer interrupt. There is a low-level set of functions allowing you to interact with the four hardware timers, but the higher-level repeating_timer set of functions is much easier to use for repeat interrupts.

The most useful functions are:

```
add_repeating_timer_us (int64_t delay_us,
      repeating_timer_callback_t callback,
          void *user_data, repeating_timer_t *out)

add_repeating_timer_ms (int32_t delay_ms,
      repeating_timer_callback_t callback,
          void *user_data, repeating_timer_t *out)

cancel_repeating_timer (repeating_timer_t *timer)
```

The first two add a repeating timer with a repeat time in microseconds or milliseconds. The second cancels a timer. The important points to note are that you need a repeating_timer struct to pass to each of these functions and this has to exist while the timer is running. The struct is used to record the details of the timer and you can mostly ignore it apart from the `user_data` field which can be used to pass data to the interrupt handler. The `callback` is a function that accepts a `repeating_timer` struct as its only parameter.

To make the motor rotate continuously we need to set up a timer which calls a `step` function at the correct interval:

```
bool step(struct repeating_timer *t)
{
    StepperBi *s = (StepperBi *)(t->user_data);
    if (s->forward)
    {
        stepForward(s);
    }
    else
    {
        stepReverse(s);
    }
    return true;
}
```

You can see that this function simply steps the motor forward or backward depending on the setting of the `dir` field. Notice that the stepper motor in use is determined by the `user_data` passed in. To make this work we need a function to set up the timer interrupt:

```
struct repeating_timer timer;

void rotate(StepperBi *s, bool dir, int speed)
{
    cancel_repeating_timer(&timer);
    s->forward = dir;
    if (speed == 0)
    {
        s->speed = 0;
        return;
    }
    s->speed = 1000 * 1000 / (4 * speed);
    add_repeating_timer_us(s->speed, step, s, &timer);
}
```

Notice that we have to deal with the case of speed set to zero separately to avoid a divide by zero exception. The speed is specified in rpm $*100$. So setting speed to 250 gives a rotation of 2.5rpm.

A main program to rotate the motor for 100ms at 2.5rpm and then stop it for another 100ms is:

```
int main()
{

    static StepperBi s1;
    StepperBiInit(&s1, 18);
    rotate(&s1, true, 250);
    while (true)
    {
        rotate(&s1, true, 250);
        sleep_ms(100);
        rotate(&s1, true, 00);
        sleep_ms(100);
    }
    return 0;
}
```

Notice that when the motor is stopped the phase is still active and so the motor is holds its position under power:

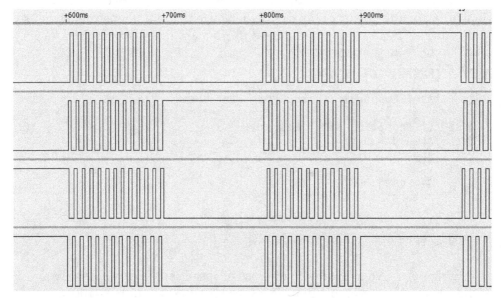

You can elaborate on this basic scheme to include more complex controls on the motor's behavior, including things like allowing it to freewheel and selecting full or half stepping.

The complete program including the timer interrupt handling is:

```c
#include <stdio.h>
#include "pico/stdlib.h"

typedef struct
{
 uint gpio;
 uint speed;
 bool forward;
 uint32_t gpiomask;
 uint phase;
} StepperBi;

uint32_t stepTable[8] =
     (uint32_t[8]){0x8, 0xC, 0x4, 0x6, 0x2, 0x3, 0x1, 0x9};
/*
    {1, 0, 0, 0},
    {1, 1, 0, 0},
    {0, 1, 0, 0},
    {0, 1, 1, 0},
    {0, 0, 1, 0},
    {0, 0, 1, 1},
    {0, 0, 0, 1},
    {1, 0, 0, 1}
*/
void StepperBiInit(StepperBi *s, uint gpio)
{
    s->gpio = gpio;

    for (int i = 0; i < 4; i++)
    {
        gpio_set_function((s->gpio) + i, GPIO_FUNC_SIO);
        gpio_set_dir((s->gpio) + i, true);
    }
    s->gpiomask = 0x0F << gpio;
    volatile uint32_t mask = stepTable[0] << gpio;
    gpio_put_masked(s->gpiomask, mask);
    s->phase = 0;
    s->speed = 0;
    s->forward = true;
}

void setPhase(StepperBi *s, uint p)
{
    uint32_t mask = stepTable[p] << (s->gpio);
    gpio_put_masked(s->gpiomask, mask);
}
```

```
void stepForward(StepperBi *s)
{
    s->phase = (s->phase + 1) % 8;
    setPhase(s, s->phase);
}

void stepReverse(StepperBi *s)
{
    s->phase = (s->phase - 1) % 8;
    setPhase(s, s->phase);
}

bool step(struct repeating_timer *t)
{
    StepperBi *s = (StepperBi *)(t->user_data);
    if (s->forward)
    {
        stepForward(s);
    }
    else
    {
        stepReverse(s);
    }
    return true;
}

struct repeating_timer timer;

void rotate(StepperBi *s, bool dir, int speed)
{
    cancel_repeating_timer(&timer);
    s->forward = dir;
    if (speed == 0)
    {
        s->speed = 0;
        return;
    }
    s->speed = 1000 * 1000 / (4 * speed);
    add_repeating_timer_us(s->speed, step, s, &timer);
}
```

```
int main()
{

    static StepperBi s1;
    StepperBiInit(&s1, 18);
    rotate(&s1, true, 250);
    while (true)
    {
        rotate(&s1, true, 250);
        sleep_ms(100);
        rotate(&s1, true, 00);
        sleep_ms(100);
    }
    return 0;
}
```

Summary

- There are a number of different types of electric motor, but DC brushed or brushless motors are the most used in the IoT.

- Brushed motors can be speed controlled using a single transistor driver and a PWM signal.

- For bidirectional control you need an H-bridge. In this case you need two PWM signals.

- Servo motors set their position in response to the duty cycle of a PWM signal.

- Brushless DC motors are very powerful and best controlled using off-the-shelf electronic modules. They are very powerful and thus dangerous if used incorrectly. They can be driven using a simple PWM signal.

- Stepper motors are a special case of a Brushless DC motor. They move in discrete steps in response to energizing different coils.

- A unipolar motor has coils that can be driven in the same direction for every step. A bipolar motor has coils that need to be driven in reverse for some steps.

- Bipolar motors need two H-bridges to operate and four GPIO lines.

- You can easily create a stepper motor driver using four GPIO lines.

Chapter 10

Getting Started With The SPI Bus

The Serial Peripheral Interface (SPI) bus can be something of a problem because it doesn't have a well-defined standard that every device conforms to. Even so, if you only want to work with one specific device it is usually easy to find a configuration that works - as long as you understand what the possibilities are.

SPI Bus Basics

The SPI bus is commonly encountered as it is used to connect all sorts of devices from LCD displays, through realtime clocks and A-to-D converters, but as different companies have implemented it in different ways, you have to work harder to implement it in any particular case. However, it does usually work, which is a surprise for a bus with no standard, or clear, specification.

The reason it can be made to work is that you can specify a range of different operating modes, frequencies and polarities. This makes the bus slightly more complicated to use, but generally it is a matter of looking up how the device you are trying to work with implements the SPI bus and then getting the Pico to work in the same way.

The SPI bus is odd in another way - it does not use bidirectional serial connections. There is a data line for the data to go from the master to the slave and a separate data line from the slave back to the master. That is, instead of a single data line that changes its transfer direction, there is one for data going out and one for data coming in. It is also worth knowing that the drive on the SPI bus is push-pull and not open-collector/drain. This provides higher speed and more noise protection as the bus is driven in both directions. There is a bidirectional mode, where a single wire is used for the data, and the Pico supports this.

In the configuration most used for the Pico, there is a single master and, at most, two slaves. The signal lines are:

♦ MOSI (Master Output Slave Input), i.e. data to the slave

♦ MISO (Master Input Slave Output), i.e. data to the master

♦ SCLK (Serial Clock), which is always generated by the master

In general, there can also be any number of SS (Slave Select), CE (Chip Enable) or CS (Chip Select) lines, which are usually set low to select which slave is being addressed. Notice that unlike other buses, I2C for example, there are no SPI commands or addresses, only bytes of data. However, slave devices do interpret some of the data as commands to do something or send some particular data.

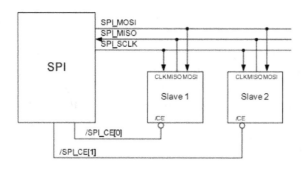

There are two other modes of operation of the SPI interface – bidirectional and LoSSI mode. The bidirectional mode simply uses a single data line, MIMO, for both input and output. The direction of the line is determined by writing a command to the slave. LoSSI mode is used to communicate with sophisticated peripherals such as LCD panels. Both of these are unsupported by the SDK and beyond the scope of this chapter. However, once you know how standard mode works, the other two are simple variations.

The data transfer on the SPI bus is also slightly odd. What happens is that the master pulls one of the chip selects low, which activates a slave. Then the master toggles the clock SCLK and both the master and the slave send a single bit on their respective data lines. After eight clock pulses, a byte has been transferred from the master to the slave and from the slave to the master. You can think of this as being implemented as a circular buffer, although it doesn't have to be.

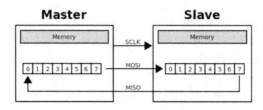

This full-duplex data transfer is often hidden by the software and the protocol used. For example, there is a read function that reads data from the slave and sends zeros or data that is ignored by the slave. Similarly, there is a write function that sends valid data, but ignores whatever the slave sends. The transfer is typically in groups of eight bits, usually most significant bit first, but this isn't always the case. In general, as long as the master supplies clock pulses, data is transferred.

Notice this circular buffer arrangement allows for slaves to be daisy-chained with the output of one going to the input of the next. This makes the entire chain one big circular shift register. This can make it possible to have multiple devices with only a single chip select, but it also means any commands sent to the slaves are received by each one in turn. For example, you could send a convert command to each A-to-D converter in turn and receive back results from each one.

The final odd thing about the SPI bus is that there are four modes which define the relationship between the data timing and the clock pulse. The clock can be either active high or low, which is referred to as clock polarity (CPOL), and data can be sampled on the rising or falling edge of the clock, which is clock phase (CPHA).

All combinations of these two possibilities gives the four modes:

SPI Mode*	Clock Polarity CPOL	Clock Phase CPHA	Characteristics
0	0	0	Clock active high data output on falling edge and sampled on rising
1	0	1	Clock active high data output on rising edge and sampled on falling
2	1	0	Clock active low data output on falling edge and sampled on rising
3	1	1	Clock active low data output on rising edge and sampled on falling

*The way that the SPI modes are labeled is common but not universal.

There is often a problem trying to work out what mode a slave device uses. The clock polarity is usually easy and the Clock phase can sometimes be worked out from the data transfer timing diagrams and:

- First clock transition in the middle of a data bit means CPHA=0
- First clock transition at the start of a data bit means CPHA=1

So to configure the SPI bus to work with a particular slave device:

1. Select the clock frequency - anything from 125MHz to 3.8kHz
2. Determine the CS polarity - active high or low
3. Set the clock mode Mode0 thru Mode3

Now we have to find out how to do this using the SDK.

Pico SPI Interfaces

The Pico has two SPI controllers, SPI0 and SPI1, that can work as a master or a slave. The connections from both controllers can be routed to different pins:

SPI0	MSIO	GP0	GP4	GP16	GP20
	CSn	GP1	GP5	GP17	GP21
	SCLK	GP2	GP6	GP18	GP22
	MOSI	GP3	GP7	GP19	GP23

SPI1	MSIO	GP8	GP12	GP24	GP28
	CSn	GP9	GP13	GP25	GP29
	SCLK	GP10	GP14	GP26	
	MOSI	GP11	GP15	GP27	

To select a pin to operate as an SPI pin all you have to do is use:

```
gpio_set_function(gpio, GPIO_FUNC_SPI);
```

For a full SPI interface you need to set the mode of one pin for one MSIO, one MOSI and one SCLK. The CSn lines are not really part of the SPI implementation. To make use of them you have to treat them like standard GPIO lines and set them high and low to select the device under program control. What this means is that you can use as many of the CSn lines with any SPI interface as you need.

The SPI Functions

Before you can make use of the SPI functions you have to include the header file:

```
#include "hardware/spi.h"
```

and you need to add the SPI library hardware_spi to the CMakeLists.txt file:

```
target_link_libraries(blinky pico_stdlib hardware_spi)
```

You might need to reconfigure the project and rebuild it.

The SPI functions can be grouped into initialization, configuration and data transfer. Let's look at each group in turn.

Initialization

There are two functions concerned with enabling and disabling the SPI bus:

```
spi_init (spi_inst_t *spi, uint baudrate)
spi_deinit (spi_inst_t *spi)
```

You can use `spi_init` to set the baud rate i.e. the clock rate, in Hertz.

It is worth mentioning at this point that the specification of the SPI controller is in terms of its hardware address rather than a 0/1 index. A macro is provided so that you can use SPI0 and SPI1 in place of the addressees. You can also use:

```
spi_get_index (spi_inst_t *spi)
```

to convert a hardware address to a 0/1 index.

Configuration

There are a number of functions that you can use to configure the way the bus works.

The `spi_set_baudrate` function is the best way of setting the baud rate because it returns the actual baud rate set, usually the closest clock rate:

```
uint  spi_set_baudrate (spi_inst_t *spi, uint baudrate)
```

The `spi_set_slave` function determines if the Pico will act as a master or slave. The default is master:

```
spi_set_slave (spi_inst_t *spi, bool slave)
```

The most important configuration function is:

```
spi_set_format (spi_inst_t *spi, uint data_bits, spi_cpol_t cpol,
                spi_cpha_t cpha, __unused spi_order_t order)
```

This lets you set the number of data bits, and the SPI mode. Notice that for the Pico the bit order can only be `SPI_MSB_FIRST`. The mode is set by specifying CPOL and CPHA using:

SPI_CPHA_0 = data latched on first clock transition

or:

SPI_CPHA_1 = data latched on second clock transition

together with:

SPI_CPOL_0 = clock active high

or:

SPI_CPOL_1 = clock active low

Data Transfer functions

Because of the way the SPI bus uses a full-duplex transfer, things are a little different from other buses when it comes to implementing functions to transfer data. The most basic transfer function is:

```
int spi_write16_read16_blocking (spi_inst_t *spi,
        const uint16_t *src, uint16_t *dst, size_t len)
```

The `src` and `dst` array have to be the same size as specified by the final parameter `len`. The `src` array is used for the data to be transmitted and the `dst` array is used for the data that is transmitted back. If you don't understand this idea of a send (source) and a receive (destination) array then see the discussion about how SPI works given earlier. Each of the arrays is composed of 16-bit elements, but only the number of bits specified in the configuration are actually sent. That is, if you set a `data_bits` to 8 then only the first eight bits of each array element are sent or received. The 16-bit half-words are used to accommodate situations where you are working with more than 8-bit transfers.

Notice that a call to any of the transfer functions is blocking, i.e. the function doesn't return until the transfer is complete. There is also no need for a timeout as all SPI transfers end after the number of clock pulses needed to transfer the specified data. Also all of the transfer functions return the number of elements read/written.

If you are only interesting in reading or writing data then you can use:

```
spi_write16_blocking (spi_inst_t *spi, const uint16_t *src, size_t
len)
spi_read16_blocking (spi_inst_t *spi, uint16_t repeated_tx_data,
uint16_t *dst, size_t len)
```

In the case of the write function the received data is simply discarded. The read function also has a parameter to specify what data you want sent. This is usually zero, but some slaves require a specific value to be sent even though it is, in principle, of no interest. Notice that both of these functions are just easier ways of calling `spi_write16_read16_blocking`.

There are also two 8-bit versions of the read/write functions:

```
spi_write_blocking (spi_inst_t *spi, const uint8_t *src, size_t len)

spi_read_blocking (spi_inst_t *spi, uint8_t repeated_tx_data,
                                    uint8_t *dst, size_t len)
```

These again are just simpler versions of `spi_write16_read16_blocking` using byte arrays rather than 16-bit arrays.

There is one final complication that you can mostly ignore. The SPI hardware is buffered. Both the MISO and MOSI connections have an 8-deep FIFO buffer and this means that you can send and receive data faster if the buffer isn't full or empty. To test the buffer's state you can use:

```
static size_t spi_is_readable(spi_inst_t * spi )
```

which returns non-zero if there is data waiting to be read and:

```
static size_t spi_is_writable(spi_inst_t * spi )
```

which returns non-zero if the buffer has space. You can use these two functions to minimize the effect of using blocking I/O functions.

Using the Data Transfer Functions

When you first start using SPI it can be difficult to get used to the idea that you send and receive data both at the same time. Indeed, you cannot receive data unless you send the same number of data elements.

The most basic of the transfer functions is spi_write16_read16_blocking and it makes the bidirectional transfer obvious. For example:

```
uint16_t wBuff[] = {'A' 'B' 'C'};
uint16_t rBuff[3];
int n = spi_write16_read16_blocking(spi0, wBuff, rBuff, 3);
```

This sends the three elements in wBuff and receives back three elements in rBuff. Whether the three elements in rBuff make any sense is a matter of what the slave sends back and they might be of no interest at all. If this is the case you might as well use:

```
uint16_t wBuff[] = {'A' 'B' 'C'};
int n=spi_write16_blocking(spi0, wBuff,3);
```

Whatever three elements the slave sends back are simply ignored. If you are using 8-bit transfers you can also use:

```
uint8_t wBuff[] = {'A' 'B' 'C'};
spi_write_blocking(spi0,wBuff,3);
```

In the same way, if what you transmit to the slave isn't of any interest, you could use:

```
uint16_t wBuff[] = {0};
uint16_t rBuff[3];
int n = spi_write16_read16_blocking(spi0, wBuff, rBuff, 3);
```

or

```
uint16_t rBuff[3];
int n=spi_read16_blocking(spi0, rBuff,3);
```

and if you are working with 8-bit data:

```
uint8_t rBuff[3];
spi_read_blocking(spi0,rBuff,3);
```

Using just these functions you should be able to deal with most SPI slaves.

Now we come to a subtle point. What is the difference between transferring multiple bytes and simply sending the bytes individually using multiple transfer calls? The answer is that each time you make a transfer call the chip select line should be activated, the data transferred and then deactivated. Using the buffer transfers, the chip select can be left active for the entire transfer, i.e. it isn't necessary to deactivate it between each byte. Sometimes this difference isn't important and you can transfer three bytes using three calls, or just one, to a transfer function. However, some slaves will abort the current multibyte operation if the chip select line is deactivated in the middle of a multibyte transfer. As the Pico requires you to activate and deactivate the chip select line manually, it is up to you to make the distinction between single and multibyte transfers.

It is important to realize that the nature of the transfer is that the first element is sent at the same time that the first element is received. That is, unlike other protocols, the whole of the send buffer isn't sent before the received data comes back. The entire transfer works a data element at a time – the first element is sent while the first element is being received, then the second element is sent at the same time as the second element is being received and so on. Not fully understanding this idea can lead to some interesting bugs.

A Loopback Example

Because of the way that data is transferred on the SPI bus, it is very easy to test that everything is working without having to add any components. All you have to do is connect MOSI to MISO so that anything sent is also received in a loopback mode.

First we have to select which pins to use and this is fairly arbitrary at this stage so we might as well use:

```
SPI0    MSIO    GP4    pin 6
        SCLK    GP6    pin 9
        MOSI    GP7    pin 10
```

We can ignore the CS line at the moment as it isn't used in a loopback. First connect pin 6 to pin 10 using a jumper wire and start a new project.

186

The program is very simple. First we initialize the SPI bus and select a clock rate of 500kHz:

```
spi_init(spi0, 500 * 1000);
```

and set the GPIO lines we are using to SPI mode:

```
gpio_set_function(4, GPIO_FUNC_SPI);
gpio_set_function(6, GPIO_FUNC_SPI);
gpio_set_function(7, GPIO_FUNC_SPI);
```

Next we configure the interface:

```
spi_set_format(spi0, 8, SPI_CPOL_0, SPI_CPHA_0, SPI_MSB_FIRST);
```

We are using 8-bit data and SPI mode 0.

Next we can send some data and receive it right back:

```
uint8_t read_data = bcm2835_spi_transfer(0xAA);
```

The hex value AA is useful in testing because it generates the bit sequence 10101010 which is easy to see on a logic analyzer.

Check that the received data matches the sent data:

```
uint16_t wBuff[1] = {0xAA};
uint16_t rBuff[1];
int n = spi_write16_read16_blocking(spi0, wBuff, rBuff, 1);
```

Finally we close the bus:

```
spi_deinit(spi0);
```

Putting all of this together gives us the complete program (remember to add hardware_spi to the CMakeLists.txt file):

```
#include <stdio.h>
#include "pico/stdlib.h"
#include "hardware/spi.h"

int main()
{
    stdio_init_all();
    spi_init(spi0, 500 * 1000);
    gpio_set_function(4, GPIO_FUNC_SPI);
    gpio_set_function(6, GPIO_FUNC_SPI);
    gpio_set_function(7, GPIO_FUNC_SPI);
    spi_set_format(spi0, 8, SPI_CPOL_0, SPI_CPHA_0, SPI_MSB_FIRST);
    uint16_t wBuff[1] = {0xAA};
    uint16_t rBuff[1];
    int n = spi_write16_read16_blocking(spi0, wBuff, rBuff, 1);
    spi_deinit(spi0);
    printf(" %X %X %d ", wBuff[0], rBuff[0], n);
}
```

If you run the program and don't get any data received back then the most likely reason is that you have connected the wrong two pins or not connected them at all.

If you connect a logic analyzer to the three pins involved – 4, 6 and 7, you will see the data transfer:

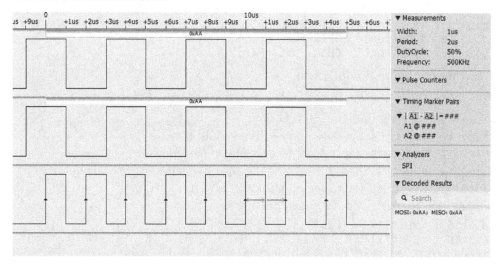

Using The CS Line

Of course there is no CS line activity on the logic analyzer because, unlike many SPI implementations, the Pico doesn't automatically control the CS line. It is up to you to initialize a CS line as a standard GPIO line and set it as appropriate during the data transfer.

For example, let's add GP5:

```
SPI0    MSIO    GP4    pin 6
        CSn     GP5    pin 7
        SCLK    GP6    pin 9
        MOSI    GP7    pin 10
```

Notice that there is no real reason to use GP5, any of the possible CSn pins would do.

Using CS active low we first have to initialize the GPIO line to output and set it high:

```
gpio_init(5);
gpio_set_dir(5, GPIO_OUT);
gpio_put(5, 1);
```

Now we can use the CS line to activate the slave by setting it low before starting the transfer and then setting it back high again afterwards:

```
gpio_put(5, 0);
int n = spi_write16_read16_blocking(spi0, wBuff, rBuff, 5);
gpio_put(5, 1);
```

If you try this out you might notice that there is a problem if you examine what is happening very carefully. The setting of the CS line occurs about $0.7\mu s$ after the first edge of the final clock pulse. This means that the CS line goes high just before the transfer is complete.

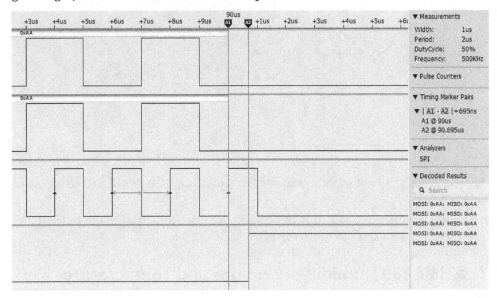

For many devices this doesn't make any difference, but it is safer to include a delay to make sure that the CS line goes high again after the end of the final clock pulse. To do this accurately you need to compute the time remaining to the end of the pulse and this depends on the clock frequency. You can set a delay using:

```
int clock = 100 * 1000;
spi_init(spi0, clock);

...

int csDelay = 1000000 / 2/clock;
gpio_put(5, 0);
int n = spi_write16_read16_blocking(spi0, wBuff, rBuff, 5);
sleep_us(csDelay);
gpio_put(5, 1);
```

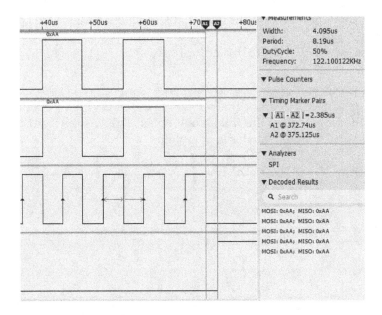

Alternatively, if speed of data transfer isn't an issue, you could just use a fixed delay of a few microseconds.

In the next chapter we will put together some functions that make the SPI bus and the CS lines easier to work with.

The BME280 Humidity, Pressure and Temperature Sensor

As an example of getting to grips with a real SPI device, we can write some code to get data from the commonly used BME280 sensor. You can also use the earlier BMP280, which is register-compatible but doesn't have a humidity sensor. Both work as an SPI and an I2C device and some of their operations as an SPI device are compromised relative to their performance as an I2C device. The BME280 is also the subject of a complete example in the Pico's SDK which implements a full interface, including the correction of raw data values. In this section we will simply implement a basic read of the raw data to show how it is done. If you want to use the device in a real application you will need the additional functions in the SDK example – or implement them yourself.

To make the SDK example easier to use we will connect the device using the same GPIO pins:

PICO	BME280
GP16 (pin 21) MISO/spi0_rx	SDO/SDO
GP17 (pin 22) Chip Select	CSB/!CS
GP18 (pin 24) SCK/spi0_sclk	SCL/SCK
GP19 (pin 25) MOSI/spi0_tx	SDA/SDI
3.3v (pin 36)	VCC
GND (pin 38)	GND

Notice that what the pins are called on a typical BME280 board varies, but you should be able to identify them.

Once you have the device connected what you need to know to send and receive data via the SPI bus varies according to the device and you have little choice but to find and read the datasheet. In this case the important table is the "memory map":

Register Name	Address	bit7	bit6	bit5	bit4	bit3	bit2	bit1	bit0	Reset state
hum_lsb	0xFE				hum_lsb<7:0>					0x00
hum_msb	0xFD				hum_msb<7:0>					0x80
temp_xlsb	0xFC		temp_xlsb<7:4>			0	0	0	0	0x00
temp_lsb	0xFB				temp_lsb<7:0>					0x00
temp_msb	0xFA				temp_msb<7:0>					0x80
press_xlsb	0xF9		press_xlsb<7:4>			0	0	0	0	0x00
press_lsb	0xF8				press_lsb<7:0>					0x00
press_msb	0xF7				press_msb<7:0>					0x80
config	0xF5		t_sb[2:0]			filter[2:0]			spi3w_en[0]	0x00
ctrl_meas	0xF4		osrs_t[2:0]			osrs_p[2:0]		mode[1:0]		0x00
status	0xF3					measuring[0]			im_update[0]	0x00
ctrl_hum	0xF2							osrs_h[2:0]		0x00
calib26..calib41	0xE1...0xF0				calibration data					individual
reset	0xE0				reset[7:0]					0x00
id	0xD0				chip_id[7:0]					0x60
calib00..calib25	0x88...0xA1				calibration data					individual

Registers:	Reserved registers	Calibration data	Control registers	Data registers	Status registers	Chip ID	Reset
Type:	do not change	read only	read / write	read only	read only	read only	write only

The important registers for our simple implementation are the first eight data registers which give the raw values of humidity, temperature and pressure. These are all read-only registers and the way that these work on the SPI bus is that first you write the address of the register you want to read and then you read as many bytes as you need. The address is auto-incremented each time you read, so sending the first address followed by eight reads transfers the contents of all of the registers.

There is one other detail to note. The most significant bit of the address byte is used to indicate a read or write operation – it has to be set to 1 for a read. If it is zero then the bytes that you send following the address are stored in the registers – the data registers are read-only. Notice that all the registers already have bit 7 set in their usual addresses and there is no need to do anything extra for a read.

So a read operation is typically:

		Control byte	Data byte	Data byte	
Start	RW	Register address (F6h)	Data register - address F6h	Data register - address F7h	Stop
CSB = 0	1	1 1 1 0 1 1 0	bit15 bit14 bit13 bit12 bit11 bit10 bit9 bit8	bit7 bit6 bit5 bit4 bit3 bit2 bit1 bit0	CSB = 1

and a write operation is:

		Control byte	Data byte		Control byte	Data byte	
Start	RW	Register address (F4h)	Data register - address F4h	RW	Register address (F5h)	Data register - adress F5h	Stop
CSB = 0	0	1 1 1 0 1 0 0	bit7 bit6 bit5 bit4 bit3 bit2 bit1 bit0	0	1 1 1 0 1 0 1	bit7 bit6 bit5 bit4 bit3 bit2 bit1 bit0	CSB = 1

Notice that the operation is started by lowering the CS line and stopped by raising the CS line. You can read or write as many values as you like and you can send another address to start the operation off at a different location.

If you look at the detailed specification of the SPI bus you will find that the CS line has to be low at least 20ns before the first clock pulse and has to remain low until at least 20ns after the final clock pulse. It also limits the clock to less than 10Mhz.

This is enough information to start to create some functions that will read the BME280's raw data registers. First we need to set the SPI hardware and the GPIO lines correctly:

```
spi_init(spi0, 500 * 1000);
gpio_set_function(16, GPIO_FUNC_SPI);
gpio_set_function(18, GPIO_FUNC_SPI);
gpio_set_function(19, GPIO_FUNC_SPI);
```

The CS line has to be set high before we start:

```
gpio_init(17);
gpio_set_dir(17, GPIO_OUT);
gpio_put(17, 1);
```

As a proof that the SPI bus is working, the first thing to try is to read the ID register which is at address 0xD0 and which returns a single byte giving the id number which should be 0x60 for the BME280 and 0x58 for the BMP280.

```
uint16_t wBuff[1] = {0xD0};
uint16_t rBuff[8];

gpio_put(17, 0);
spi_write_blocking(spi0, wBuff, 1);
sleep_ms(10);
spi_read_blocking(spi0, 0, rBuff, 1);
sleep_us(1);
gpio_put(17, 1);

printf("Chip ID is 0x%x\n", rBuff[0]);
```

As long as this works we can move on to read the raw data. If it doesn't work then either you have connected the device incorrectly or the device is broken.

We first have to set up what measurements we want to make and exactly how. This is controlled by two registers - 0xF4 controls pressure and temperature and 0xF2 controls humidity. You can see how the different bits in these registers set the accuracy and rate of measurement in the datasheet, but for general use we can set both registers using:

```
    gpio_put(17, 0);
    sleep_us(1);
    wBuff[0] = 0xF2;
    wBuff[1] = 0x1;
    spi_write_blocking(spi0, wBuff, 2);
    wBuff[0] = 0xF4;
    wBuff[1] = 0x27;
    spi_write_blocking(spi0, wBuff, 2);
    gpio_put(17, 1);
    sleep_us(1);
```

This sets the humidity, temperature and pressure measurement to x1 over-sampling and normal mode sampling, which reads the sensors at a regular interval set by another register.

To read the raw data we can use the same technique of writing a register address, but this time we read eight items of data:

```
wBuff[0]=0xF7;
gpio_put(17, 0);
spi_write_blocking(spi0, wBuff, 1);
sleep_ms(10);
spi_read_blocking(spi0, 0, rBuff, 8);
sleep_us(1);
gpio_put(17, 1);
```

We can now put the bytes read from the device together to get the three readings:

```
uint32_t pressure = ((uint32_t) rBuff[0] << 12) |
                    ((uint32_t) rBuff[1] << 4) | (rBuff[2] >> 4);
uint32_t temperature = ((uint32_t) rBuff[3] << 12) |
                    ((uint32_t) rBuff[4] << 4) | (rBuff[5] >> 4);
uint32_t humidity = (uint32_t) rBuff[6] << 8 | rBuff[7];
```

Putting all this together with some `printf` statements to display the data gives the complete program (remember to add hardware_spi to the CMakeLists.txt file):

```
#include <stdio.h>
#include "pico/stdlib.h"
#include "hardware/spi.h"

int main()
{
    stdio_init_all();
    spi_init(spi0, 500 * 1000);
    spi_set_format(spi0, 8, SPI_CPOL_0, SPI_CPHA_0, SPI_MSB_FIRST);

    gpio_set_function(16, GPIO_FUNC_SPI);
    gpio_set_function(18, GPIO_FUNC_SPI);
    gpio_set_function(19, GPIO_FUNC_SPI);
    gpio_init(17);
    gpio_set_dir(17, GPIO_OUT);
    gpio_put(17, 1);
    sleep_ms(1);
    uint8_t wBuff[1] = {0xD0};
    uint8_t rBuff[8];

    gpio_put(17, 0);
    sleep_us(1);
    spi_write_blocking(spi0, wBuff, 1);
    spi_read_blocking(spi0, 0, rBuff, 1);
    sleep_us(1);
    gpio_put(17, 1);
    printf("Chip ID is 0x%x\n", rBuff[0]);
    gpio_put(17, 0);
    sleep_us(1);
    wBuff[0] = 0xF2;
    wBuff[1] = 0x1;
    spi_write_blocking(spi0, wBuff, 2);
    wBuff[0] = 0xF4;
    wBuff[1] = 0x27;
    spi_write_blocking(spi0, wBuff, 2);
    gpio_put(17, 1);
    sleep_us(1);
```

```
    wBuff[0] = 0xF7;
    gpio_put(17, 0);
    sleep_us(1);
    spi_write_blocking(spi0, wBuff, 1);

    spi_read_blocking(spi0, 0, rBuff, 8);
    sleep_us(1);
    gpio_put(17, 1);

    uint32_t pressure = ((uint32_t)rBuff[0] << 12) |
            ((uint32_t)rBuff[1] << 4) | (rBuff[2] >> 4);
    uint32_t temperature = ((uint32_t)rBuff[3] << 12) |
            ((uint32_t)rBuff[4] << 4) | (rBuff[5] >> 4);
    uint32_t humidity = (uint32_t)rBuff[6] << 8 | rBuff[7];

    printf("Humidity = %d\n", humidity);
    printf("Pressure = %d\n", pressure);
    printf("Temp. = %d\n", temperature);
}
```

If you try this out you will be disappointed to discover that the raw values aren't easy to interpret as real values. They are readings from the internal A-to-D converter and they have to be converted using the compensation formulas before they can be used.

Of course, it makes sense to factor out into functions the repetitive parts of the code to make it easier to extend the program. In particular, a read_registers function is sensible and this is used in the SDK example:

```
static void read_registers(uint8_t reg, uint8_t *buf, uint16_t len)
{
    gpio_put(17, 0);
    spi_write_blocking(spi_default, &reg, 1);
    spi_read_blocking(spi_default, 0, buf, len);
    sleep_us(1);
    gpio_put(17, 1);
    sleep_ms(10);
}
```

If you want to make use of the BME280 for accurate measurements then it is essential that you read the compensation data and use it to compute corrected values. This isn't difficult, but the calculations are complicated and you can find them fully implemented in the example included in the SDK. Now that you know the general logic of working with the device, the rest should be easier to understand.

Problems

The SPI bus is often a real headache because of the lack of a definitive standard, but in most cases you can make it work. The first problem is in discovering the characteristics of the slave device you want to work with. In general, this is solved by a careful reading of the datasheet or perhaps some trial and error, see the next chapter for an example.

If you are working with a single slave then generally things work once you have the SPI bus configuration set correctly. Things are more difficult when there are multiple devices on the same bus. The Pico has enough CS lines to handle eight devices, more if you only want to use a single SPI interface. Typically you will find SPI devices that don't switch off properly when they are not being addressed. In principle, all SPI devices should present high impedance outputs (i.e. tri-state buffers) when not being addressed, but some don't. If you encounter a problem you need to check that the selected slave is able to control the MISO line properly.

Summary

- The SPI bus is often problematic because there is no SPI standard.

- Unlike other serial buses, it makes use of unidirectional connections.

- The data lines are MOSI (master output slave input) and MISO (master input slave output).

- In addition, there is a clock line, output from master, and a number of select lines that you have to drive under program control.

- Timing for the select lines is a problem as you have to include a delay that makes sure that it remains low until the end of the final clock pulse.

- Data is transferred from the master to the slave and from the slave to the master on each clock pulse, arranged as a circular buffer.

- The Pico has two SPI devices which can work with almost any of the GPIO lines.

- The SDK provides all the functions you need to set up the SPI bus and transfer data one byte or multiple bytes at a time.

- You can test the SPI bus using a simple loopback connection.

- Working with a single slave is usually fairly easy, working with multiple slaves can be more of a problem.

- The BME280 is included as a complete example as part of the SDK but serves as a good example of how the SPI bus works.

Chapter 11

A-To-D and The SPI Bus

The SPI bus can be difficult to make work at first, but once you know what to look for about how the slave claims to work it gets easier. To demonstrate how it is done, let's add eight channels of 12-bit A-to-D using the MCP3008.

The Pico has a single A-to-D Converter (ADC) with analog inputs, four of which can be used via external pins. Before moving on to look at the use of SPI to add more A-to-D converters, let's take a look at those the Pico already has. If you are only interested in the detail of using the SPI bus, skip to that section.

Pico ADC

The Pico has a single onboard ADC which has four multiplexed inputs. Three are available on the external pins and one is used for an internal temperature sensor. You can see from the diagram that pins GP26, GP27, GP28 and GP29 can be used as analog inputs.

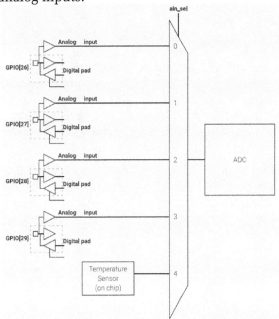

The ADC is a successive approximation converter. You don't need to know how it works to use it, but it isn't difficult to understand. The input voltage is compared to a standard voltage, VREF. The idea is that first a voltage equal to VREF/2 is generated and the input voltage is compared to this. If it is lower then the most significant bit is a 0 and if it is equal or greater then it is a 1. At the next step the voltage generated is VREF/2+VREF/4 and the comparison is repeated to generate the next bit. Successive approximation converters are easy to build, but they are slow. The Pico's ADC needs 96 clock cycles to create a 12-bit result, which gives a maximum sampling rate of 500kS/s with a default clock of 48MHz.

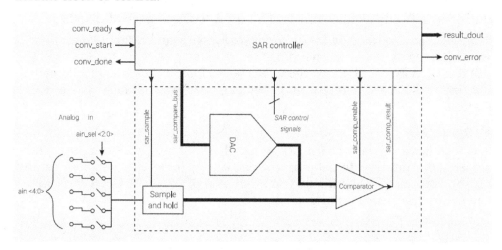

The Pico's ADC is very useful, but it isn't as accurate as you might hope. Although it has 12 bits, the claimed effective accuracy is only 9 bits and most of this loss of precision is due to the way the reference voltage is supplied and to noise due to its integration with other digital devices. According to the documentation, you can improve the accuracy by modifying the reference voltage:

> For much improved ADC performance, an external 3.0V shunt reference, such as LM4040, can be connected from the ADC_VREF pin to ground. Note that if doing this the ADC range is limited to 0-3.0V signals (rather than 0-3.3V), and the shunt reference will draw continuous current through the 200R filter resistor (3.3V-3.0V)/200 = ~1.5mA.

The ADC can be set to do conversions continuously, reading each of the possible inputs in a round-robin fashion, storing the results in an 8-deep FIFO (the documentation says 4-deep) buffer. Alternatively, you can simply start a conversion on a given input when you need the data.

The simplest way of using the ADC is to perform a single read of a single input under software control. Before making use of it, you have to initialize it:

```
adc_init (void)
```

You also have to initialize the pins you are going to use in a special analog input mode:

```
adc_gpio_init (uint gpio)
```

 and select the ADC input used with that GPIO line:

```
adc_select_input (uint input)
```

You can include the internal temperature sensor as an input using:

```
adc_set_temp_sensor_enabled(bool enable)
```

Once you have selected the input you are going to read, you can start a conversion and get the result using:

```
static uint16_t adc_read (void)
```

The simplest A-to-D program you can write is:

```
#include <stdio.h>
#include "pico/stdlib.h"
#include "hardware/adc.h"
int main()
{
 stdio_init_all();
 adc_init();
 adc_gpio_init(26);
 adc_gpio_init(27);

 while (1) {
   const float conversion_factor = 3.3f / (1 << 12);
   adc_select_input(0);
   uint16_t result = adc_read();
   printf("Raw value 0: 0x%03x, voltage: %f V\n",
                        result, result * conversion_factor);
   adc_select_input(1);
   result = adc_read();
   printf("Raw value 1: 0x%03x, voltage: %f V\n",
                        result, result * conversion_factor);
   sleep_ms(500);
 }
}
```

You also need to add `hardware_adc` to the `CmakeLists.txt` file:

```
target_link_libraries(MyProg pico_stdlib hardware_adc)
```

You have to initialize each of the GPIO lines you want to use. Then you can select which input to read and read it.

Reading the ADC in this way is often the best way to work, but occasionally you need to read the inputs one after another. In this case the fact that there is a buffer that can store four readings comes in useful.

To set round-robin mode you need to use:

```
adc_set_round_robin (uint input_mask)
```

The mask specifies which inputs are included in the measurement in the obvious way - bit 0 controls input 0 and so on. You also have to set up the way the FIFO buffer works:

```
adc_fifo_setup(bool en,bool dreq_en,uint16_t  dreq_thresh,bool
err_in_fifo, bool byte_shift )
```

The first parameter enables the FIFO. The next two and the final parameter set up DMA to transfer results automatically from the buffer to another location and this is beyond the scope of this book. The fourth parameter determines if bit 15 of the result is used for an error flag.

Once you have set the inputs to be read, you can use:

```
adc_run (bool run)
```

which starts the automatic reading. Each reading is stored in the FIFO buffer. If you don't read the buffer to retrieve a value then it just sits there until the buffer fills and it is discarded. Notice the buffer doesn't contain the last four readings, but the first read before the buffer fills.

You can read the buffer using:

```
static uint16_t adc_fifo_get (void)
static uint16_t adc_fifo_get_blocking (void)
```

The difference is that the blocking function will wait until there is data ready to read.

You can also find out the state of the buffer using:

```
static bool adc_fifo_is_empty (void)
static uint8_t adc_fifo_get_level (void)
```

and you can empty the buffer using:

```
adc_fifo_drain (void)
```

The simplest round-robin-reading program is:

```c
#include <stdio.h>
#include "pico/stdlib.h"
#include "hardware/adc.h"

int main()
{
    stdio_init_all();

    adc_init();
    adc_gpio_init(26);
    adc_gpio_init(27);
    adc_set_round_robin(0x03);
    adc_fifo_setup(true,false,0,false,false);
    adc_run(true);
    const float conversion_factor = 3.3f / (1 << 12);
    while (1)
    {
        uint16_t result = adc_fifo_get();
        printf("Raw value 0: 0x%03x, voltage: %f V\n",
                       result, result * conversion_factor);
        int level = adc_fifo_get_level();
        printf("level: %d \n", level);
    }
}
```

This just reads inputs 0 and 1 as fast as possible, given the need to print the results. If you try this out you will see that you do get input 0 followed by input 1 reported alternately, but you will also see that the level reported is always 8. This is because the time to print the values takes longer than a conversion and the buffer fills and values are discarded.

You can slow down the clock rate, and hence the conversion rate, by setting the clock divider:

```c
adc_set_clkdiv (float clkdiv)
```

The divider is a 16-bit integer with a 4-bit fractional part. With the default 48MHz clock the slowest sampling rate is approximately one sample every 1.366ms or 732 samples per second.

Even if you add:

```c
adc_set_clkdiv((float)0xFFFF);
```

to the program you will still find that you cannot read and print the result quickly enough to avoid the buffer overflowing. This isn't unreasonable as the idea of using an automatic system is to record data faster than the Pico could normally process it.

If you are going to rely on the round-robin-reading method you need to make use of some even more advanced features of the ADC to implement either an IRQ handler or a DMA transfer of data. To enable the IRQ handler you need to use:

```
adc_irq_set_enabled (bool enabled)
```

The interrupt is active when the buffer reaches the threshold set for a DMA transfer, even if DMA isn't in use.

The MCP3008 SPI ADC

An alternative to using the Pico's built-in ADC with its noise and stability problems is to use an external chip. The MCP3000 family is a low-cost versatile SPI-based set of A-to-D converters. Although the MCP3008, with eight analog inputs at 10-bit precision, and the MCP3004, with four analog inputs at 10-bit precision, are the best known, there are other devices in the family, including ones with 12-bit and 13-bit precision and differential inputs, at around the same sort of cost - $1 to $2.

In this chapter the MCP3008 is used because it is readily available and provides a good performance at low cost, but the other devices in the family work in the same way and could be easily substituted.

The MCP3008 is available in a number of different packages but the standard 16-pin PDIP is the easiest to work with using a prototyping board. You can buy it from the usual sources including Amazon, see Resources on this book's webpage. Its pinouts are fairly self-explanatory:

```
CH0 ▢1        16▢ V_DD
CH1 ▢2        15▢ V_REF
CH2 ▢3   M    14▢ AGND
CH3 ▢4   C    13▢ CLK
CH4 ▢5   P    12▢ D_OUT
CH5 ▢6   3    11▢ D_IN
CH6 ▢7   0    10▢ CS/SHDN
CH7 ▢8   0    9▢  DGND
         8
```

You can see that the analog inputs are on the left and the power and SPI bus connections are on the right. The conversion accuracy is claimed as 10 bits, but how many of these bits correspond to reality and how many are noise depends on how you design the layout of the circuit.

You need to take great care if you need high accuracy. For example, you will notice that there are two voltage inputs, VDD and VREF. VDD is the supply voltage that runs the chip and VREF is the reference voltage that is used to compare the input voltage. Obviously, if you want highest accuracy, VREF, which has to be lower than or equal to VDD, should be set by an accurate low-noise voltage source. However, in most applications VREF and VDD are simply connected together and the usual, low- quality, supply voltage is used as the reference. If this isn't good enough then you can use anything from a

Zener diode to a precision voltage reference chip such as the TL431. At the very least, however, you should add a 1μF capacitor to ground connected to the VDD pin and the VREF pin.

The MC3000 family is based on the same type of ADC as the Pico's built-in device, a successive approximation converter.

You can see that successive approximation fits in well with a serial bus as each bit can be obtained in the time needed to transmit the previous bit. However, the conversion is relatively slow and a sample-and-hold circuit has to be used to keep the input to the converter stage fixed. The sample-and-hold takes the form of a 20pF capacitor and a switch. The only reason you need to know about this is that the conversion has to be completed in a time that is short compared to the discharge time of the capacitor. So, for accuracy, there is a minimum SPI clock rate as well as a maximum.

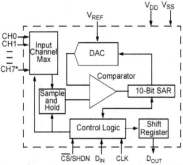

Also, to charge the capacitor quickly enough for it to follow a changing voltage, it needs to be connected to a low-impedance source. In most cases this isn't a problem, but if it is you need to include an op amp. If you are using an op amp buffer then you might as well implement an anti-aliasing filter to remove frequencies from the signal that are too fast for the ADC to respond to. How all this works takes us into the realm of analog electronics and signal processing and well beyond the core subject matter of this book.

You can also use the A-to-D channels in pairs, i.e. in differential mode, to measure the voltage difference between them. For example, in differential mode you measure the difference between CH0 and CH1, i.e. what you measure is CH1-CH0. In most cases, you want to use all eight channels in single-ended mode. In principle, you can take 200k samples per second, but only at the upper limit of the supply voltage, i.e. VDD=5V, falling to 75k samples per second at its lower limit of VDD=2.7V.

The SPI clock limits are a maximum of 3.6MHz at 5V and 1.35MHz at 2.7V. The clock can go slower, but because of the problem with the sample-and-hold mentioned earlier, it shouldn't go below 10kHz. How fast we can take samples is discussed later in this chapter.

Connecting To The Pico

The connection from the MCP3008 to the Pico's SPI bus is very simple and can be seen in the diagram below.

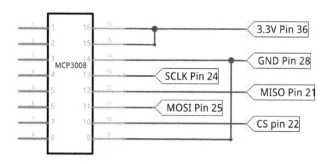

Pico	MCP3008
GPIO 16 (pin 21) MISO	Pin 12
GPIO 17 (pin 22) Chip Select	Pin 10
GPIO 18 (pin 24) SCLK	Pin 13
GPIO 19 (pin 25) MOSI	Pin 11
3.3v (pin 36)	Pins 15 and 16
GND (pin 38)	Pins 14 and 9

The only additional component that is recommended is a $1\mu F$ capacitor connected between pins 15 and 16 to ground, which is mounted as close to the chip as possible. As discussed in the previous section, you might want a separate voltage reference for pin 15 rather than just using the 3.3V supply.

Basic Configuration

Now we come to the configuration of the SPI bus. We have some rough figures for the SPI clock speed - around 10kHz to a little more than 1.35MHz. So a clock frequency of 500kHz seems a reasonable starting point.

From the datasheet, the chip select has to be active low and, by default, data is sent most significant bit first for both the master and the slave. The only puzzle is what mode to use? This is listed in the datasheet as mode 0 0 with clock active high or mode 1 1 with clock active low. For simplicity we will use mode 0 0.

We now have enough information to initialize the slave:

```
spi_init(spi0, 500 * 1000);
spi_set_format (spi0,8, SPI_CPOL_0,SPI_CPHA_0, SPI_MSB_FIRST);
gpio_set_function(16, GPIO_FUNC_SPI);
gpio_set_function(18, GPIO_FUNC_SPI);
gpio_set_function(19, GPIO_FUNC_SPI);

gpio_init(17);
gpio_set_dir(17, GPIO_OUT);
gpio_put(17, 1);
```

The Protocol

Now we have the SPI initialized and ready to transfer data, but what data do we transfer? As already discussed in the previous chapter, the SPI bus doesn't have any standard commands or addressing structure. Each device responds to data sent in different ways and sends data back in different ways. You simply have to read the datasheet to find out what the commands and responses are.

Reading the datasheet might be initially confusing because it says that you have to send five bits to the slave - a start bit, a bit that selects its operating mode single or differential, and a 3-bit channel number. The operating mode is 1 for single-ended and 0 for differential.

So to read Channel 3, i.e. 011, in single-ended mode you would send the slave:

11011xxx

where an x can take either value. In response, the slave holds its output in a high impedance state until the sixth clock pulse, then sends a zero bit on the seventh, followed by bit 9 of the data on the eighth clock pulse.

That is, the slave sends back:

xxxxxx0b9

where x means indeterminate. The remaining nine bits are sent back in response to the next nine clock pulses. This means you have to transfer three bytes to get all ten bits of data. This all makes reading the data in 8-bit chunks confusing.

The datasheet suggests a different way of doing the job that delivers the data more neatly packed into three bytes. What it suggests to send a single byte is:

00000001

At the same time, the slave transfers random data, which is ignored. The final 1 is treated as the start bit. If you now transfer a second byte with most significant bit indicating single or differential mode, then a 3-bit channel address and the remaining bits set to 0, the slave will respond with the null and the top two bits of the conversion. Now all you have to do to get the final eight bits of data is to read a third byte:

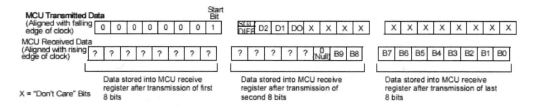

This way you get two neat bytes containing the data with all the low-order bits in their correct positions.

Using this information we can now write some instructions that read a given channel. For example, to read Channel 0 we first send a byte set to 0x01 as the start bit and ignore the byte the slave transfers. Next we send 0x80 to select single-ended and Channel 0 and keep the byte the slave sends back as the two high-order bits. Finally, we send a zero byte (0x00) so that we get the low-order bits from the slave:

```
uint16_t wBuff[3] = {0x01, 0x80, 0x00};
uint16_t rBuff[3];
gpio_put(17, 0);
int n = spi_write16_read16_blocking(spi0, wBuff, rBuff, 3);
sleep_us(1);
gpio_put(17, 1);
```

Notice you cannot send the three bytes one at a time using transfer because that results in the CS line being deactivated between the transfer of each byte.

To get the data out of rBuff we need to do some bit manipulation:

```
int data = ((int)rBuff[1] & 0x03) << 8 | (int)rBuff[2];
```

The first part of the expression extracts the low three bits from the first byte the slave sent and, as these are the most significant bits, they are shifted up eight places. The rest of the bits are then ORed with them to give the full 10-bit result. To convert to volts we use:

```
float volts = (float) data * 3.3f / 1023.0f;
```

assuming that VREF is 3.3V.

In a real application you would also need to convert the voltage to some other quantity, like temperature or light level.

If you connect a logic analyzer to the SPI bus you will see something like:

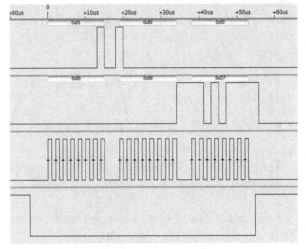

You can see the commands and the response, in this case a reading of 0.693V.

The complete program is (remember to add hardware_spi to the CMakeLists.txt file):

```c
#include <stdio.h>
#include "pico/stdlib.h"
#include "hardware/spi.h"
int main()
{
    stdio_init_all();
    spi_init(spi0, 500 * 1000);
    spi_set_format(spi0, 8, SPI_CPOL_0, SPI_CPHA_0, SPI_MSB_FIRST);
    gpio_set_function(16, GPIO_FUNC_SPI);
    gpio_set_function(18, GPIO_FUNC_SPI);
    gpio_set_function(19, GPIO_FUNC_SPI);
    gpio_init(17);
    gpio_set_dir(17, GPIO_OUT);

    gpio_put(17, 1);
    sleep_ms(1);
    uint16_t wBuff[3] = {0x01, 0x80, 0x00};
    uint16_t rBuff[3];
    gpio_put(17, 0);
    int n = spi_write16_read16_blocking(spi0, wBuff, rBuff, 3);
    sleep_us(1);
    gpio_put(17, 1);
    int data = ((int)rBuff[1] & 0x03) << 8 | (int)rBuff[2];
    float volts = (float)data * 3.3f / 1023.0f;
    printf("%f V\n", volts);
}
```

Some Packaged Functions

This all works, but it would be good to have a function that read the ADC on a specified channel:

```
float readADC(uint8_t chan)
{
    uint16_t wBuff[] = {0x01, (0x08 | chan) << 4, 0x00};
    uint16_t rBuff[3];
    gpio_put(17, 0);
    int n = spi_write16_read16_blocking(spi0, wBuff, rBuff, 3);
    sleep_us(1);
    gpio_put(17, 1);
    int data = ((int)rBuff[1] & 0x03) << 8 | (int)rBuff[2];
    return (float)data * 3.3f / 1023.0f;
}
```

Notice that this only works if the SPI bus has been initialized and set up correctly. An initialization function is something like:

```
void SPI_init()
{
    spi_init(spi0, 500 * 1000);
    spi_set_format(spi0, 8, SPI_CPOL_0, SPI_CPHA_0, SPI_MSB_FIRST);
    gpio_set_function(16, GPIO_FUNC_SPI);
    gpio_set_function(18, GPIO_FUNC_SPI);
    gpio_set_function(19, GPIO_FUNC_SPI);

    gpio_init(17);
    gpio_set_dir(17, GPIO_OUT);
    gpio_put(17, 1);
    sleep_ms(1);
}
```

With these two functions, the main program is very simple:

```
int main()
{
    stdio_init_all();
    SPI_init();
    float volts = readADC(0);
    printf("%f V\n", volts);
}
```

How Fast

Once you have the basic facilities working, the next question is always how fast does something work. In this case we need to know what sort of data rates we can achieve using this ADC. The simplest way of finding this out is to use the fastest read loop for a channel:

```
for(;;){
    int data=readADC(0x5);
}
```

With the clock of 500kHz the sampling rate is measured to be 17kHz. This is perfectly reasonable as it takes at least 24 clock pulses to read the data. Most of the time in the loop is due to the 24 clock pulses, so there is little to be gained from optimization.

Increasing the clock rate to 1MHz pushes the sampling rate to 32kHz, which is just fast enough to digitize audio, as long as you don't waste too much time in the loop in processing.

Changing the clock rate to 2Mhz pushes the sampling up to 55kHz, which is fast enough for most audio, but notice that this is more than the recommended clock rate at 3.3V.

Also notice that as the clock rate goes up, you have to ensure that the voltage source is increasingly low-impedance to allow the sample-and-hold to charge in a short time.

Summary

- The Pico has a single ADC with four inputs. It is subject to a lot of noise from the power supply and circuits around it which reduces its accuracy.

- You can read individual input lines or set a round-robin read to make regular measurements.

- Making SPI work with any particular device has four steps:

  1. Discover how to connect the device to the SPI pins. This is a matter of identifying pinouts and mostly what chip selects are supported.

  2. Find out how to configure the Pi's SPI bus to work with the device. This is mostly a matter of clock speed and mode.

  3. Identify the commands that you need to send to the device to get it to do something and what data it sends back as a response.

  4. Find, or work out, the relationship between the raw reading, the voltage and the quantity the voltage represents.

- The MCP3000 range of A-to-D converters is very easy to use via SPI.

- You can read data at rates as fast as 55kHz which is fast enough for some audio applications.

Chapter 12

Using The I2C Bus

The I2C, standing for I-Squared-C or Inter IC, bus is one of the most useful ways of connecting moderately sophisticated sensors and peripherals to any processor. The only problem is that it can seem like a nightmarish confusion of hardware, low-level interaction and high-level software. There are few general introductions to the subject because at first sight every I2C device is different, but there are shared principles that can help you work out how to connect and talk to a new device.

The I2C bus is a serial bus that can be used to connect multiple devices to a controller. It is a simple bus that uses two active wires: one for data and one for a clock. Despite there being lots of problems in using the I2C bus, because it isn't well standardized and devices can conflict and generally do things in their own way, it is still commonly used and too useful to ignore.

The big problem in getting started with the I2C bus is that you will find it described at many different levels of detail, from the physical bus characteristics and protocol to the details of individual devices. It can be difficult to relate all of this together and produce a working project. In fact, you only need to know the general workings of the I2C bus, some general features of the protocol, and know the addresses and commands used by any particular device.

To explain and illustrate these idea we really do have to work with a particular device to make things concrete. However, the basic stages of getting things to work, the steps, the testing and verification, are more or less the same irrespective of the device.

I2C Hardware Basics

The I2C bus is very simple from the hardware point of view. It has just two signal lines, SDA and SCL, the data and clock lines respectively. Each of these lines is pulled up by a suitable resistor to the supply line at whatever voltage the devices are working - 3.3V and 5V are common choices. The size of the pull-up resistors isn't critical, but 4.7K is typical as shown in the circuit diagram.

You simply connect the SDA and SCL pins of each of the devices to the pull-up resistors. Of course, if any of the devices have built-in pull-up resistors you can omit the external resistors. More of a problem is if multiple devices each have pull-ups. In this case you need to disable all but one.

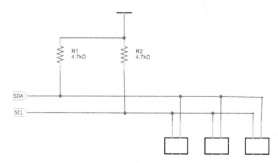

The I2C bus is an open collector bus. This means that it is actively pulled down by a transistor set to on. When the transistor is off, however, the bus returns to the high voltage state via the pull-up resistor. The advantage of this approach is that multiple devices can pull the bus low at the same time. That is, an open collector bus is low when one or more devices pulls it low and high when none of the devices is active.

The SCL line provides a clock which is used to set the speed of data transfer, one data bit is presented on the SDA line for each pulse on the SCL line. In all cases, the master drives the clock line to control how fast bits are transferred. The slave can, however, hold the clock line low if it needs to slow down the data transfer. In most cases the I2C bus has a single master device, the Pico in our case, which drives the clock and invites the slaves to receive or transmit data. Multiple masters are possible, but this is advanced and usually not necessary.

All you really need to know is that all communication usually occurs in 8-bit packets. The master sends a packet, an address frame, which contains the address of the slave it wants to interact with. Every slave has to have a unique address, which is usually 7 bits, but it can be 10 bits, and the Pico does support this. In the rest of this chapter we will use 7-bit addressing because it is commonly supported.

One of the problems in using the I2C bus is that manufacturers often use the same address, or same set of selectable addresses, and this can make using particular combinations of devices on the same bus difficult or impossible.

The 7-bit address is set as the high-order 7 bits in the byte and this can be confusing as an address that is stated as 0x40 in the datasheet results in 0x80 being sent to the device. The low-order bit of the address signals a write or a read operation depending on whether it is a 0 or a 1 respectively. After sending an address frame it then sends or receives data frames back from the slave. There are also special signals used to mark the start and end of an exchange of packets, but the library functions take care of these.

This is really all you need to know about I2C in general to get started, but it is worth finding out more of the details as you need them. You almost certainly will need them as you debug I2C programs.

The clock SCL and data SDA lines rest high. The master signals a Start bit by pulling the SDA line down – S in the diagram below. The clock is then pulled low by the master, during which time the SDA line can change state. The bit is read in the middle of the following high period of the clock pulse B1, B2 and so on in the diagram. This continues until the last bit has been sent when the data line is allowed to rise while the clock is high, so sending a stoP bit – P in the diagram. Notice that when data is being transmitted the data line doesn't change while the clock is high. Any change in the data line when the clock is high sends a start or a stop bit, i.e. clock high and falling data line is a start bit and clock high and rising data line is a stop bit:

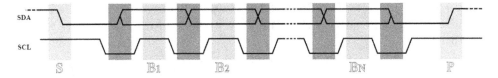

The clock speed was originally set at 100kHz, standard mode, but then increased to 400kHz in fast mode. In practice, devices usually specify a maximum clock speed that they will work with.

The Pico I2C

The Pico has two I2C controllers, I2C0 and I2C1, that can work as a master or a slave. The connections from both controllers can be routed to different pins:

I2C0	SDA	GP0	GP4	GP8	GP12	GP16	GP20		GP28
	SCL	GP1	GP5	GP9	GP13	GP17	GP21		

I2C1	SDA	GP2	GP6	GP10	GP14	GP18	GP22	GP26
	SCL	GP3	GP7	GP11	GP15	GP19		GP27

To select a pin to operate as an SPI pin all you have to do is use:

```
gpio_set_function(gpio, GPIO_FUNC_I2C);
```

For a full I2C interface, you need to set the mode of one pin for one SDA and one SCL. You should ensure that only one GPIO line is enabled for a particular I2C function. You also either have to set the GPIO lines to pull-up or preferably provide an external pull-up resistor.

The I2C Functions

There are I2C functions for initialization, configuration and for writing and reading to the registers. Let's look at each group in turn.

Initialization

There are two functions concerned with enabling and disabling the I2C bus:

```
uint   i2c_init (i2c_inst_t *i2c, uint baudrate)
i2c_deinit (i2c_inst_t *i2c)
```

You can use the i2c_init function to set the baud rate, i.e. the clock rate, in Hertz.

It is worth mentioning at this point that the specification of the I2C controller is in terms of its hardware address rather than an 0/1 index. A macro is provided so that you can use i2c0 and ic21 in place of the addressees. You can also use:

```
static uint i2c_hw_index (i2c_inst_t *i2c)
```

to convert a hardware address to a 0/1 index.
You also need to add:
```
#include "hardware/i2c.h"
```
and edit CMakeLists.txt to include:
```
target_link_libraries(myProg pico_stdlib hardware_i2c)
```

Configuration

There are a number of functions that you can use to configure the way the bus works.

The i2ci_set_baudrate function is the best way of setting the baud rate because it returns the actual baud rate set, usually the closest clock rate.

```
uint i2c_set_baudrate (i2c_inst_t *i2c, uint baudrate)
```

The Pico doesn't support the most recent high speed modes and the maximum clock rate is 1MHz.

The i2c_set_slave function determines if the Pico will act as a master or slave. The default is master.

```
i2c_set_slave_mode (i2c_inst_t *i2c, bool slave, uint8_t addr)
```

You also have to specify the address that the slave will respond to.

Write

There are a number of very similar write functions in the SDK. The most basic is:

```
int i2c_write_blocking (i2c_inst_t *i2c, uint8_t addr,
                const uint8_t *src, size_t len, bool nostop)
```

The first parameter specifies the I2C hardware to use and the second gives the address of the slave you are trying to write to. The next two specify a buffer of bytes to be sent and its length. The return value is the number of bytes written.

The final parameter, nostop, needs some explanation. When you use this function it first sends an address frame, a byte containing the address of the device you specified. Notice that the 7-bit address has to be shifted into the topmost bits and the first bit has to be zeroed for a write operation. So when you write to a device with an address of 0x40, you will see 0x80 on a logic analyzer, i.e. 0x40<<1. After the address frame as many data frames are sent as specified in src and len.

The final parameters control how the stop bit is sent or not. The usual write transaction is:

```
START|ADDR|ACK|DATA0|ACK|
          DATA1|ACK|
            . . . .
        DATAn|ACK|STOP
```

Notice that it is the slave that sends the ACK bit and, if the data is not received correctly, it can send NAK instead. Also notice that there is a single STOP bit at the end of the transaction and this is what you get if you set nostop to false. If you set nostop to true then the final stop bit isn't sent and the next data transfer can continue as part of the same transaction.

Notice that multibyte transfer is quite different from sending single bytes one at a time:

```
START|  ADDR  |ACK|DATA0|ACK|STOP
START|  ADDR  |ACK|DATA1|ACK|STOP
      . . .
START|  ADDR  |ACK|DATAn|ACK|STOP
```

Notice that there are now multiple ADDR frames sent as well as multiple START and STOP bits. What this means in practice is that you have to look at a device's datasheet and send however many bytes it needs as a single operation. You cannot rely on being able to send the same number of bytes broken into chunks.

The other write functions work in the same way but with slight variations. There are two functions which allow you to specify a timeout:

```
int i2c_write_timeout_us (i2c_inst_t *i2c, uint8_t addr,
                    const uint8_t *src, size_t len,
                        bool nostop, uint timeout_us)
int i2c_write_blocking_until (i2c_inst_t *i2c, uint8_t addr,
                    const uint8_t *src, size_t len,
                        bool nostop, absolute_time_t until)
```

The first specifies the timeout in microseconds and the second will time out when a time is reached.

The hardware also supports a 16-element buffer on both receive and send. The standard functions make use of this by default and hence return immediately if the buffers aren't full. You can find the state of the write buffer using:

```
static size_t i2c_get_write_available (i2c_inst_t *i2c)
```

and you can send data to the buffer using:

```
i2c_write_raw_blocking (i2c_inst_t *i2c,
                        const uint8_t *src, size_t len)
```

Writing To A Register

A very standard interaction between master and slave is writing data to a register. This isn't anything special and, as far as the I2C bus is concerned, you are simply writing raw data. However, datasheets and users tend to think in terms of reading and writing internal storage locations, i.e. registers in the device. In fact, many devices have lots of internal storage, indeed some I2C devices, for example I2C EPROMS, are nothing but internal storage.

In this case a standard transaction to write to a register is:

1. Send address frame
2. Send a data frame with the command to select the register
3. Send a data frame containing the byte, or word, to be written to the register

So, for example, you might use:

```
uint8_t buf[]={registerAddress,data};
int i2c_write_blocking (i2c, addr,buf,2, false);
```

Notice the command that has to be sent depends on the device and you have to look it up in its datasheet. Also notice that there is a single START and STOP bit at the beginning and end of the transaction.

Read

The read functions are similar to the write functions. The most important is:

```
int i2c_read_blocking (i2c_inst_t *i2c, uint8_t addr,
                            uint8_t *dst, size_t len, bool nostop)
```

and the parameters mean the same things as for the corresponding write function. This sends an address frame and then reads as many bytes from the slave as specified. As in the case of write, the address supplied is shifted up one bit and the lower-order bit set to 1 to indicate a read operation. So, if the current slave is at address 0x40, the read sends a read address of 0x81 – this is important to remember if you are viewing the transaction on a logic analyzer.

The main problem with the simple read function is that, if the slave doesn't send the data, it can block forever. There are two timeout functions:

```
static int i2c_read_timeout_us (i2c_inst_t *i2c, uint8_t addr,
                    uint8_t *dst, size_t len,
                    bool nostop, uint timeout_us)
int i2c_read_blocking_until (i2c_inst_t *i2c, uint8_t addr,
                    uint8_t *dst, size_t len,
                    bool nostop, absolute_time_t until)
```

The first will time out after the specified number of microseconds and the second times out when the time is reached.

The read channel has a 16-element buffer and you can determine how many free entries there are using:

```
static size_t i2c_get_read_available (i2c_inst_t *i2c)
```

and you can send data directly to the buffer using:

```
i2c_read_raw_blocking (i2c_inst_t *i2c, uint8_t *dst, size_t len)
```

The read transaction is:

```
START|ADDR|ACK|DATA0|ACK|
             |DATA1|ACK|
             |DATA2|ACK|
        . . .
             |DATAn|NAK|STOP
```

The master sends the address frame and the slave sends the ACK after the address to acknowledge that it has been received and it is ready to send data. Then, the slave sends bytes, one at a time, and the master sends ACK in response to each byte. Finally, the master sends a NAK to indicate that the last byte has been read and then a STOP bit. That is, the master controls how many bytes are transferred.

As in the case of the write functions, a block transfer of n bytes is different from transferring n bytes one at a time and you can suppress the final stop bit by setting nostop to true.

Reading A Register

As for writing to a register, reading from a register is a very standard operation, but it is slightly more complicated in that you need both a write and a read operation. That is, to read a register you need a write operation to send the address of the register to the device and then a read operation to get the data that the device sends as the contents of the register. So, for example, you would use something like:

```
char buf[]={registerAddress};
i2c_write_blocking(i2c0, 0x40, buf, 1, false);
i2c_read_blocking(i2c0, 0x40, buf, 1, false);
```

If the register sends multiple bytes then you can usually read these one after another as a block transfer without sending an address frame each time. Notice that we don't suppress the stop bit between the read and the write to make it a single transaction.

In theory, and mostly in practice, a register read of this sort can work with a stop-start separating the write and the read operation, which is what you get if you use separate write and read function calls without suppressing the stop bit. That is, the transfer sequence is:

```
START|ADDR|ACK|REGADDR|ACK|STOP|
START|ADDR|ACK|DATA1|ACK|
            |DATA2|ACK|

            . . .
            |DATAn|NAK|STOP
```

If you look at the end of the write and the start of the read using a logic analyzer, you will see that there is a STOP and START bit between them.

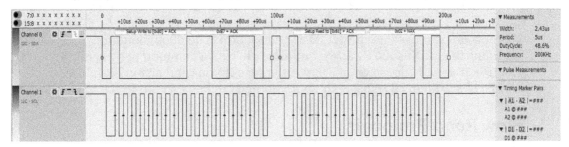

For some devices this is a problem. A STOP bit is a signal that another transaction can start and this might allow another master to take over the bus. To avoid this some devices demand a repeated START bit between the write and the read and no STOP bit. This is referred to as a "repeated start bit" or a "restart" transaction.

The sequence for a repeated start bit register read is:

```
START|ADDR|ACK|REGADDR|ACK|
START|ADDR|ACK|DATA0|ACK|
             |DATA1|ACK|
    ...
             |DATAn|NAK|STOP
```

Notice that there is only one STOP bit.

In theory, either form of transaction should work, but in practice you will find that some slave devices state that they need a repeated start bit and no stop bits in continued transactions. In this case you need to be careful how you send and receive data. For example, to read a register from a device that requires repeated START bits but no STOP bit you would use:

```
char buf[]={registerAddress};
i2c_write_blocking(i2c0, 0x40, buf, 1, true);
i2c_read_blocking(i2c0, 0x40, buf, 1, false);
```

You can see in the logic analyzer display that there is now just a single START bit between the write and the read.

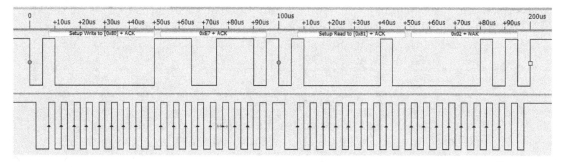

Very few devices need a repeated start transaction. The documentation mentions the MLX90620 IR array, but this is hardly a common peripheral. In practice, it usually doesn't make any difference if you send a stop bit in the middle of a write/read transaction, but you need to know about it just in case.

Slow Read Protocols

The I2C clock is mostly controlled by the master and this raises the question of how we cope with the speed that a slave can or cannot respond to a request for data.

There are two broad approaches to waiting for data on the I2C bus. The first is simply to request the data and then perform reads in a polling loop. If the device isn't ready with the data, then it sends a data frame with a NAK bit set.

In this case the SDK read function returns a negative error value rather than the number of bytes read. So all we have to do is test for a negative response. Of course, the polling loop doesn't have to be "tight". The response time is often long enough to do other things and you can use the I2C bus to work with other slave devices while the one you activated gets on with trying to get the data you requested. All you have to do is to remember to read its data at some later time.

The second way is to allow the slave to hold the clock line low after the master has released it – so called "clock stretching". In most cases the master will simply wait before moving on to the next frame while the clock line is held low. This is very simple and it means you don't have to implement a polling loop, but also notice that your program is frozen until the slave releases the clock line.

Many devices implement both types of slow read protocol and you can use whichever suits your application.

A Real Device

Using an I2C device has two problems - the physical connection between master and slave and figuring out what the software has to do to make it work. Here we'll work with the HTU21D/Si7021 and the information in its datasheet to make a working temperature humidity sensor using the I2C functions we've just met.

 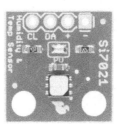

First the hardware. The HTU21D Humidity and Temperature sensor is one of the easiest of I2C devices to use. Its only problem is that it is only available as a surface-mount package. To overcome this you could solder some wires onto the pads or buy a general breakout board. However, it is much simpler to buy the HTU21D breakout board because this has easy connections and built-in pull-up resistors. The HTU21D has been replaced by the Si7021, which is more robust than the original and works in the same way, but the HTU21D is still available from many sources.

If you decide to work with some other I2C device you can still follow the steps given, modifying what you do to suit it. In particular, if you select a device that only works at 5V you might need a level converter.

Given that the HTU21D has pull-up resistors you don't need to enable the onboard pull-ups provided by the Pico. If you notice any irregularity in the signal at higher frequencies then adding some additional pull-ups might help.

You can use a prototype board to make the connections and this makes it easier to connect other instruments such as a logic analyzer. Given that the pinouts vary according to the exact make of the device, you need to compare the suggested wiring with the breakout board you are actually using.

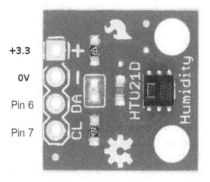

Pico	HTU21
SDA GP4 pin 6	SDA/DA
SCK GP5 pin 7	SCL/CL
3.3v pin 36	VCC/VIN/+
GND pin 38	GND/-

First Program

After wiring up any I2C device, the first question that needs to be answered is, does it work? Unfortunately for most complex devices finding out if it works is a multi-step process. Our first program aims to read some data back from the HTU21D, any data will do.

If you look at the datasheet you will find that the device address is 0x40 and that it supports the following commands/registers:

Command	Code	Comment
Trigger Temperature Measurement	0xE3	Hold master
Trigger Humidity Measurement	0xE5	Hold master
Trigger Temperature Measurement	0xF3	No Hold master
Trigger Humidity Measurement	0xF5	No Hold master
Write user register	0xE6	
Read user register	0xE7	
Soft Reset	0xFE	

The easiest of these to get started with is the Read user register command. The user register gives the current setup of the device and can be used to set the resolution of the measurement.

Notice that the codes that you send to the device can be considered as addresses or commands. In this case you can think of sending 0xE7 as a command to read the register or the read address of the register, it makes no difference. In most cases, the term "command" is used when sending the code makes the device do something, and the term "address" is used when it simply makes the device read or write specific data.

To read the user register we have to write a byte containing 0xE7 and then read the byte the device sends back. This involves sending an address frame, a data frame, and then another address frame and reading a data frame. The device seems to be happy if you send a stop bit between each transaction or just a new start bit.

A program to read the user register is fairly easy to put together. The address of the device is 0x40, so its write address is 0x80 and its read address is 0x81. Recall that bus addresses are shifted one bit to the left and the base address is the write address and the read address is base address+1.

As the I2C functions adjust the address as needed, we simply use `0x40` as the device's address, but it does affect what you see if you sample the data being exchanged (remember to add hardware_i2c to the CMakeLists.txt file):

```
#include <stdio.h>
#include "pico/stdlib.h"
#include "hardware/i2c.h"

int main()
{
    stdio_init_all();

    i2c_init(i2c0, 100 * 1000);

    gpio_set_function(4, GPIO_FUNC_I2C);
    gpio_set_function(5, GPIO_FUNC_I2C);
    uint8_t buf[] = {0xE7};

    i2c_write_blocking(i2c0, 0x40, buf, 1, false);
    i2c_read_blocking(i2c0, 0x40, buf, 1, false);
    printf("User Register = %X \r\n", buf[0]);
}
```

This sends the address frame `0x80` and then the data byte `0xE7` to select the user register. Next it sends an address frame `0x81` to read the data.

If you run the program you will see:

```
Register = 2
```

This is the default value of the register and it corresponds to a resolution of 12 bits and 14 bits for the humidity and temperature respectively and a supply voltage greater than 2.25V.

The I2C Protocol In Action

If you have a logic analyzer that can interpret the I2C protocol connected, what you will see is:

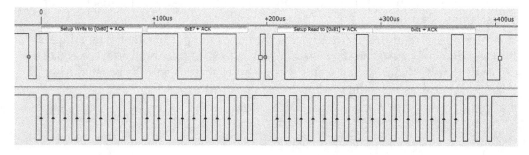

You can see that the `write_byte` function sends an address packet set to the device's 7-bit address `0x40` as the high-order bits with the low-order bit set to zero to indicate a write, i.e `0x80`. After this you get a data packet sent containing `0xE7`, the address of the register. After a few microseconds it sends the address frame again, only this time with the low-order bit set to 1 to indicate a read. It then receives back a single byte of data from the device, `0x02`. Also notice the start and stop bits at the end of each byte.

This all demonstrates that the external device is working properly and we can move on to getting some data of interest.

Reading The Raw Temperature Data

Now we come to reading one of the two quantities that the device measures – temperature. If you look back at the command table you will see that there are two possible commands for reading the temperature:

Command	Code	Comment
Trigger Temperature Measurement	0xE3	Hold master
Trigger Temperature Measurement	0xF3	No Hold master

What is the difference between Hold master and No Hold master? This was discussed earlier in a general context under the section Slow Read Protocols. The device cannot read the temperature instantaneously and the master can either opt to be held waiting for the data, i.e. Hold master, or released to do something else and poll for the data until it is ready, i.e No Hold master.

Hold master option works by allowing the device to stretch the clock pulse by holding the line low after the master has released it. In this mode the master will wait until the device releases the line. Not all masters support this mode, but the Pico does and this makes it the simpler option. To read the temperature using the Hold master mode you simply send 0xE3 and then read three bytes. The simplest program that will work is:

```
#include <stdio.h>
#include "pico/stdlib.h"
#include "hardware/i2c.h"
int main()
{
    stdio_init_all();
    i2c_init(i2c0, 100 * 1000);
    gpio_set_function(4, GPIO_FUNC_I2C);
    gpio_set_function(5, GPIO_FUNC_I2C);
    uint8_t buf[4] = {0xE3};
    i2c_write_blocking(i2c0, 0x40, buf, 1, true);
    i2c_read_blocking(i2c0, 0x40, buf, 3, false);
    uint8_t msb = buf[0];
    uint8_t lsb = buf[1];
    uint8_t check = buf[2];
    printf("msb %d \n\r lsb %d \n\r checksum %d \n\r",
                                    msb, lsb, check);
};
```

The buffer is unpacked into three variables with more meaningful names:
msb - most significant byte, lsb - least significant byte, check - checksum

If you try this out you should find that it works and it prints something like:
```
msb 97
lsb 232
checksum 217
```
with the temperature in the 20°C range.

The logic analyzer reveals what is happening. First we send the usual address frame and write the 0xE3. Then, after a short pause, the read address frame is sent and the clock line is held low by the device (lower trace):
The clock line is held low by the device for over 42ms while it gets the data ready. It is released and the three data frames are sent:

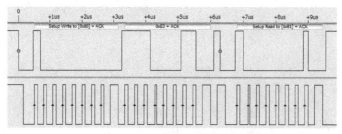

This response is a long way down the logic analyzer trace so keep scrolling until you find it.

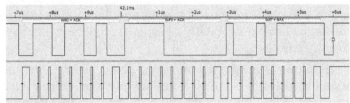

Notice that we suppress the stop bit between the write and the read to make it a single transaction.

Processing The Data

Our next task isn't really directly related to the problem of using the I2C bus, but it is a very typical next step. The device returns the data in three bytes, but the way that this data relates to the temperature isn't simple.

If you read the datasheet you will discover that the temperature data is the 14-bit value that results from putting together the most and least significant bytes and zeroing the bottom two bits. The bottom two bits are used as status bits, bit zero currently isn't used and bit one is a 1 if the data is a humidity measurement and a 0 if it is a temperature measurement.

To put the two bytes together we use:

```
unsigned int data16=((unsigned int) msb << 8) |
                         (unsigned int) (lsb & 0xFC);
```

This zeros the bottom two bits, shifts the `msb` up eight bits and ORs the two together. The result is a 16-bit temperature value with the bottom two bits zeroed. Now we have a raw temperature value but we have still have to convert it to standard units. The datasheet gives the formula:

```
Temperature in °C= -46.85 + 175.72 * data16 / 216
```

The only problem in implementing this is working out 2^{16}. You can work out 2^x with the expression `1<<x`, i.e. shift `1` x places to the right.

This gives:

```
float temp = (float)(-46.85 +(175.72 * data16 /(float)(1<<16)));
```

As 2^{16} is a constant that works out to 65536 it is more efficient to write:

```
float temp = (float)(-46.85 +(175.72 * data16 /(float)65536));
```

Now all we have to do is print the temperature:

```
printf("Temperature %f C \n\r", temp);
```

The full listing is at the end of this chapter.

Reading Humidity

The nice thing about I2C and using a particular I2C device is that it gets easier. Once you have seen how to do it with one device, the skill generalizes and, once you know how to deal with a particular device, other aspects of the device are usually similar.

While clock stretching is simple it sometimes doesn't work with some slave and master combinations. It is worth knowing how the alternative method works. For this reason let's implement the humidity reading using polling. We also find out how to use the No Hold master mode of reading the data, which is sometimes useful.

We write the 0xF5 once to the slave and then repeatedly attempt to read the three-byte response. If the slave isn't ready it simply replies with a NAK which the SDK function signals by returning a negative error value:

```
buf[0] = 0xF5;
i2c_write_blocking(i2c0, 0x40, buf, 1, true);
while (i2c_read_blocking(i2c0, 0x40, buf, 3, false) < 0)
{
    sleep_ms(1);
};
```

This polls repeatedly until the slave device returns an ACK, when the data is loaded into the buffer. Once we have the data, the formula to convert the 16-bit value to percentage humidity is:

RH= -6 + 125 * data16 / 216

Putting all this together, and reusing some variables from the previous parts of the program, we have:

```
buf[0] = 0xF5;
i2c_write_blocking(i2c0, 0x40, buf, 1, true);
while (i2c_read_blocking(i2c0, 0x40, buf, 3, false) < 0)
{
    sleep_ms(1);
};
msb = buf[0];
lsb = buf[1];
check = buf[2];
printf("msb %d \n\r lsb %d \n\r checksum %d \n\r",
                                        msb, lsb, check);
data16 = ((unsigned int)msb << 8) | (unsigned int)(lsb & 0xFC);
float hum = -6 + (125.0 * (float)data16) / 65536;
printf("Humidity %f %% \n\r", hum);
```

The only unusual part of the program is using %% to print a single % character, which is necessary because % means something in printf. We also need to implement the crcCheck function.

Checksum Calculation

Although computing a cyclic redundancy checksum, CRC, isn't specific to I2C, it is another common task. The datasheet explains that the polynomial used is:

$$X^8+X^5+X^4+1$$

Once you have this information you can work out the divisor by writing a binary number with a one in each location corresponding to a power of X in the polynomial. In this case the 8th, 5th, 4th and 1st bit. Hence the divisor is:

```
0x0131
```

What you do next is roughly the same for all CRCs. First you put the data that was used to compute the checksum together with the checksum value as the low-order bits:

```
uint32_t data32 = ((uint32_t)msb << 16)|
                     ((uint32_t) lsb <<8) |  (uint32_t) check;
```

Now you have three bytes, i.e 24 bits, in a 32-bit variable. Next you adjust the divisor so that its most significant non-zero bit aligns with the most significant bit of the three bytes. As this divisor has a 1 at bit eight, it needs to be shifted 15 places to the right to move it to be the 24th bit:

```
uint32_t divisor = ((uint32_t) 0x0131) <<15;
```

Now that you have both the data and the divisor aligned, you step through the topmost 16 bits, i.e. you don't process the low-order eight bits which hold the received checksum. For each bit you check to see if it is a 1. If it is you replace the data with the data XOR divisor. In either case you shift the divisor one place to the right:

```
for (int i = 0; i < 16; i++){
  if( data32 & (uint32_t)1<<(23 - i))data32 =data32 ^ divisor;
  divisor=divisor >> 1;
};
```

When the loop ends, if there was no error, the data32 should be zeroed and the received checksum is correct and as computed on the data received.

A complete function to compute the checksum, with some optimization, is:

```
uint8_t crcCheck(uint8_t msb, uint8_t lsb, uint8_t check){
 uint32_t data32 = ((uint32_t)msb << 16)|((uint32_t) lsb <<8)|
                     (uint32_t) check;
 uint32_t divisor = 0x988000;
 for (int i = 0 ; i < 16 ; i++){
   if( data32 & (uint32_t)1<<(23 - i) ) data32 ^= divisor;
   divisor>>= 1;
 };
 return (uint8_t) data32;
}
```

It is rare to get a CRC error on an I2C bus unless it is overloaded or subject to a lot of noise.

Complete Listing

The complete program for reading temperature and humidity, including checksums, is:

```c
#include <stdio.h>
#include "pico/stdlib.h"
#include "hardware/i2c.h"
uint8_t crcCheck(uint8_t msb, uint8_t lsb, uint8_t check)
{
    uint32_t data32 = ((uint32_t)msb << 16) | ((uint32_t)lsb << 8) |
                                                (uint32_t)check;

    uint32_t divisor = 0x988000;
    for (int i = 0; i < 16; i++)
    {
        if (data32 & (uint32_t)1 << (23 - i))
            data32 ^= divisor;
        divisor >>= 1;
    };
    return (uint8_t)data32;
}

int main()
{
    stdio_init_all();

    i2c_init(i2c0, 100 * 1000);

    gpio_set_function(4, GPIO_FUNC_I2C);
    gpio_set_function(5, GPIO_FUNC_I2C);

    uint8_t buf[4] = {0xE3};
    i2c_write_blocking(i2c0, 0x40, buf, 1, true);
    i2c_read_blocking(i2c0, 0x40, buf, 3, false);
    uint8_t msb = buf[0];
    uint8_t lsb = buf[1];
    uint8_t check = buf[2];
    printf("msb %d \n\r lsb %d \n\r checksum %d \n\r",
                                            msb, lsb, check);
    unsigned int data16 = ((unsigned int)msb << 8) |
                            (unsigned int)(lsb & 0xFC);
    printf("crc = %d\n\r", crcCheck(msb, lsb, check));
    float temp = (float)(-46.85 + (175.72 * data16 / (float)65536));
    printf("Temperature %f C \n\r", temp);
```

```
        buf[0] = 0xF5;
        i2c_write_blocking(i2c0, 0x40, buf, 1, true);
        while (i2c_read_blocking(i2c0, 0x40, buf, 3, false) < 0)
        {
            sleep_ms(1);
        };

        msb = buf[0];
        lsb = buf[1];
        check = buf[2];
        printf("msb %d \n\r lsb %d \n\r checksum %d \n\r",
                                            msb, lsb, check);
        printf("crc = %d\n\r", crcCheck(msb, lsb, check));
        data16 = ((unsigned int)msb << 8) | (unsigned int)(lsb & 0xFC);
        float hum = -6 + (125.0 * (float)data16) / 65536;
        printf("Humidity %f %% \n\r", hum);
}
```

Notice that we used clock stretching in reading the temperature and polling in reading the humidity. In practice, you would choose one method according to your needs.

Of course this is just the start. Once you have the device working and supplying data it is time to write your code in the form of functions that return the temperature and the humidity and generally make the whole thing more useful and easier to maintain. This is often how this sort of programming goes. First you write a lot of inline code so that it works as fast as it can, then you move blocks of code to functions to make the program more elegant and easy to maintain, checking at each refactoring that it all still works.

Also remember that you need to add hardware_i2c to the CMakeLists.txt file

Not all devices used standard bus protocols. In Chapter 14 we'll look at a custom serial protocol that we have to implement for ourselves.

Summary

- The I2C bus is simple yet flexible and is one of the most commonly encountered ways of connecting devices.

- The I2C bus uses two wires – a data line and a clock.

- The Pico has two I2C interfaces.

- Each I2C interface can be connected to a pair of GPIO lines.

- The I2C protocol isn't standardized and you have to take account of variations in the way devices implement it.

- There are single byte transfer operations and multibyte transfers which differ in when a stop bit is sent.

- The low-level protocol can be made slightly more high-level by thinking of it as a single write or read a register operation.

- Sometimes a device cannot respond immediately and needs to keep the master waiting for data. There are two ways to do this, polling and clock stretching.

- The HTU21D is a simple I2C device, but getting it working involves using polling or stretching.

- Computing a check sum is an involved, but common, operation.

Chapter 13

Using The PIO

The most interesting and attractive feature of the Pico is arguably its PIO – Programmable I/O hardware. So far we have used direct access to the GPIO lines or to some built-in hardware that controls them such as PWM, I2C or SPI. If you want to connect to a device that these standards apply to then your problem is solved. If, on the other hand, you have a device that doesn't use one of these standards then you are faced with the task of constructing your own implementation of the interface. For example, the DHT22 temperature and humidity sensor uses its own protocol for delivering its data and the 1-Wire bus is commonly encountered, but not often supported, in hardware. You can even go beyond any standard and implement your own custom data transfer protocol.

The traditional way to approach any custom or unsupported protocol is to use "bit banging". This is simply the act of writing a program which controls GPIO lines to simulate the hardware that might be used to implement the protocol. Basically what you have to do is set GPIO lines high and low as dictated by the timing of the protocol and then read data at set times. This is easy in theory, but getting the timings right is harder that it appears and synchronization between state changes is particularly challenging. In addition there is the problem that bit banging ties up the processor. In many cases this doesn't matter. In other cases you can use one core to implement the protocol and another to process the data. However the Pico's PIOs provide a general-purpose solution to the problem that offers advantages that go well beyond the traditional solutions.

The Pico documentation on the PIO even suggests that if you find yourself working on a bit-banging solution then you should stop and start again using the PIO. I wouldn't go this far because the PIO solution is more complex and specialized and if a simple bit-banging solution works you need a motivation to transfer your attention to the PIO. This said, it is worth spending time learning about the PIO if you anticipate ever making use of it. With the right approach it isn't as difficult as it first appears.

PIO Basic Concepts

The problem with getting to grips with the PIO is that there are two distinct views of it – inside and outside. You can also add to this the extra complication of setting up a project that makes use of it, but that is a one-time problem. The best way to think about the PIO is as a black box that performs some transaction using GPIO lines and presents and accepts data from the processor – exactly like other I/O subsystems PWM, SPI, I2C etc. The only difference is that the transaction it performs is programmable.

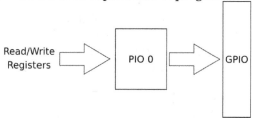

This the same situation as for the I2C or SPI hardware – once set up you communicate with the PIO by reading and writing registers and it is associated with a number of GPIO lines.

As you might guess from the illustration there is more than one PIO. The Pico has two, PIO0 and PIO1, and each can be programmed independently of the other. To make things simple, we will use PIO0 but everything translates to PIO1 if you need to use it.

You communicate with the PIO by reading and writing registers, but, as with other hardware modules, the SDK provides functions to do this for you. Not all of the examples that you will encounter make full use of the SDK functions and there is certainly more than one way to write a program to work with a PIO. In this book we will make use of the SDK functions, explaining a little about what they are doing.

Configuring GPIO for PIO Output

The first and most important thing to master is that the PIO doesn't have instructions that work with particular GPIO lines. You don't write a PIO program that sets the output of GP2, say. Instead you specify which GPIO lines are to be included in a number of groups. Each PIO has four different "state machines" that can be set to run a program stored in the PIO. Each state machine has its own set of GPIO lines that it works with and at the simplest each state machine can perform the same sort of task on different GPIO pins. So for example, if you programmed the PIO to be an SPI controller then you could define four different SPI interfaces, each to a different set of pins. It is also possible to run each state machine from a different program, but more of this later.

236

Each state machine has two sets of output lines:

> **OUT** - Lines in the OUT group are specified by a base and a count, e.g. base is GP4 and count is 2 gives GP4 and GP5. They are controlled by instructions that transfer data from the processor to the state machine. That is, they are lines you set by writing data to the state machine. Typically the lines in the OUT group are what you would think of as data lines.
>
> You can set the OUT group using:
>
> ```
> sm_config_set_out_pins (pio_sm_config *c, uint out_base,
>                          uint out_count)
> ```
>
> which modifies a configuration struct c which you use later to configure the state machine using pio_sm_init. The out_base parameter gives the first GPIO line in the group and the out_count parameter gives you the number of lines in the group. By default all of the OUT pins are set to high impedance mode and have to be explicitly set to act as outputs.
>
> **SET** – Specified by a base and a count e.g. base is GP4 and count is 2 gives GP4 and GP5. The SET group of GPIO lines are controlled by instructions running on the state machine. That is they are lines you set within the PIO program. Typically the lines in the SET group are used for what you would think of as clock lines.
>
> You can set the SET group using:
>
> ```
> sm_config_set_set_pins (pio_sm_config *c, uint set_base,
>                          uint set_count)
> ```
>
> which again modifies a configuration struct c which you use later to configure the state machine using pio_sm_init. The set_base parameter gives the first GPIO line in the group and the set_count parameter gives you the number of lines in the group. By default all of the SET pins are set to high impedance mode and have to be explicitly set to act as outputs.

A third group of output lines, SIDESET, is also available and while it turns out to be very useful it is slightly more difficult to understand. We will return to it later.

Notice that a PIO program doesn't write to a particular GPIO line but to one of the groups of lines and these are defined by writing to registers or, better, using the SDK functions in your C program. Also notice that the groups of GPIO lines are associated with different PIO instructions. The OUT group is used by the out instruction and the SET group is used by the set instruction.

PIO Blinky

Now it is time to write and run our first PIO program and in the grand tradition we will, eventually, write a Blinky program – the Hello World of hardware.

The PIO is programmed using a special assembly language and we will return to its main features later, but for now you can most probably understand the meaning of our first simple program:

```
.program squarewave
    set pindirs, 1    ; Set pin to output
again:
    set pins, 1       ; Drive pin high
    set pins, 0       ; Drive pin low
    jmp again         ; Set PC to label `again`
```

The first instruction sets pin 1 in the SET group of pins to be an active output, i.e. it changes from a high impedance state to an output. This is more complicated than it seems. More of exactly how this works in the section on Output to the GPIO.

The loop that follows this repeatedly changes the SET group of pins from high to low. Notice that from this program you cannot tell which pins are actually being used – this is set in your C program via the PIO registers or the equivalent SDK functions.

The program is simple, but now we have to convert it into machine code by either hand-assembling it, which is possible but tedious, or passing though an assembler. The SDK has an assembler includes and it has a CMake function that will invoke the assembler and transfer its machine code into C array that can be loaded into the PIO. The C array and other useful things are presented to your program in a header file that you include in your program. The line that you need to add to the CmakeLists file are:

```
pico_generate_pio_header(pio ${CMAKE_CURRENT_LIST_DIR}/sqwave.pio)
```

This assumes that the name of the executable is pio and that the assembly language is stored in a file called sqwave.pio stored in the project's folder. When the project is built this generates the file sqwave.pio.h. i.e. whatever the name of the assembly file is with .h as an extension.

If you are going to use the SDK functions to configure and interact with the PIO you also need:

```
target_link_libraries(pio pico_stdlib hardware_pio)
```

assuming that your executable is called pio.

A complete `CmakeLists.txt` for a project called `pioBlinky` with the main C program in `pio.c` and the assembler in `sqwave.pio.h` is:

```
cmake_minimum_required(VERSION 3.13)

set(CMAKE_C_STANDARD 11)
set(CMAKE_CXX_STANDARD 17)

include(pico_sdk_import.cmake)
pico_sdk_init()

project(pioBlinky C CXX ASM)
add_executable(pio
 pio.c
)
pico_generate_pio_header(pio ${CMAKE_CURRENT_LIST_DIR}/sqwave.pio)

target_link_libraries(pio  pico_stdlib hardware_pio)
pico_add_extra_outputs(pio)
```

Remember you also need to copy `pico_sdk_import.cmake` into the folder.

Now all we need is a C program to make use of the assembler – to load it and set the state machine running. We have to include the header file that the assembler generated:

```
#include "sqwave.pio.h"
```

This adds the definition of the machine code to your program:

```
static const uint16_t squarewave_program_instructions[] = {
            //     .wrap_target
    0xe081, //  0: set     pindirs, 1
    0xe001, //  1: set     pins, 1
    0xe000, //  2: set     pins, 0
    0x0001, //  3: jmp     1
            //     .wrap
};
```

You could write some code to load the contents of the array into a PIO, but the header file also creates a struct that can be passed to an SDK function that will load the code for you:

```
static const struct pio_program squarewave_program = {
    .instructions = squarewave_program_instructions,
    .length = 4,
    .origin = -1,
};
```

To load the code all we have to do is:

```
uint offset = pio_add_program(pio0, &squarewave_program);
```

In this case we have decided to use pio0.

Now we have the code loaded into pio0 the next job is to pick one of the four possible state machines to execute and configure it. To select a state machine it is better to let the SDK select the first free machine:

```
uint sm = pio_claim_unused_sm(pio0, true);
```

The final parameter will cause the program to fail if there are no state machines available. Set the final parameter to false and the return value is negative rather than a state machine index in case of error.

With the state machine that we are going to use settled, we can now configure it. You could do this directly, but the simplest and best way to do the job is to use the SDK. This allows you to set up a struct with all of the configuration values set and then initialize the state machine in one go. First we need a default configuration so we only need to change the values that matter:

```
pio_sm_config c = squarewave_program_get_default_config(offset);
```

Now we have to set the configuration as promised. We need to specify which pins are going to be in the SET group:

```
sm_config_set_set_pins(&c, 2, 1);
```

and in this case we have selected just one pin, GP2, as the group starts at GP2 and has just one pin. This means that our set instruction in the PIO program will toggle just pin GP2. We also have to set the GPIO function to GPIO_FUNC_PIO0 to let the processor know that this the pin is being controlled by the PIO. Instead of using the standard:

```
gpio_set_function(2, GPIO_FUNC_PIO0);
```

you can use the specific PIO function to do the same job:

```
pio_gpio_init(pio0, 2);
```

Finally we can load the configuration into the state machine and start it running:

```
pio_sm_init(pio0, sm, offset, &c);
pio_sm_set_enabled(pio0, sm, true);
```

If you now look at the output of GP2 you will see a square wave.

The complete program is but remember that it needs the PIO program and the CMakeLists.txt file:

```
#include "pico/stdlib.h"
#include "hardware/pio.h"

#include "sqwave.pio.h"

int main()
{
    uint offset = pio_add_program(pio0, &squarewave_program);

    uint sm = pio_claim_unused_sm(pio0, true);
    pio_sm_config c = squarewave_program_get_default_config(offset);

    sm_config_set_set_pins(&c, 2, 1);
    pio_gpio_init(pio0, 2);

    pio_sm_init(pio0, sm, offset, &c);
    pio_sm_set_enabled(pio0, sm, true);
    return 0;
}
```

We do have a square wave producing program but it isn't suitable as a Blinky example. At the moment the clock rate is set to produce a square wave at around 40MHz and we need to bring down the frequency to something more reasonable so that we can see an LED blink on and off.

Clock Division And Timing

There are a number of ways of controlling the speed with which things happen, the most direct and preferable is to change the clock frequency by specifying a divider. The PIO clock can be divided down using a 16-bit divider – 8-bit integer/8-bit fractional. In most cases, you should avoid using a fractional divider as it introduces extra periods to make the frequency average out to the fractional part. This can make the PIO subject to jitter, which decreases the reliability.

You can set the clock divider using either of:

```
pio_sm_set_clkdiv (PIO pio, uint sm, float div)
pio_sm_set_clkdiv_int_frac (PIO pio, uint sm,
                    uint16_t div_int, uint8_t div_frac)
```

If you add:

```
sm_config_set_clkdiv_int_frac(&c,255,0);
```

then you will get the lowest clock frequency using the default clock, i.e. 500kHz.

This brings us to another important idea. Most of the timing in PIO programs is linked to the time an instruction takes to complete and most instructions take one clock cycle. This can cause difficulties in that execution paths may not be equal in time when you want them to be. For example, consider our simple PIO program:

```
.program squarewave
    set pindirs, 1   ; Set pin to output
again:
    set pins, 1      ; Drive pin high
    set pins, 0      ; Drive pin low
    jmp again        ; Set PC to label `again`
```

The first set pins takes 1 clock cycle, the second takes one clock cycle but the jmp instruction also takes one clock cycle meaning that the GPIO line is high for one clock cycle and low for two clock cycles. There are a number of ways of changing timings. For example, you could include a nop instruction which wastes a single clock cycle but also uses one memory slot. Alternatively you could specify a delay as part of the instruction – all PIO instructions can have a delay in clock cycles specified as [n] at the end of the instruction. So our new program:

```
.program squarewave
    set pindirs, 1   ; Set pin to output
again:
    set pins, 1 [1]  ; Drive pin high
    set pins, 0      ; Drive pin low
    jmp again        ; Set PC to label `again`
```

Holds the line high for two clock cycles and low for two clock cycles.

With the maximum clock divider this gives a square wave output at around 120kHz which is still too fast for flashing an LED. The maximum delay you can specify in any instruction is 31 clock cycles so even:

```
.program squarewave
    set pindirs, 1   ; Set pin to output
again:
    set pins, 1 [31] ; Drive pin high
    set pins, 0 [30] ; Drive pin low
    jmp again        ; Set PC to label `again`
```

only brings the clock down to 7.5kHz.

In general you should try to choose a clock frequency that makes timing of pulses using just per instruction delays to adjust the relative timings. Each instruction and delay takes one clock cycle so this is the natural unit of measurement to use.

In our case we need a much longer delay than 32 clock cycles instruction delays can produce – we need a spin wait loop.

Writing Loops

One of the things you will most likely have to do is write the equivalent of a for or while loop in PIO assembler and it might not be obvious how to do this because it doesn't have control structures like C. To write a loop you need to know that each state machine has two scratch 32-bit storage registers called x and y. You can store values and use values in these registers from various sources using the in, out, set or mov instructions. If you want to set a register, x say, to a constant value then you need to use:

```
set x,31
```

where 31 is the maximum value you can set because the instruction is limited to a 5-bit immediate value.

You can use the registers to implement a for loop with up to 32 repeats. The jmp instruction can test the value of a register for zero and auto-decrement it after the test. This means an n repeat for loop can be constructed as:

```
set x,n
loop: nop
jump x--, loop
```

Using this you can slow the rate at which the GPIO line is toggled by repeating the nop 32 times. However, even if you use:

```
set x,n
loop: nop [31]
jump x--, loop
```

the effective rate of toggling the GPIO line is still too great to see an LED flash. To slow it down even more you need two nested loops.

The complete PIO program is:

```
.program squarewave
    set pindirs, 1
again:
    set pins, 1
    set x, 31
 loop1:
    set y,31
    loop2:
       nop [31]
       jmp y--,loop2
    jmp x--,loop1

    set pins, 0
    set x, 31
loop3:
    set y,31
  loop4:
     nop [31]
     jmp y--,loop4
  jmp x--,loop3
  jmp again
```

You can see the two nested loops – loop1/loop2 and loop3/loop4. This is not a good design, but it is a working Blinky program and there are many optimizations you can apply to reduce the size of the program. If you try it you will find it runs at about 7.2Hz and if you change the GPIO line to GP25 you will see the onboard LED flash.

The need for a pair of nested loops to slow things down is due to the simple fact that we can only set the x or y register to a maximum of 31 because the PIO assembly instructions only have space for a 5-bit literal field. There is another way to set the x and y register using data transferred into the PIO program from the C program and this brings us to the subject of data input.

Data To The PIO

Just like any of the I/O subsystems in the Pico, you can send data to the PIO from your C program. There are more basic ways to do this job, but the SDK provides easy-to-use functions. The Pico provides a 3-element, 32-bit FIFO buffer, the TX FIFO, for input to the state machine and, usually, output to the GPIO lines. You can write data to the TX FIFO using:

```
pio_sm_put (PIO pio, uint sm, uint32_t data)
pio_sm_put_blocking (PIO pio, uint sm, uint32_t data)
```

The difference is that the first function doesn't wait for free space in the FIFO and returns without making any changes apart from setting the TXOVER flag if the FIFO is full. The second blocks until there is space to store the data. You can find out the current state of the FIFO using:

```
static bool pio_sm_is_tx_fifo_full (PIO pio, uint sm)
static bool pio_sm_is_tx_fifo_empty (PIO pio, uint sm)
static uint pio_sm_get_tx_fifo_level (PIO pio, uint sm)
```

The PIO program can read data from the TX FIFO using the pull instruction which moves the first item of data from the FIFO into the Output Shift Register OSR. Usually the OSR is then used to drive the OUT group of lines, more of this later. However, the mov instruction can be used to move the OSR to a range of destinations including the x and y registers. This means we can use the TX FIFO buffer to set the x or y register to a full 32-bit value.

Using this we can create a Blinky program that just uses one loop and can create time delays in excess of 30 minutes. The PIO program is:

```
.program squarewave
    set pindirs, 1
    pull block
again:
    set pins, 1
    mov x, osr
 loop1:
    jmp x--,loop1
    set pins, 0
    mov x, osr
 loop2:
    jmp x--,loop2
jmp again
```

Notice the way the OSR is used as a way of storing the loop count so that it can be used to reset the x register each time. If you needed to use the OSR for something else this wouldn't be possible and you would have to use the y register or some other method. Also notice that the pull block instruction causes the PIO program to wait until there is some data in the TX FIFO to start things off.

The C program is:

```c
#include "pico/stdlib.h"
#include "hardware/pio.h"

#include "sqwave.pio.h"

int main()
{

    uint offset = pio_add_program(pio0, &squarewave_program);

    uint sm = pio_claim_unused_sm(pio0, true);
    pio_sm_config c = squarewave_program_get_default_config(offset);

    sm_config_set_set_pins(&c, 2, 1);
    pio_gpio_init(pio0, 2);

    sm_config_set_clkdiv_int_frac(&c, 255, 0);
    pio_sm_init(pio0, sm, offset, &c);
    pio_sm_set_enabled(pio0, sm, true);

    pio_sm_put_blocking(pio0, sm, 0xFFFF);
    return 0;
}
```

The only real difference is the `pio_sm_put_blocking` function at the end
which stores 0xFFFF in the TX FIFO to start the PIO running. If you run this
program you will find that the frequency is 3.7Hz. If you change the pin from
GP2 to GP25 you will also see the onboard LED flash.

This is a way of passing a single parameter to a PIO program. If you want to
pass two or more parameters then it can be done, but things become more
complicated.

Output To GPIO

The use of the Output Shift Register, OSR, to store a value that is moved to
the x register is reasonable but it isn't the usual role for the OSR. It is the link
between values passed to the state machine and the state of the GPIO lines.
We have already seen that the SET group of GPIO lines can be controlled
using the `set` command, now we move on to consider how the OUT group of
GPIO lines can be controlled using the `out` command. Recall that the OUT
group is a set of GPIO lines specified by a starting number and number of
lines:

```c
sm_config_set_out_pins (pio_sm_config *c, uint out_base,
                                          uint out_count)
```

The data in the OSR can be moved to the OUT group of pins using the `out` instruction:

```
out pins, n
```

where n is the number of bits shifted to the OUT group. The bits that are shifted out are used to set the first n GPIO lines in the OUT group and any remaining lines are set to zero. Notice that while we use the term "shift" this applies only to what happens to the contents of the OSR register. The n bits are presented to the n GPIO lines in one operation – i.e. all of the GPIO lines change their state at the same time. The "shift" simply means that the data in the OSR register is moved to remove the n bits used. You can set the direction of the shift so as to make either the most significant or least significant bits the ones that are used in the OSR register first:

```
sm_config_set_out_shift (pio_sm_config *c,  bool shift_right,
                    bool autopull, uint pull_threshold)
```

The last two parameters control the automatic loading of the OSR, see later.

In general, 32 bits are sent to the destination of the `out` command, the lower n bits coming from the OSR and the remaining bits being zero. Of course usually only the lower n bits are actually useful. If you repeat the `out` instruction the next n bits are used and so on until the shift register is empty when all 32 bits have been shifted out. A simple PIO program example will help clarify. In this case we will send the bits from a 32-bit value to two GPIO pins just to show how things work:

```
.program squarewave
    set pindirs, 3
    pull block
again:
    out pins,2
    jmp again
```

You can see that all the program does is to pull a single 32-bit value from the TX FIFO into the OSR and then uses the `out` instruction to send pairs of bits to the first two pins in the OUT group of pins.

This seems simple, but the `set pindir` is more complicated than you might expect. The `set` instruction sets the direction of the SET group of pins. The literal value used in the instruction is used as a mask to set the pin directions. This means that it can only set the direction of the first five GPIO lines in the SET group. This usually isn't a problem as using more than five GPIO lines for output is uncommon. However, the `out` instruction sends the data from the OSR to the first two GPIO lines in the OUT group, not the SET group. You can see that the `set` instruction only enables the first two lines of the OUT group if they are the same in both groups.

The key thing is that the GPIO lines are controlled by a single 32-bit register which ignores pin mappings and it doesn't matter how you set a bit, the GPIO line is enabled. You could use an out instruction to set the bits in the OUT group, but this would require data from your C program to be placed in the TX FIFO.

Another solution is to configure the pindir from the C program using:

```
pio_sm_set_consecutive_pindirs (PIO pio,  uint sm,
              uint pin_base,  uint pin_count,  bool is_out)
```

or

```
pio_sm_set_pindirs_with_mask (PIO pio, uint sm,
                uint32_t pin_dirs,  uint32_t pin_mask)
```

The first sets the GPIO pins starting at GPpin_base and ending at GPpin_base+pin_count to high impedance or output according to is_out. The second uses a mask to set the directions of the pins corresponding to ones in the mask to the state specified in pin_dirs. Notice that in both cases you are working with the entire 32 GPIO lines, not any of the PIO groups. These functions should be used to initialize the PIO before it is enabled.

Now we have the PIO program, all that remains is the C program which sends some "random" data:

```c
#include "pico/stdlib.h"
#include "hardware/pio.h"
#include "sqwave.pio.h"

int main()
{

    uint offset = pio_add_program(pio0, &squarewave_program);

    uint sm = pio_claim_unused_sm(pio0, true);
    pio_sm_config c = squarewave_program_get_default_config(offset);
    sm_config_set_set_pins(&c, 2, 2);
    sm_config_set_out_pins(&c, 2, 2);
    pio_gpio_init(pio0, 2);
    pio_gpio_init(pio0, 3);

    sm_config_set_clkdiv_int_frac(&c, 255, 0);
    pio_sm_init(pio0, sm, offset, &c);
    pio_sm_set_enabled(pio0, sm, true);

    pio_sm_put_blocking(pio0, sm, 0xFEDCBA98);
    return 0;
}
```

Notice that we need to set the SET and the OUT pins to be the same as we use both `set` and `out` instructions in the PIO program. The final instruction sends some arbitrary data to the TX FIFO and this is output two bits at a time to the two GPIO lines, GP2 and GP3:

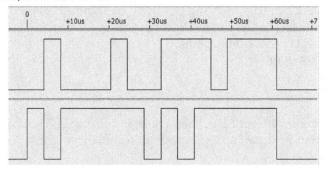

The output stops when the OSR is empty but the `out` instruction keeps sending zeros to the GPIO lines.

If you want to keep the data flowing, you have to keep refilling the OSR. For example, you could change the C program to send data to the buffer whenever there was a free space:

```
while (true)
{
    pio_sm_put_blocking(pio0, sm, 0xFEDCBA98);
}
```

Now the PIO program can read new data from the TX FIFO whenever it wants to:

```
.program squarewave
    set pindirs, 3   ; Set pin to output
    pull block

again:
  out pins,2
  out pins,2
  out pins,2
      pull block

  jmp again
```

In this case we send the first three pairs of bits to the output pins and then read the TX FIFO into the OSR to get new data.

Of course, usually you would use all of the data in the OSR before reloading it. This standard task can be done automatically with the `autopull` which reloads the OSR whenever its contents fall below a threshold.

You set `autopull` using the last two parameters of:

```
sm_config_set_out_shift (pio_sm_config *c,  bool shift_right,
                         bool autopull, uint pull_threshold)
```

If you set `autopull` to true then the OSR will be reloaded from the TX FIFO when it contents fall below the `pull_threshold`.
Using this the PIO program becomes:

```
.program squarewave
again:
  out pins,2
  jmp again
```

On this occasion no attempt has been made to set the OUT group of pins to output – this will be done in the C program to illustrate how this works.

```
#include "pico/stdlib.h"
#include "hardware/pio.h"
#include "sqwave.pio.h"

int main()
{
    uint offset = pio_add_program(pio0, &squarewave_program);
    uint sm = pio_claim_unused_sm(pio0, true);
    pio_sm_config c = squarewave_program_get_default_config(offset);
    sm_config_set_set_pins(&c, 2, 2);
    sm_config_set_out_pins(&c, 2, 2);
    pio_gpio_init(pio0, 2);
    pio_gpio_init(pio0, 3);
    pio_sm_set_consecutive_pindirs(pio0, sm, 2, 2, true);
    sm_config_set_clkdiv_int_frac(&c, 255, 0);
    sm_config_set_out_shift (&c, true, true, 6);
    pio_sm_init(pio0, sm, offset, &c);
    pio_sm_set_enabled(pio0, sm, true);
    while (true)
    {
        pio_sm_put_blocking(pio0, sm, 0xFEDCBA98);
    }
    return 0;
}
```

Notice that now:

```
pio_sm_set_consecutive_pindirs(pio0, sm, 2, 2, true);
```

sets GP2 and GP3 to output before the state machine starts. If you run this program you will find that it does the same job as the previous program, but in fewer instructions and fewer clock cycles.

There are some minor points of how `autopull` works we've not covered, but you now have the general principles.

Side Effects

Now we have encountered most of the idea behind PIO output to the GPIO lines but there is one more additional feature – set-side as a side effect. As well as being able to explicitly set GPIO lines using `set` or `out`, we can also arrange for any instruction to set GPIO lines as part of its execution. In this sense, the setting of the GPIO lines is a "side effect" of the instruction. Side effects are usually thought of as something to avoid in a standard program – you want an instruction to do what it appears to do and nothing more. In the case of PIO programming, however, side effects are very useful because they allow you to set GPIO lines according to where the program is in its execution. That is, they can be used to signal to the outside world the state of the program. At a more utilitarian level, being able to set a GPIO line as a side effect of another instruction can save both time and instructions.

The only downside of side effects is that they are coded using the space in the PIO instruction that is normally used to specify a delay. There is a 5-bit field used to code the delay and the side effect and you can trade bits for each purpose. The default is that all five bits are used to specify a delay and this makes it possible to specify up to 31 clock cycles of delay. You can allocate bits to be used to set sides using:

```
.side_set count opt pindirs
```

where count is the number of set-side bits to allocate, opt means that the set-side is optional on an instruction and `pindirs` is the option to set the pin directions as a side effect. Setting `pindirs` as a side effect is useful if you need to change a line from `out` to `in` as the program progresses.

Alternatively you can use the SDK to set the same options when you configure the state machine:

```
sm_config_set_sideset (pio_sm_config *c, uint bit_count,
                                  bool optional, bool pindirs)
```

Both ways of setting the options apply to the entire program.

Obviously you should choose to use as few set-side bits as possible if you want to make use of a delay. The `side_set` directive has to come at the start of the program and it remains in effect for the entire program.

In addition to setting the number of `side_set` bits you also need to set the SIDESET GPIO group using:

```
sm_config_set_sideset_pins (pio_sm_config *c, uint sideset_base)
```

This sets the start of the SIDESET group and you can specify any number of contiguous GPIO lines that the number of set-side bits allows.

Finally to include a GPIO line to set as a side effect you can add:

side *value*

after any instruction and the value will be used to set the SETSIDE pins (or their directions).

To show how all this works the simplest thing to do is write the square wave generator again, but this time using nothing but set-side options:

```
.program squarewave
.side_set 1 opt
again:
  nop side 1
  jmp   again side 0
```

The side_set directive specifies a single bit, which means that the SETSIDE group of GPIO lines is effectively a single line. The nop has a side effect of setting the side effect lines to 1 and the jmp sets it back to 0.

The main program to make use of this is fairly standard, but we need to set the SETSIDE group to start at GP2 if this is the line we want to toggle:

```
#include "pico/stdlib.h"
#include "hardware/pio.h"
#include "sqwave.pio.h"

int main()
{
    uint offset = pio_add_program(pio0, &squarewave_program);

    uint sm = pio_claim_unused_sm(pio0, true);
    pio_sm_config c = squarewave_program_get_default_config(offset);
    sm_config_set_sideset_pins(&c,2);
    pio_gpio_init(pio0, 2);
    pio_sm_set_consecutive_pindirs(pio0, sm, 2, 1, true);
    sm_config_set_clkdiv_int_frac(&c, 255, 0);
    pio_sm_init(pio0, sm, offset, &c);

    pio_sm_set_enabled(pio0, sm, true);
    return 0;
}
```

If you run this program you will find that pin GP2 is toggled in a 50% square wave at around 245kHz, without a single out or set instruction in sight. Notice that the rising edge occurs when the loop starts and the falling edge when the loop ends.

As an example of using more than one GPIO line as a side effect consider:

```
.program squarewave
.side_set 2 opt
again:
  nop side 2
  jmp  again side 1
```

Now we have set aside two bits to control set-side GPIO lines, which means we can control two of them. First we write 2, 10 in binary, to the pair of lines and then 1, or 01, which switches the lines in anti-phase – when one is high the other is low. The main program has to be changed to configure two GPIO lines:

```
sm_config_set_sideset_pins(&c,2);
pio_gpio_init(pio0, 2);
pio_gpio_init(pio0, 3);
```

Set-side lines can overlap with OUT and SET lines and if such instructions set the same GPIO line, the set-side instruction has precedent.

Input

Now we have described most of the general ideas of PIO output to GPIO lines, it is time to consider input from GPIO lines. The good news is that this is easy to understand as long as you have followed the ideas involved in output. The only problem is that, in practice, input is always harder than output and in the case of PIO programming you have to rethink how things work. The reason is that you don't have any edge-triggered events or timers. Everything you do has to be conditioned on the state of the system and raw timings based on how long instructions take to execute.

The basic mechanisms of input are the same as output. There is a 4-element, 32-bit RX FIFO buffer that you can read from your C program using:

```
static uint32_t pio_sm_get_blocking (PIO pio, uint sm)
static uint32_t pio_sm_get (PIO pio, uint sm)
```

Obviously the first function blocks until there is some data to read and the second returns at once, either with data or with an undefined value.

You can find the current state of the RX FIFO using:

```
static bool pio_sm_is_rx_fifo_full (PIO pio, uint sm)
static bool pio_sm_is_rx_fifo_empty (PIO pio, uint sm)
static uint pio_sm_get_rx_fifo_level (PIO pio, uint sm)
```

Data gets into the RX FIFO from the PIO via the Input Shift Register, ISR, which is the input equivalent of the OSR.

To transfer data from the GPIO lines you use the `in` instruction,

```
in pins,n
```

The `in` instruction moves n bits from the IN GPIO group into the ISR shifting up any data that is already present. You can also use it to transfer n bits from the x or y registers and a few other sources. The IN group of GPIO lines is defined in the C program using:

```
sm_config_set_in_pins (pio_sm_config *c, uint in_base)
```

As in the case of the SETSIDE group, you only have to specify a base number as you can read from any GPIO line, even if it is an output. What this means is that an `in` instruction can read all of the 32 GPIO lines and only the numbering of the lines changes. For example, after:

```
sm_config_set_in_pins (&c,10);
```

which sets the base to GP10, the instruction:

```
in pins,3
```

will transfer the state of GP10, GP11 and GP12 to the ISR.

Once you have sufficient bits in the ISR, you can transfer the entire 32-bit value to the RX FIFO using the `push` instruction:

```
push block
```

This waits for a free space in the RX FIFO and clears the ISR ready for further use. You can also use `autopush` to transfer data to the RX FIFO automatically when a bit count threshold is reached. You can set the direction in which the ISR is shifted and the use of auto-push and threshold using:

```
static void sm_config_set_in_shift (pio_sm_config *c,
        bool shift_right,  bool autopush, uint push_threshold)
```

As the simplest example, let's read GP2 and use its state to control the on-board LED. This isn't a useful program, but it is a good illustration of the basics. The PIO program is simply:

```
.program light
again:
  in pins,1
  push block
  jmp  again
```

You can see that this simply read the state of the first INPUT pin and pushes it to the RX FIFO. Of course, after four reads and pushes, the RX FIFO will be full and the program will stall.

The C program simply has to set things up, read the data and set the on-board LED accordingly:

```c
#include "pico/stdlib.h"
#include "hardware/pio.h"
#include "light.pio.h"

int main()
{

    uint offset = pio_add_program(pio0, &light_program);

    uint sm = pio_claim_unused_sm(pio0, true);
    pio_sm_config c = light_program_get_default_config(offset);

    sm_config_set_in_pins(&c, 2);
    pio_gpio_init(pio0, 2);

    pio_sm_set_consecutive_pindirs(pio0, sm, 2, 1, false);
    sm_config_set_clkdiv_int_frac(&c, 255, 0);

    pio_sm_init(pio0, sm, offset, &c);
    pio_sm_set_enabled(pio0, sm, true);

    gpio_init(25);
    gpio_set_dir(25, GPIO_OUT);
    while (true)
    {
        uint32_t flag = pio_sm_get_blocking(pio0, sm);
        if (flag == 0)
        {
            gpio_put(25, 0);
        }
        else
        {
            gpio_put(25, 1);
        }
    }

    return 0;
}
```

Notice the use of `pio_sm_set_consecutive_pindirs` to set GP2 to input. This is necessary for the program to work. If you set GP2 to high and low you will see the LED turn on and off. The problem with the program is that you have no idea when it reads the input line. All you can say is that the speed of `readin` is controlled by how fast the C program makes room for new data in the RX FIFO.

Edges

This is all there is to using input, but the big problem is when do you read the state of the GPIO lines? When you are implementing a data transfer protocol, it is usual that you output something and then wait a given time before reading. Alternatively, data is read in response to a clock state transition, often an edge, but we have no direct way of responding to an input edge.

The solution to the problem takes us a little way beyond the simple `in` instruction. The PIO supports a conditional wait and a conditional jump, based on the state of a GPIO line. The instruction:

```
wait state pin n
```

will wait until the pin indexed by n in the INPUT group is in the specified state. Notice that n=0 is the first pin in the group.

You can also select the pin by absolute GPIO number:

```
wait state gpio n
```

will wait until GP*n* is in the specified state. You can also wait on an IRQ, but this is beyond the scope of this first look at the PIO system.

The conditional jump:

```
jmp pin target
```

jumps to the target if the pin specified by

```
sm_config_set_jmp_pin (pio_sm_config *c, uint pin)
```

is a **1** and pin is a raw GPIO number and not specified by the INPUT group.

The `wait` instruction is about synchronizing the program to the outside world and the `jmp` is about determining what processing should occur according to the state of the outside world. For example, if you need to start a process based on the start of a rising edge you could use:

```
wait 0 pin 0
wait 1 pin 0
```

This works by waiting for the GPIO line to go to zero and hence, when the second wait ends, you know that a rising edge has just occurred. For this to be accurate the clock rate should be high compared to the pulses being input. Notice that if you read the line after the second wait, the state will be one clock cycle after the rising edge. In general, whatever you do as a result of the edge will occur some number of clock cycles after the edge. This need for a high clock rate to localize the edge can make other aspects of timing difficult.

For example, we can generate a pulse that is close to the rising edge of an input pulse train. The PIO program is:

```
.program squarewave
again:
    wait 0 pin 0
    wait 1 pin 0
    set pins, 1
    set pins, 0
jmp  again
```

This waits on the first pin in the INPUT group to change from 0 to 1, i.e. a rising edge, and then toggles the first pin in the SET group.

The C program to make this work, using GP2 as the input and GP3 as the output, is:

```c
#include "pico/stdlib.h"
#include "hardware/pio.h"
#include "sqwave.pio.h"
int main()
{
    uint offset = pio_add_program(pio0, &squarewave_program);
    uint sm = pio_claim_unused_sm(pio0, true);
    pio_sm_config c = squarewave_program_get_default_config(offset);
    sm_config_set_set_pins(&c, 3, 1);
    sm_config_set_in_pins(&c, 2);
    pio_gpio_init(pio0, 2);
    pio_gpio_init(pio0, 3);
    pio_sm_set_consecutive_pindirs(pio0, sm, 2, 1, false);
    pio_sm_set_consecutive_pindirs(pio0, sm, 3, 1, true);
    sm_config_set_clkdiv_int_frac(&c, 255, 0);
    pio_sm_init(pio0, sm, offset, &c);
    pio_sm_set_enabled(pio0, sm, true);
    return 0;
}
```

With the clock set to a low rate, you can see that the marker pulse isn't very close to the rising edge:

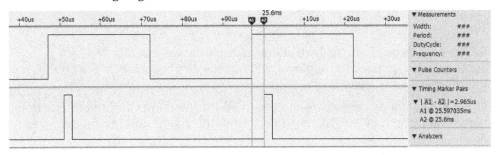

257

If you increase the clock rate to its maximum, the displacement becomes very small – 45n:

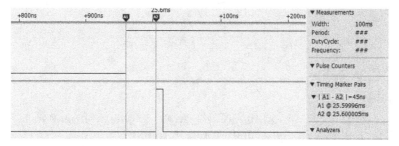

To see the problem, consider the task of moving the marker to the middle of the pulse where you might want to sample the line's state. At maximum clock rate this might be too many cycles to use a simple delay. A slower clock rate is easier, but less accurate in its alignment with the edge.

Advanced PIO

This first look at the PIO and its use has covered the main topics to make it possible for you to write PIO programs and use them from C. It isn't complete and there are many additional features that you still have to discover. Most of these features are about optimization. For example, nearly all PIO programs take the form of an infinite loop and this is a waste of one of the scarce 32 instruction locations and introduces a clock cycle delay. As an alternative you can place:

```
.wrap_target
```

before the instruction that you want to restart the program at and:

```
.wrap
```

after the last instruction. For example, our previous program can be written

```
.program squarewave
.wrap_target
    wait 0 pin 0
    wait 1 pin 0
    set pins, 1
    set pins, 0
.wrap
```

In this case there is no `jmp` instruction as the program counter is automatically set back to the target when it reaches the `wrap`. It is as if the program's address space was circular.

Other topics not discussed are the use of DMA, interrupts and the interaction between multiple PIOs. This is all very straightforward and logical once you have mastered the basics.

Now we move on to discover how the PIO can do useful work for us.

Summary

- The PIO and the state machine are special processors designed to interact with the outside world.

- You can use a PIO attempt to implement any otherwise unsupported protocol.

- The Pico has two PIOs each with four state machines.

- The GPIO lines associated with the PIO are determined by a set of groups – OUT, SET, IN and SETSIDE. GPIO lines also have to be set to PIO mode before they will work in any of the groups.

- You can set the clock frequency that the PIO uses to execute instructions one per clock cycle.

- The clock should be set to a frequency that is suitable for the sort of pulses the PIO is working with.

- It is easy to toggle a GPIO line but slightly harder to make it slow enough to flash an LED. To do this you need to implement a busy wait loop.

- The OSR and ISR are used to send data to and receive data from the GPIO lines.

- There are two FIFO stacks which can be used to send data to the OSR and ISR from the processor.

- Every instruction can change the state of GPIO lines in the SETSIDE group as a side effect of its execution.

- Working with edges isn't natural for the state machine but it can be achieved using wait instructions.

Chapter 14

The DHT22 Sensor
Implementing A Custom Protocol

In this chapter we make use of all the ideas introduced in earlier chapters to create a raw interface with the low-cost DHT11/22 temperature and humidity sensor. It is an exercise in implementing a custom protocol directly in C using bit banging and then using the PIO. Given the documentations advises against using it, you might be wondering why we start with bit banging? The answer is that bit banging is easier to debug and it is usually a good idea to implement it first if possible, if only to prove that the device in question works and you know how it works.

The DHT22

The DHT22 is a more accurate version of the DHT11 and it is used in this project. The software will work with both versions and also with the AM2302, which is equivalent to the DHT22.

Model AM2302/DHT22
Power supply 3.3-5.5V DC
Output signal digital signal via 1-wire bus
Sensing element Polymer humidity capacitor
Operating range
 humidity 0-100%RH;
 temperature -40~80Celsius
Accuracy
 humidity +-2%RH(Max +-5%RH);
 temperature +-0.5Celsius
Resolution or sensitivity
 humidity 0.1%RH;
  temperature 0.1Celsius
Repeatability
  humidity +-1%RH;
  temperature +-0.2Celsius

The device will work at 3.3V and it makes use of a 1-wire open collector-style bus, which makes it very easy to make the physical connection to the Pico.

The 1-wire bus used isn't standard and is only used by this family of devices, so we have little choice but to implement the protocol in C.

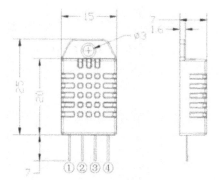

The pinouts are:

1. VDD
2. SDA serial data
3. not used
4. GND

and the standard way of connecting the device is:

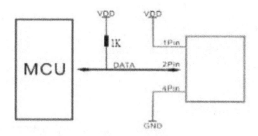

Although the recommended pull-up resistor is 1K, a higher value works better with the Pico - typically 4.7K, but larger will work.

The serial protocol is also fairly simple:

1. The host pulls the line low for between 0.8ms and 29ms, usually 1ms.

2. It then releases the bus which is pulled high.

3. After between 20μs and 200μs, usually 30μs, the device starts to send data by pulling the line down for around 80μs and then lets it float high for another 80μs.

4. Next 40 bits of data are sent using a 70μs high for a 1 and a 26μs high for a 0 with the high pulses separated by around 50μs low periods.

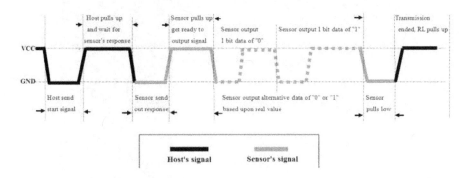

What we have to do is pull the line low for 1ms or so to start the device sending data and this is very easy. Then we have to wait for the device to pull the line down and let it pull up again for about 160μs and then read the time that the line is high or low 40 times.

A 1 corresponds to 70μs and a 0 corresponds to 26 to 28μs. This is within the range of pulse measurements that can be achieved using standard library functions. There is also a 50μs low period between each data bit and this can be used to do some limited processing. The time between falling edge transitions is therefore 120μs for a 1 and 76μs for a 0.

When trying to work out how to decode a new protocol it often helps to try to answer the question, "how can I tell the difference between a 0 and a 1?"

If you have a logic analyzer it can help to look at the waveform and see how you work it out manually. In this case, despite the complex-looking timing diagram, the difference comes down to a short versus a long pulse!

The Electronics

Exactly how you build the circuit is a matter of preference. The basic layout can be seen below.

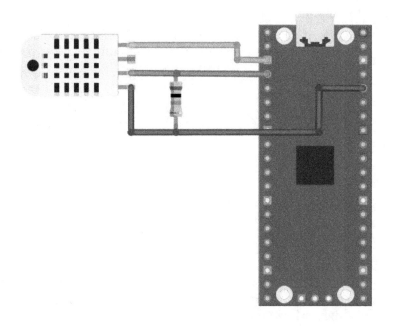

Pico	DHT22
3.5V OUT pin 36	VDD pin 1
GP2 pin 4	SDA serial data pin 2
GND pin 3	GND pin 4

It is very easy to create this circuit using a prototyping board and some jumper wires. You can also put the resistor close to the DHT22 to make a sensor package connected to the Pico using three cables.

The Software

With the hardware shown above connected to the Pico, the first thing that we need to do is establish that the system is working. The simplest way to do this is to pull the line down for 1ms and see if the device responds with a stream of pulses. These can be seen on a logic analyzer or an oscilloscope, both are indispensable tools. If you don't have access to either tool then you will just have to skip to the next stage and see if you can read in some data.

The simplest code that will do the job is:

```c
#include <stdio.h>
#include "pico/stdlib.h"
#include "hardware/gpio.h"

int main()
{
    stdio_init_all();
    gpio_init(2);
    gpio_set_dir(2, GPIO_OUT);
    gpio_put(2, 1);
    sleep_ms(1);
    gpio_put(2, 0);
    sleep_ms(1);
    gpio_set_dir(2, GPIO_IN);
    return 0;
}
```

Setting the line initially high, to ensure that it is configured as an output, we then set it low, wait for around 1ms and then change its direction to input and so allow the line to be pulled high.

There is no need to set the line's pull-up mode because the Pico is the only device driving the line until it releases the line by changing direction to input. When a line is in input mode it is high impedance and this is why we need an external pull-up resistor in the circuit.

As long as the circuit has been correctly assembled and you have a working device, you should see something like:

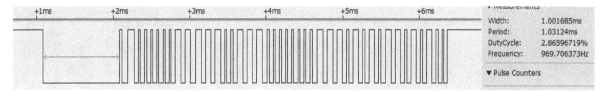

265

Reading the Data

With preliminary flight checks complete, it is time to read the 40-bit data stream. The first thing to do is wait for the low that the device sends before the start bit and then wait for the start bit:

```
for (int i = 0; i < 2; i++)
{
    while (gpio_get(2) == 1){};
    while (gpio_get(2) == 0){};
}
```

The for loop waits for two falling edges.

Next we can start to read in the data. A total of 40 bits, i.e. 5 bytes, is difficult to work with in standard variable types. A good compromise is to read in the first 32 bits into a 32-bit unsigned integer and then read the final byte into a byte variable. The reason is that the fifth byte is a checksum, so we have separated out the data and the checksum, but there are many different ways to organize this task.

First we read the 32 data bits:

```
uint32_t t2;
uint32_t data = 0;
uint32_t t1 = time_us_32();
for (int i = 0; i < 32; i++)
{
    while (gpio_get(2) == 1){};
    while (gpio_get(2) == 0){};
    t2 = time_us_32();
    data = data << 1;
    data = data | ((t2 - t1) > 100);
    t1 = t2;
}
```

You can see the general idea is to simply find the time between falling edges and then treat anything bigger then 100μs as a 1. In practice, the measured times between falling edges is 80μs for a 0 and 120μs and 100 is a threshold halfway between the two. The bits are shifted into the variable data so that the first byte transmitted is the high-order byte.

Next we need to read the checksum byte:

```
uint8_t checksum = 0;
for (int i = 0; i < 8; i++)
{
    while (gpio_get(2) == 1){};
    while (gpio_get(2) == 0){};
    t2 = time_us_32();
    checksum = checksum << 1;
    checksum = checksum | (t2 - t1) > 100;
    t1 = t2;
}
```

This works in the same way. At the end of this we have 32 data bits in data and eight checksum bits in checksum and all we have to do is process the data to get the temperature and humidity.

Extracting the Data

You can process the data without unpacking it into individual bytes, but it is easier to see what is happening if we do:

```
uint8_t byte1 = (data >> 24 & 0xFF);
uint8_t byte2 = (data >> 16 & 0xFF);
uint8_t byte3 = (data >> 8 & 0xFF);
uint8_t byte4 = (data & 0xFF);
```

The first two bytes are the humidity measurement and the second two the temperature.

The checksum is just the sum of the first four bytes reduced to eight bits and we can test it using:

```
printf("Checksum %X %X\n",checksum,(byte1+byte2+byte3+byte4)&0xFF);
```

If you don't want to unpack the data then you can use:

```
printf("Checksum %X %X\n", checksum, ((data & 0xFF) +
            (data >> 8 & 0xFF) + (data >> 16 & 0xFF) +
                        (data >> 24 & 0xFF)) & 0xFF);
```

If the two values are different, there has been a transmission error. The addition of the bytes is done as a full integer and then it is reduced back to a single byte by the AND operation. If there is a checksum error, the simplest thing to do is get another reading from the device. Notice, however, that you shouldn't read the device more than once every two seconds.

The humidity and temperature data are also easy to reconstruct as they are transmitted high byte first and 10 times the actual value.

Extracting the humidity data is easy:

```
float humidity = (float)((byte1 <<8)| byte2) / 10.0;
printf("Humidity= %f %\n", humidity);
```

The temperature data is slightly more difficult in that the topmost bit is used to indicate a negative temperature. This means we have to test for the most significant bit and flip the sign of the temperature if it is set:

```
float temperature;
int neg = byte3 & 0x80;
byte3 = byte3 & 0x7F;
temperature = (float)(byte3 << 8 | byte4) / 10.0;
if (neg > 0)
    temperature = -temperature;
printf("Temperature= %f C\n", temperature);
```

This completes the data processing.

The program as presented works, but it would benefit from refactoring into functions. A complete, refactored, listing including a main program can be seen below. This is just one way to break the program down into functions and exactly how to do it depends on many factors.

```
#include <stdio.h>
#include "pico/stdlib.h"
#include "hardware/gpio.h"

inline static void WaitFallingEdge(uint gpio)
{
    while (gpio_get(gpio) == 1){};
    while (gpio_get(gpio) == 0){};
}

uint32_t getData(uint gpio)
{
    uint32_t t2;
    uint32_t data = 0;
    uint32_t t1 = time_us_32();
    for (int i = 0; i < 32; i++)
    {
        WaitFallingEdge(2);
        t2 = time_us_32();
        data = data << 1;
        data = data | ((t2 - t1) > 100);
        t1 = t2;
    }
    return data;
}
```

```
uint8_t getCheck(uint gpio)
{
    uint8_t checksum = 0;
    uint32_t t2;
    uint32_t t1 = time_us_32();
    for (int i = 0; i < 8; i++)
    {
        WaitFallingEdge(2);
        t2 = time_us_32();
        checksum = checksum << 1;
        checksum = checksum | (t2 - t1) > 100;
        t1 = t2;
    }
    return checksum;
}

void dhtInitalize(uint gpio){
    gpio_init(gpio);
    gpio_set_dir(gpio, GPIO_OUT);
    gpio_put(gpio, 1);
    sleep_ms(1);
    gpio_put(gpio, 0);
    sleep_ms(1);
    gpio_set_dir(gpio, GPIO_IN);
    for (int i = 0; i < 2; i++)
    {
        WaitFallingEdge(gpio);
    }
}

typedef struct
{
    float temperature;
    float humidity;
    bool error;
} dhtData;
```

```
void dhtread(uint gpio, dhtData *reading)
{
    dhtInitalize(gpio);
    uint32_t data = getData(gpio);
    uint8_t checksum = getCheck(gpio);
    uint8_t byte1 = (data >> 24 & 0xFF);
    uint8_t byte2 = (data >> 16 & 0xFF);
    uint8_t byte3 = (data >> 8 & 0xFF);
    uint8_t byte4 = (data & 0xFF);

    reading->error= (checksum != ((byte1 + byte2 + byte3 + byte4)
                                                    & 0xFF));
    reading->humidity = (float)((byte1 << 8) | byte2) / 10.0;

    int neg = byte3 & 0x80;
    byte3 = byte3 & 0x7F;
    reading->temperature = (float)(byte3 << 8 | byte4) / 10.0;
    if (neg > 0)
        reading->temperature = -reading->temperature;
}

int main()
{
    stdio_init_all();

    printf("data^^^^^\n");
    dhtData reading;
    dhtread(2, &reading);
    printf("Humidity= %f %\n", reading.humidity);
    printf("Temperature= %f C\n", reading.temperature);
    return 0;
}
```

DHT22 Using the PIO – Counting

The DHT22 is not well suited to working with the PIO. The reason is that its protocol doesn't use fixed time slots for each bit or synchronization via a separate clock, two situations where it is usually possible to write compact PIO programs to send and receive data. The DHT22 relies on the length of the slot used to transmit a single bit to code zero or one and this means that decoding is a matter of measuring the time between edges. The PIO doesn't have access to a timer and implementing an instruction clock counter isn't straightforward – but it can be done. The following PIO program does exactly this, but it is a long program and it only just satisfies the constraints placed on it to work. After presenting the obvious algorithm with a slightly difficult implementation, a simpler and more direct but less obvious method is implemented.

Before going into details, it is worth explaining what the constraints are and what makes PIO access worth the effort. The bit-banging solution given earlier works and is perfectly good. However, it demands the full attention of the processor while the data is being read in. If an interrupt occurs during reading, the data will be corrupt. On the other hand, if you can implement a PIO program that reads in the data the processor is free to do something else until it wants to use the data and interrupts have no effect. This all depends on the PIO being able to read the data from the device and keep it stored ready for when the processor wants to read it. If you consider this for a few moments, this means that you can hold data in the 4-word FIFO buffer and an additional word in the ISR, making a total of 160 bits of temporary storage, which seems to be more than enough for the 40 bits that the DHT22 produces. However, for a timing-based protocol, things are more complicated.

We can write a loop that counts instruction cycles when the input line is high and this count can be up to 32 bits in resolution. However, there is no easy way to convert the 32-bit count into single bits by applying a threshold as in the bit-banging example. What this means is that we are forced to send the bit counts, rather than the decoded bits back to the processor. A little arithmetic reveals that we can store the counts for all 40 bits as long as the count is represented as a 4-bit number. We can store the first 32-bits, the data in the four word FIFO buffer with the counts for each byte, in a single element. The final byte can be stored in the ISR until the processor reads the FIFO register and frees up space. A count of 4 bits is enough to tell the difference between the times for a zero and a one and this makes the whole scheme possible, as long as we adjust the clock frequency correctly.

What all this means is that we can write a PIO program that can be set to read the data from the DHT22 and store the result in the FIFO and the ISR until the processor is ready to read it. The downside is that the processor has to convert the timing counts to bits and pack the results into bytes before processing the humidity, temperature and checksum – a small price to pay.

With all this worked out we can write the PIO program. The first problem is that we have to send a 1ms initialization pulse:

```
.program dht
        set pins, 1
        set pindirs, 1
again:
        pull block
        set pins, 0
        mov x, osr
loop1:
        jmp x--,loop1
        set pindirs, 0
```

This uses a data value written to the state machine by the C program to execute a delay loop that takes 1ms. It also serves to start the conversion. Also notice that the low pulse is terminated by setting the pin to input. Next we have to wait for two rising edges to pass before we get to the data pulses:

```
wait 1 pin 0
wait 0 pin 0
wait 1 pin 0
wait 0 pin 0
```

Finally we can start reading in the four bytes of data:

```
        set y,31
bits:
        wait 1 pin 0
        set x, 0
loop2:
        jmp x--,continue
continue: jmp pin,loop2
        in x,4
        jmp y--,bits
```

The bits loop processes all 32 bits. The inner loop2 processes each bit in turn. The x register is set to zero and then decremented using a forward jump to the end of the loop. Notice that it doesn't matter if the jump is taken, the next instruction is always continue. Decrementing the x register when it is already at zero seems to increment it, but as this is not part of the PIO specification there is a small danger that this behavior might change. Once the loop has completed, the 4-bit count is transferred to the ISR and the next bit starts. Notice that it is assumed that auto-push is set so that the FIFO is automatically added to when the ISR is full.

We have to repeat the process for the checksum:

```
        set y,7
check:
        wait 1 pin 0
        set x, 0
loop3:
        jmp x--,continue2
continue2: jmp pin,loop3
        in x,4
        jmp y--,check
jmp again
```

Notice that if the C program hasn't read the FIFO then this blocks and waits for free space. Finally, we jump back to the start of the program to wait for the C program to write to the FIFO.

The C program to make all this work is fairly straightforward, but it involves a lot of bit manipulation to convert the counts into bits:

```c
uint8_t getByte(PIO pio, uint sm)
{
    uint32_t count = pio_sm_get_blocking(pio0, sm);
    uint8_t byte = 0;
    for (int i = 0; i < 8; i++)
    {
        byte = byte << 1;
        if (((count >> i * 4) & 0x0F) > 8)
        {
            byte = byte | 1;
        }
    }
    return byte;
}
```

This reads a word from the PIO and converts it into a byte by comparing each 4-bit count with a threshold, i.e. 8.

Using this function we can obtain the five bytes needed to compute the humidity, temperature and checksum as per the previous program. All that is needed to complete the program is a function to get the data in a useful form and an initialization function.

The complete program is:

```c
#include <stdio.h>
#include "pico/stdlib.h"
#include "hardware/gpio.h"
#include "hardware/pio.h"
#include "DHT.pio.h"
uint dhtInitalize(PIO pio, int gpio)
{
    uint offset = pio_add_program(pio, &dht_program);

    uint sm = pio_claim_unused_sm(pio, true);
    pio_gpio_init(pio, gpio);
    pio_sm_config c = dht_program_get_default_config(offset);
    sm_config_set_clkdiv_int_frac(&c, 128, 0);
    sm_config_set_set_pins(&c, gpio, 1);
    sm_config_set_in_pins(&c, gpio);
    sm_config_set_jmp_pin(&c, gpio);
    sm_config_set_in_shift(&c, true, true, 32);
    pio_sm_init(pio0, sm, offset, &c);

    pio_sm_set_enabled(pio0, sm, true);
    return sm;
}
```

```c
uint8_t getByte(PIO pio, uint sm)
{
    uint32_t count = pio_sm_get_blocking(pio0, sm);
    uint8_t byte = 0;
    for (int i = 0; i < 8; i++)
    {
        byte = byte << 1;
        if (((count >> i * 4) & 0x0F) > 8)
        {
            byte = byte | 1;
        }
    }
    return byte;
}

typedef struct
{
    float temperature;
    float humidity;
    bool error;
} dhtData;

void dhtread(PIO pio, uint sm, dhtData *reading)
{
    pio_sm_put_blocking(pio, sm, 1000);
    uint8_t byte1 = getByte(pio, sm);
    uint8_t byte2 = getByte(pio, sm);
    uint8_t byte3 = getByte(pio, sm);
    uint8_t byte4 = getByte(pio, sm);
    uint8_t checksum = getByte(pio, sm);
    reading->error = (checksum == (byte1 + byte2 + byte3 + byte4) &
                                                        0xFF);
    reading->humidity = (float)((byte1 << 8) | byte2) / 10.0;
    int neg = byte3 & 0x80;
    byte3 = byte3 & 0x7F;
    reading->temperature = (float)(byte3 << 8 | byte4) / 10.0;
    if (neg > 0) reading->temperature = -reading->temperature;
}
int main()
{
    stdio_init_all();
    uint sm = dhtInitalize(pio0, 2);
    dhtData reading;
    dhtread(pio0, sm, &reading);
    printf("Humidity= %f %\n", reading.humidity);
    printf("Temperature= %f C\n", reading.temperature);
    return 0;
}
```

The initialization program is the only function of additional interest as most of the rest of the program follows the previous example. The function dhtInitalize(PIO pio, int gpio) sets the clock frequency so that instructions take $2\mu s$. This gives a count in the region of 4 to 13 and the threshold is set accordingly. At this clock speed, you also need to set the x register to 1000 to get the 1ms initialization pulse. It also sets the auto-push to 32 bits and a right shift. Notice that as well as the SET and IN groups, you have to set the jump pin to the GPIO line being used or the counting loop doesn't work.

The PIO program is:

```
.program dht
    set pins, 1
    set pindirs, 1
again:
  pull block
  set pins, 0
mov x, osr
loop1:
    jmp x--,loop1
set pindirs, 0
wait 1 pin 0
wait 0 pin 0
wait 1 pin 0
wait 0 pin 0

        set y,31
bits:
        wait 1 pin 0
        set x, 0
loop2:
        jmp x--,continue
continue: jmp pin,loop2
        in x,4
        jmp y--,bits

        set y,7
check:
        wait 1 pin 0
        set x, 0
loop3:
        jmp x--,continue2
continue2: jmp pin,loop3
        in x,4
        jmp y--,check
jmp again
```

See the next section for the CMakeLists.txt file used.

DHT22 Using the PIO – Sampling

A simpler alternative way for decoding the data is to ignore the fact that it is the width of each bit's frame that defines a zero, a short frame, or a one a long frame, and notice that if you sample at a suitable fixed time from the rising edge of a pulse then you will get a zero in a zero frame and a one in a one frame:

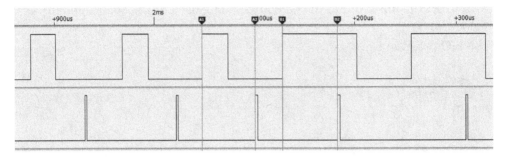

You can see the sampling times from the pulses on the lower trace of the logic analyzer and the fact that you do indeed get a 0 in a zero frame and a 1 in a one frame. You can also see that the time to sample from the rising edge is constant, even if the sampling period varies.

Surprisingly, the PIO program to implement this sampling isn't significantly simpler than the previous program, but the entire four data bytes can now be packed into a single FIFO entry and the checksum byte can occupy a second entry.

The PIO program starts off in the same way:

```
.program dht
    set pins, 1
    set pindirs, 1
again:
  pull block
  set pins, 0
mov x, osr
loop1:
    jmp x--,loop1
set pindirs, 0
wait 1 pin 0
wait 0 pin 0
wait 1 pin 0
wait 0 pin 0
```

The waits' position is at the state of the data and now we can wait for a rising edge and then delay until the sample time:

```
set y,31
bits:
   wait 1 pin 0 [25]
    in pins,1
    wait 0 pin 0
 jmp y--,bits
```

This too is very similar, only now we don't keep a count but simply add the single bit sampled from the input line to the ISR. When all 32 bits have been added, the autopush moves the data to the FIFO.

The eight checksum bits are just as easy to process and the complete PIO program is:

```
.program dht
 set pins, 1
 set pindirs, 1
again:
 pull block
 set pins, 0
mov x, osr
loop1:
 jmp x--,loop1
set pindirs, 0
wait 1 pin 0
wait 0 pin 0
wait 1 pin 0
wait 0 pin 0

set y,31
bits:
 wait 1 pin 0 [25]
 in pins,1
 wait 0 pin 0
 jmp y--,bits

 set y,7
check:
wait 1 pin 0 [25]
 in pins,1
 wait 0 pin 0
 jmp y--,check
push block
jmp again
```

Notice that we have to manually push the ISR because it doesn't fill up just the 8 bits of the checksum.

The C program is also very like the previous program, but we have to change the clock frequency and the shift direction to make decoding the bytes from the 32-bit word easier:

```
sm_config_set_clkdiv_int_frac(&c, 255, 0);
sm_config_set_in_shift(&c, false, true, 32);
```

We need a slower clock speed to make the delay position the sample point about $50\mu s$ from the rising edge – recall that the delay is limited to 32 clock cycles.

The dhtread function now might as well read the FIFO and decode the data directly as it is a much simpler task:

```
void dhtread(PIO pio, uint sm, dhtData *reading)
{
    pio_sm_put_blocking(pio, sm, 500);
    uint32_t data = pio_sm_get_blocking(pio0, sm);
    uint8_t byte1 = (data >> 24 & 0xFF);
    uint8_t byte2 = (data >> 16 & 0xFF);
    uint8_t byte3 = (data >> 8 & 0xFF);
    uint8_t byte4 = (data & 0xFF);
    uint8_t checksum = pio_sm_get_blocking(pio0, sm) & 0xFF;
```

Notice the need to change the value sent to the input to account for the slower clock rate – 500 now produces a 1ms initialization pulse. The rest of the program is unchanged as we now have the four data bytes and the checksum as before. This program is simpler to implement and can be extended to a protocol that needs to read in more than 40 bits at a time.

Complete Listing

```
#include <stdio.h>
#include "pico/stdlib.h"
#include "hardware/gpio.h"
#include "hardware/pio.h"
#include "DHT.pio.h"
uint dhtInitalize(PIO pio, int gpio)
{
    uint offset = pio_add_program(pio, &dht_program);
    uint sm = pio_claim_unused_sm(pio, true);
    pio_gpio_init(pio, gpio);
    pio_sm_config c = dht_program_get_default_config(offset);
    sm_config_set_clkdiv_int_frac(&c, 255, 0);
    sm_config_set_set_pins(&c, gpio, 1);
    sm_config_set_in_pins(&c, gpio);
    sm_config_set_in_shift(&c, false, true, 32);
    pio_sm_init(pio0, sm, offset, &c);
    pio_sm_set_enabled(pio0, sm, true);
    return sm;
}
```

```c
typedef struct
{
    float temperature;
    float humidity;
    bool error;
} dhtData;

void dhtread(PIO pio, uint sm, dhtData *reading)
{
    pio_sm_put_blocking(pio, sm, 500);

    uint32_t data = pio_sm_get_blocking(pio0, sm);
    uint8_t byte1 = (data >> 24 & 0xFF);
    uint8_t byte2 = (data >> 16 & 0xFF);
    uint8_t byte3 = (data >> 8 & 0xFF);
    uint8_t byte4 = (data & 0xFF);
    uint8_t checksum = pio_sm_get_blocking(pio0, sm) & 0xFF;

    reading->error = (checksum != ((byte1 + byte2 + byte3 + byte4) &
                                                    0xFF));
    reading->humidity = (float)((byte1 << 8) | byte2) / 10.0;

    int neg = byte3 & 0x80;
    byte3 = byte3 & 0x7F;
    reading->temperature = (float)(byte3 << 8 | byte4) / 10.0;
    if (neg > 0)
        reading->temperature = -reading->temperature;
}

int main()
{
    stdio_init_all();
    uint sm = dhtInitalize(pio0, 2);
    dhtData reading;
    dhtread(pio0, sm, &reading);
    printf("Humidity= %f %\n", reading.humidity);
    printf("Temperature= %f C\n", reading.temperature);
    return 0;
}
```

The full PIO program is:

```
.program dht
    set pins, 1
    set pindirs, 1
again:
  pull block
  set pins, 0
mov x, osr
loop1:
    jmp x--,loop1
set pindirs, 0
wait 1 pin 0
wait 0 pin 0
wait 1 pin 0
wait 0 pin 0

set y,31
bits:
   wait 1 pin 0 [25]
    in pins,1
    wait 0 pin 0
 jmp y--,bits

 set y,7
check:
wait 1 pin 0 [25]
    in pins,1
    wait 0 pin 0
 jmp y--,check
push block
jmp again
```

Assuming that the C file is called DHT.c and the PIO file is called DHT.PIO, the Cmakelists.txt file is:

```
cmake_minimum_required(VERSION 3.13)
set(CMAKE_C_STANDARD 11)
set(CMAKE_CXX_STANDARD 17)
include(pico_sdk_import.cmake)
project(dht C CXX ASM)
pico_sdk_init()
add_executable(dht
 DHT.c
 )
pico_generate_pio_header(dht ${CMAKE_CURRENT_LIST_DIR}/DHT.pio)
target_link_libraries(dht  pico_stdlib hardware_pio)
pico_add_extra_outputs(dht)
```

Summary

- The DHT22 is a low-cost temperature and humidity sensor.

- It uses a custom single wire bus which is not compatible with the 1-Wire bus.

- Its asynchronous protocol is easy to implement directly in user space.

- A very simple checksum is used to detect errors.

- It is possible to implement the protocol as defined in the data sheet using a PIO by using counting loops to time each pulse.

- A better use of the PIO is to notice that the protocol can be decoded by testing the state of the line a fixed time after the rising edge.

Chapter 15
The 1-Wire Bus And The DS1820

The 1-Wire bus is a proprietary bus that is very easy to use and has a lot of useful devices you can connect to it, including the iButton security devices, memory, data loggers, fuel gauges and more. However, probably the most popular of all 1-Wire devices is the DS18B20 temperature sensor - it is small, very cheap and very easy to use. This chapter show you how to work with it, but first let's deal with the general techniques needed to work with the 1-Wire bus.

Programming in C on the Pico gives you more than enough speed to implement a bit-banging driver, which for many purposes is sufficient. However, the 1-Wire protocol is easy enough to implement using the PIO. In this chapter we look at the basic ideas of the 1-Wire bus, implement a bit banging program for its most popular device and extend this to a PIO program.

The Hardware

One-wire devices are very simple and only use a single wire to transmit data:

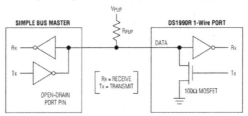

The 1-Wire device can pull the bus low using its Tx line and can read the line using its Rx line. The reason for the pull-up resistor is that both the bus master and the slave can pull the bus low and it will stay low until they both release the bus.

The device can even be powered from the bus line by drawing sufficient current through the pull-up resistor - so called parasitic mode. Low power devices work well in parasitic mode, but some devices have such a heavy current draw that the master has to provide a way to connect them to the power line - so called strong pull-up. In practice, parasitic mode can be difficult to make work reliably for high-power devices.

In normal-powered mode there are just three connections - V power, usually 3.3V for the Pico, Ground and Data:

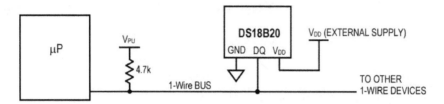

The pull-up resistor varies according to the device, but anything from 2.2K to 4.7kΩ works. The longer the bus, the lower the pull-up resistor has to be to reduce "ringing". There can be multiple devices on the bus and each one has a unique 64-bit lasered ROM code, which can be used as an address to select the active devices.

For simplicity, it is better to start off with a single device and avoid the problem of enumerating the devices on the bus, although once you know how everything works this isn't difficult to implement. To get started, select a 1-wire device that you want to work with and set it up ready to talk to the Pico, in this case the DS18B20 is explained. The functions described in this chapter should work with any 1-wire device.

Initialization

Every transaction with a 1-wire device starts with an initialization handshake. First we have to work out how to configure the GPIO line. This example assumes that the 1-wire device is connected to GP2.

You might think that we have to initialize the GPIO line so that it works in pull-up mode. This isn't necessary and the default push-pull mode will do. The reason is that, in the case of the 1-wire bus, the master controls when other devices send their data. Typically the master sends a pulse and then the slaves respond by pulling the line low. As long as the master doesn't drive the line during the period when the slaves are responding, everything is fine.

What we do in practice is to configure the GPIO line for output only when the master needs to drive the line. Once the master is finished the GPIO line is set back to input and the pull-up resistor is allowed to pull the line back up. After this, any slave wanting to send data is free to pull the line low.

The first transaction we need is the initialization pulse. This is simply a low pulse that lasts at least 480μs, a pause of 15μs to 60μs follows and then any and all of the devices on the bus pull the line low for 60μs to 240μs.

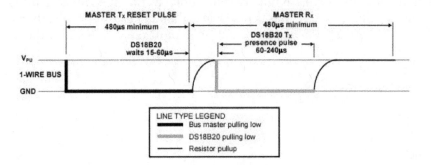

The suggested timings are set the line low for $480\mu s$ and read the line after $70\mu s$ followed by a pause of $410\mu s$.

This is fairly easy to implement as a function:

```
int presence(uint8_t pin)
{
    gpio_set_dir(2, GPIO_OUT);
    gpio_put(pin, 1);
    sleep_ms(1);
    gpio_put(pin, 0);
    sleep_us(480);
    gpio_set_dir(pin, GPIO_IN);
    sleep_us(70);
    int b = gpio_get(pin);
    sleep_us(410);
    return b;
}
```

We pull the line low for $480\mu s$ and then let it be pulled back up by changing the line to input, i.e. high impedance. After a $70\mu s$ wait, which is right at the start of the guaranteed period when the line should be low if there is an active device on the bus, we read the input line and then wait another $410\mu s$ to complete the data slot.

The timings in this case are not critical as long as the line is read while it is held low by the slaves, which is never less than 60μs and is typically as much as 100μs. If there is a device, the function should return a 0 and if there are no devices it should return a 1.

```c
#include <stdio.h>
#include "pico/stdlib.h"
#include "hardware/gpio.h"
int main()
{
    stdio_init_all();
    gpio_init(2);

    if (presence(2) == 1)
    {
        printf("No device \n");
    }
    else
    {
        printf("Device present \n");
    }
    return 0;
}
```

If you try this partial program and have a logic analyzer with a 1-wire protocol analyzer you will see something like:

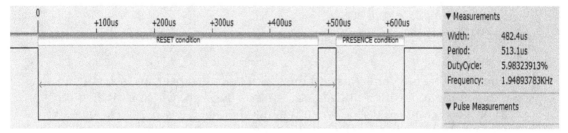

Seeing a presence pulse is the simplest and quickest way to be sure that your hardware is working.

Writing Bits

Our next task is to implement the sending of some data bits to the device. The 1-Wire bus has a very simple data protocol. All bits are sent using a minimum of 60μs for a read/write slot. Each slot must be separated from the next by a minimum of 1μs.

The good news is that timing is only critical within each slot. You can send the first bit in a time slot and then take your time before you send the next bit as the device will wait for you. This means you only have to worry about timing within the functions that read and write individual bits.

To send a 0 you have to hold the line low for most of the slot. To send a 1 you have to hold the line low for just between 1μs and 15μs and leave the line high for the rest of the slot. The exact timings can be seen below:

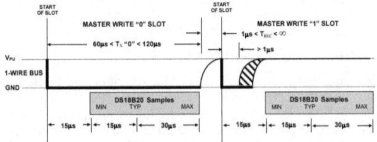

It seems reasonable to use the typical timings given in the datasheets. So for a 0 we hold the line low for 60μs then let it go high for the remainder of the slot, 10μs. To send a 1 we hold the line for 6μs and then let it go high for the remainder of the slot, 64μs. As the only time critical operations are the actual setting of the line low and then back to high, there is no need to worry too much about the speed of operation of the entire function so we might as well combine writing 0 and 1 into a single writeBit function:

```
void writeBit(uint8_t pin, int b)
{
    int delay1, delay2;
    if (b == 1)
    {
        delay1 = 6;
        delay2 = 64;
    }
    else
    {
        delay1 = 60;
        delay2 = 10;
    }
    gpio_set_dir(pin, GPIO_OUT);
    gpio_put(pin, 0);
    sleep_us(delay1);
    gpio_set_dir(pin, GPIO_IN);
    sleep_us(delay2);
}
```

The code at the start of the function simply increases the time between slots slightly. Notice that once again we return the GPIO line to input, i.e. high impedance, rather than driving the line high at the end of the transaction. This allows the line to be pulled high ready for any response from the slave.

You can see two ones followed by two zeros in the following logic analyzer trace:

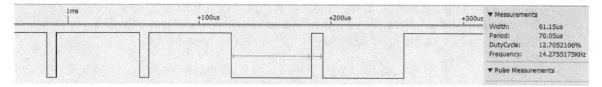

A First Command - Writing Bytes

After discovering that there is at least one device connected to the bus, the master has to issue a ROM command. In many cases the ROM command used first will be the Search ROM command, which enumerates the 64-bit codes of all of the devices on the bus. After collecting all of these codes, the master can use Match ROM commands with a specific 64-bit code to select the device the master wants to talk to.

While it is perfectly possible to implement the Search ROM procedure, it is simpler to work with the single device by using commands which ignore the 64-bit code and address all of the devices on the bus at the same time. Of course, this only works as long as there is only one device on the bus. If there is only one device then we can use the Skip ROM command 0xCC to tell all the devices on the bus to be active.

We now need a function that can send a byte. As we have a writeBit function this is easy:

```
void sendskip(uint8_t pin){
 writeBit(pin 0);
 writeBit(pin 0);
 writeBit(pin 1);
 writeBit(pin 1);
 writeBit(pin 0);
 writeBit(pin 0);
 writeBit(pin 1);
 writeBit(pin 1);
}
```

Notice that 0xCC is 1100 1100 in binary and the 1-Wire bus sends the least significant bit first. If you try this out you should find it works, but the device doesn't respond because it is waiting for another command. Again, as the time between writing bits isn't critical, we can take this first implementation of the function and write something more general, if slightly slower.

The `writeByte` function will write the low eight bits of an `int` to the device:

```c
void writeByte(uint8_t pin, int byte) {
    int i;
    for (i = 0; i < 8; i++) {
        if (byte & 1) {
            writeBit(pin, 1);
        } else {
            writeBit(pin, 0);
        }
        byte = byte >> 1;
    }
}
```

Using this we can send a Skip ROM command using:

```c
writeByte(2, 0xCC);
```

You can see the pattern of bits sent on a logic analyzer:

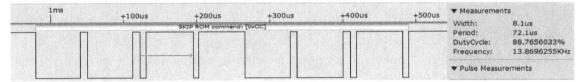

Reading Bits

We already know how the master sends a 1 and a 0. The protocol for the slave device is exactly the same except that the master still provides the slot's starting pulse. That is, the master starts a 60μs slot by pulling the bus down for at least 1μs. Then the slave device either holds the line down for a further 15μs minimum or it simply allows the line to float high. See below for the exact timings:

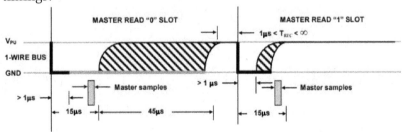

So all we have to do to read bits is to pull the line down for more than 1μs and then sample the bus after pausing long enough for the line to be pulled up or held low. The datasheet gives 6μs for the master's pulse and a 9μs pause.

In practice, a final delay of $2\mu s$ seems to work best and allows for the time to change the line's direction:

```
uint8_t readBit(uint8_t pin)
{
    gpio_set_dir(pin, GPIO_OUT);
    gpio_put(pin, 0);
    sleep_us(8);
    gpio_set_dir(pin, GPIO_IN);
    sleep_us(2);
    uint8_t b = gpio_get(pin);
    sleep_us(60);
    return b;
}
```

A logic analyzer shows the typical pattern of bits from the device:

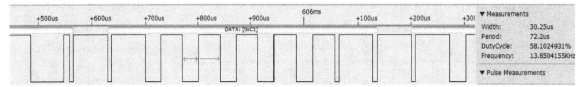

By adding some commands to toggle a line after the sample is taken, we can see how the timing works:

You might think that sampling so close to the rising edge of the timing pulse is a bad idea, but the timing of the sample tends to drift longer not shorter and this short timing reduces the error rate.

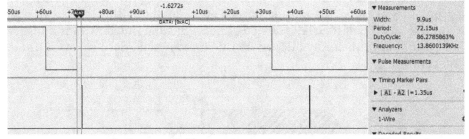

Finally, we need a function that will read a byte. As in the case of writing a byte, there is no time criticality in the time between reading bits so we don't need to take extra special care in constructing the function:

```
int readByte(uint8_t pin) {
    int byte = 0;
    int i;
    for (i = 0; i < 8; i++) {
        byte = byte | readBit(pin) << i;
    };
    return byte;
}
```

The only difficult part is to remember that the 1-Wire bus sends the least significant bit first and so this has to be shifted into the result from the right. The sequence is:

- Test to see if a device is present:
    ```
    presence(uint8_t pin)
    ```
- Write a byte:
    ```
    void writeByte(uint8_t pin, int byte)
    ```
- Read a byte:
    ```
    int readByte(uint8_t pin)
    ```

These functions will be used in the next two chapters to work with real 1-wire devices.

These are not the only functions we need to work with the 1-Wire bus. We need to be able to compute the CRC error checks that are commonly used to confirm that data has been transmitted correctly and we need to perform a ROM search to discover what devices are connected to the bus, but this is beyond the scope of this introduction. For details of a general C implementation, see *Raspberry Pi IOT in C, Second Edition*, ISBN:9781871962635.

Computing The CRC

We have already encountered the idea and implementation of a CRC (Cyclic Redundancy Checksum) in Chapter 12. The 1-Wire bus uses the same CRC for all its devices and therefore we need to implement it just once. This is perhaps not in the most efficient way, but it will work. For low data rate applications high efficiency isn't needed and you can make use of a direct implementation. The 1-Wire datasheet specifies the CRC used in 1-wire devices as a shift register rather than as a polynomial equation:

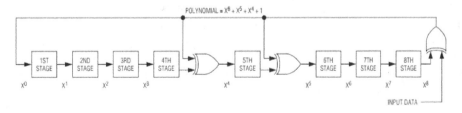

However, this is equivalent to a generator polynomial that defines the CRC as it is simply the hardware implementation of the calculation.

In this case it is:

$X^8 + X^5 + X^4 + 1$

The first question to answer is, what is the connection between binary values, polynomials and shift-registers? The answer is that you can treat a binary number as the coefficients of a polynomial, for example 101 is $1*X^2+0*X+1$. Each bit position corresponds to a power of X. Using this notation creates a very simple relationship between multiplying by X and a left-shift.

For example:

$(1*X^2 + 0*X+ 1)*X = 1*X^3 + 0*X^2 + 1X + 0$

corresponds to:

101 <<1 == 1010

You can see that this extends to multiplying one polynomial by another and even polynomial division, all accomplished by shifting and XOR (eXclusive OR).

The CRC is the remainder when you divide the polynomial that represents the data by the generator polynomial. The computation of the remainder is what the shift register specified on the datasheet does. The fact that the division can be implemented so simply in hardware is what makes this sort of CRC computation so common. All the hardware has to do is zero the shift register and feed the data into it. When all the data has been shifted in, what is left in the shift register is the CRC, i.e. the remainder.

To check the data you have received, all you have to do is run it through the shift register again and compare the computed CRC with the one received. A better trick is also to run the received CRC through the shift register. If there have been no errors, this will result in 0.

You can look into the theory of CRCs, bit sequences and polynomials further, it is interesting and practically useful, but we now know everything we need to if we want to implement the CRC used by 1-Wire devices. All we have to do is implement the shift register in software.

From the diagram, what we have to do is take each bit of the input data and XOR it with the least significant bit of the current shift register. If the input bit is 0, the XORs in the shift register don't have any effect and the CRC just has to be moved one bit to the right. If the input bit is 1, we have to XOR the bits at positions 3 and 4 with 1 and put a 1 in at position 7 to simulate shifting a 1 into the register, i.e. XOR the shift register with 10001100.

So the algorithm for a single byte is:

```
for (j = 0; j < 8; j++) {
        temp = (crc ^ databyte) & 0x01;
        crc >>= 1;
        if (temp)
                crc ^= 0x8C;
                databyte>>= 1;
        }
}
```

First we XOR the data with the current CRC and extract the low-order bit into temp. Then we right-shift the CRC by one place. If the low-order result stored in temp was a 1, we have to XOR the CRC with 0x8C to simulate the XORs in the shift register and shift in a 1 at the most significant bit. Then shift the data one place right and repeat for the next data bit.

With this worked out, we can now write a crc8 function that computes the CRC for the entire eight bytes of data:

```
uint8_t crc8(uint8_t *data, uint8_t len) {
    uint8_t i;
    uint8_t j;
    uint8_t temp;
    uint8_t databyte;
    uint8_t crc = 0;
    for (i = 0; i < len; i++) {
        databyte = data[i];
        for (j = 0; j < 8; j++) {
            temp = (crc ^ databyte) & 0x01;
            crc >>= 1;
            if (temp)
            crc ^= 0x8C;
            databyte >>= 1;
        }
    }
    return crc;
}
```

With this in place we can now check the CRC of any data a 1-Wire bus device sends us.

The DS18B20 Hardware

Now let's put all of this to work with the most popular 1-Wire device, the DS18B20. It is available in a number of formats, but the most common makes it look just like a standard BJT (Bipolar Junction Transistor) which can sometimes be a problem when you are trying to find one. You can also get them made up into waterproof sensors complete with cable.

No matter how packaged, they will work at 3.3V or 5V.

The basic specification of the DS18B20 is:

- Measures temperatures from -55°C to +125°C (-67°F to +257°F)
- ±0.5°C accuracy from -10°C to +85°C
- Thermometer resolution is user-selectable from 9 to 12 bits
- Converts temperature to 12-bit digital word in 750ms (max)

It can also be powered from the data line, allowing the bus to operate with only two wires - data and ground. However, this "parasitic power" mode is difficult to make work reliably and best avoided in an initial design. To supply it with enough power during a conversion, the host has to connect it directly to the data line by providing a "strong pull-up" - essentially a transistor. In normal-powered mode there are just three connections:

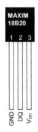

Ground needs to be connected to the system ground, VDD to 3.3V and DQ to the pull-up resistor of an open collector bus.

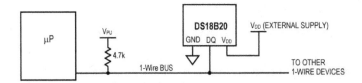

While you can have multiple devices on the same bus, for simplicity it is better to start off with a single device until you know that everything is working.

You can build the circuit in a variety of ways. You can solder the resistor to the temperature sensor and then use some longer wires with clips to connect to the Pico. You could also solder directly to the Pico or use a prototyping board.

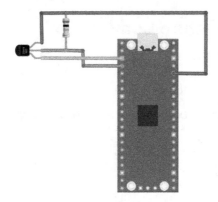

Initialization

Every transaction with the a 1-wire device starts with an initialization handshake. The master holds the bus low for at least $480\mu s$, a pause of $15\mu s$ to $60\mu s$ follows, and then any and all of the devices on the bus pull the line low for $60\mu s$ to $240\mu s$.

For this we need the `presence` function:

```
int main()
{
    stdio_init_all();
    gpio_init(2);
    if (presence(2) == 1)
    {
        printf("No device \n");
    }
      read temperature
  ...
```

If you try this partial program and have a logic analyzer with a 1-wire protocol analyzer, you will see something like:

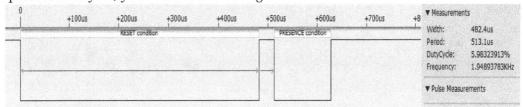

Seeing a presence pulse is the simplest and quickest way to be sure that your hardware is working. From this point it is just a matter of using the functions developed in the previous chapters to work with the commands defined in the datasheet.

Initiating Temperature Conversion

As there is only one device on the 1-Wire bus, we can use the Skip ROM command (0xCC) to signal it to be active:

```
writeByte(2, 0xCC);
```

You can see the pattern of bits sent on a logic analyzer:

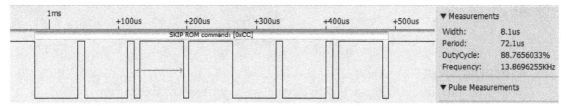

Our next task is to send a Convert command, 0x44, to start the DS18B20 making a temperature measurement. Depending on the resolution selected, this can take as long as 750ms. How the device tells the master that the measurement has completed depends on the mode in which it is operating, but using an external power line, i.e. not using parasitic mode, the device sends a 0 bit in response to a bit read until it is completed when it sends a 1.

This is how 1-Wire devices that need time to get data ready slow down the master until they are ready. The master can read a single bit as often as it likes and the slave will respond with a 0 until it is ready with the data.

As we already have a readBit function this is easy. The software polls for the completion by reading the bus until it gets a 1 bit:

```
int convert(uint8_t pin)
{
    writeByte(pin, 0x44);
    int i;
    for (i = 0; i < 500; i++)
    {
        sleep_ms(10);
        if (readBit(pin) == 1)
            break;
    }
    return i;
}
```

You can of course test the return value to check that the result has been obtained. If `convert` returns `500` then the loop times out. When the function returns, the new temperature measurement is stored in the device's scratchpad memory and now all we have to do is read this.

Reading the Scratchpad

The scratchpad memory has nine bytes of storage in total and does things like control the accuracy of conversion and provide status information. In our simple example the only two bytes of any great interest are the first two, which hold the result of a temperature conversion. However, as we are going to check the CRC for error detection, we need to read all nine bytes.

All we have to do is issue a Read Scratchpad, `0xBE`, command and then read the nine bytes that the device returns. To send the new command we have to issue a new initialization pulse and a Skip ROM, `0xCC`, command followed by a Read Scratchpad command, `0xBE`:

```
presence(2);
writeByte(2, 0xCC);
writeByte(2, 0xBE);
```

Now the data is ready to read. We can read all nine bytes of it or just the first two that we are interested in. The device will keep track of which bytes have been read. If you come back later and read more bytes you will continue the read from where you left off. If you issue another initialization pulse then the device aborts the data transmission.

As we do want to check the CRC for errors, we will read all nine bytes:

```
uint8_t data[9];
    for (int i = 0; i < 9; i++)
    {
        data[i] = readByte(2);
    }
```

Now we have all of the data stored in the scratchpad and the CRC byte, we can check for errors:

```
uint8_t crc = crc8(data, 9);
```

As before, `crc` will be `0` if there are no transmission errors. The `crc8` function was given earlier.

Getting The Temperature

To obtain the temperature measurement we need to work with the first two bytes, which are the least and most significant bytes of the 12-bit temperature reading:

```
int t1 = data[0];
int t2 = data[1];
```

t1 holds the low-order bits and t2 the high-order bits.

All we now have to do is to put the two bytes together as a 16-bit two's complement integer. As the Pico supports a 16-bit int type, we can do this very easily:

```
int16_t temp1 = (t2 << 8 | t1);
```

Notice that this only works because int16_t really is a 16-bit integer. If you were to use:

```
int temp1= (t2<<8 | t1);
```

temp1 would be correct for positive temperatures but it would give the wrong answer for negative values because the sign bit isn't propagated into the top 16 bits. If you want to use a 32-bit integer, you will have to propagate the sign bit manually:

```
if(t2 & 0x80) temp1=temp1 | 0xFFFF0000;
```

Finally, we have to convert the temperature to a scaled floating-point value. As the returned data gives the temperature in centigrade with the low-order four bits giving the fractional part, it has to be scaled by a factor of 1/16:

```
float temp = (float) temp1 / 16;
```

Now we can print the CRC and the temperature:

```
printf("CRC %hho \n\r ", crc);
printf("temperature = %f C \n", temp);
```

A Temperature Function

Packaging all of this into a single function is easy:

```
float getTemperature(uint8_t pin) {
    if (presence(pin) == 1) return -1000;
    writeByte(pin, 0xCC);
    if (convert(pin) == 500) return -3000;
    presence(pin);
    writeByte(pin, 0xCC);
    writeByte(pin, 0xBE);
    int i;
    uint8_t data[9];
    for (i = 0; i < 9; i++) {
        data[i] = readByte(pin);
    }
    uint8_t crc = crc8(data, 9);
    if(crc!=0) return -2000;
    int t1 = data[0];
    int t2 = data[1];
    int16_t temp1 = (t2 << 8 | t1);
    float temp = (float) temp1 / 16;
    return temp;
}
```

Notice that the function returns -1000 if there is no device, -2000 if there is a CRC error and -3000 if the device fails to provide data. These values are outside the range of temperatures that can be measured.

The Complete Program

The complete program to read and display the temperature is:

```c
#include <stdio.h>
#include "pico/stdlib.h"
#include "hardware/gpio.h"

int presence(uint8_t pin)
{
    gpio_set_dir(2, GPIO_OUT);
    gpio_put(pin, 1);
    sleep_ms(1);
    gpio_put(pin, 0);
    sleep_us(480);
    gpio_set_dir(pin, GPIO_IN);
    sleep_us(70);
    int b = gpio_get(pin);
    sleep_us(410);
    return b;
}

void writeBit(uint8_t pin, int b)
{
    int delay1, delay2;
    if (b == 1)
    {
        delay1 = 6;
        delay2 = 64;
    }
    else
    {
        delay1 = 60;
        delay2 = 10;
    }
    gpio_set_dir(pin, GPIO_OUT);
    gpio_put(pin, 0);
    sleep_us(delay1);
    gpio_set_dir(pin, GPIO_IN);
    sleep_us(delay2);
}
```

```c
void writeByte(uint8_t pin, int byte)
{
    for (int i = 0; i < 8; i++)
    {
        if (byte & 1)
        {
            writeBit(pin, 1);
        }
        else
        {
            writeBit(pin, 0);
        }
        byte = byte >> 1;
    }
}
uint8_t readBit(uint8_t pin)
{
    gpio_set_dir(pin, GPIO_OUT);
    gpio_put(pin, 0);
    sleep_us(8);
    gpio_set_dir(pin, GPIO_IN);
    sleep_us(2);
    uint8_t b = gpio_get(pin);
    sleep_us(60);
    return b;
}
int readByte(uint8_t pin)
{
    int byte = 0;
    int i;
    for (i = 0; i < 8; i++)
    {
        byte = byte | readBit(pin) << i;
    };
    return byte;
}
int convert(uint8_t pin)
{
    writeByte(pin, 0x44);
    int i;
    for (i = 0; i < 500; i++)
    {
        sleep_ms(10);
        if (readBit(pin) == 1)
            break;
    }
    return i;
}
```

```c
uint8_t crc8(uint8_t *data, uint8_t len)
{
    uint8_t i;
    uint8_t j;
    uint8_t temp;
    uint8_t databyte;
    uint8_t crc = 0;
    for (i = 0; i < len; i++)
    {
        databyte = data[i];
        for (j = 0; j < 8; j++)
        {
            temp = (crc ^ databyte) & 0x01;
            crc >>= 1;
            if (temp)
                crc ^= 0x8C;

            databyte >>= 1;
        }
    }

    return crc;
}

float getTemperature(uint8_t pin) {
    if (presence(pin) == 1) return -1000;
    writeByte(pin, 0xCC);
    if (convert(pin) == 500) return -3000;
    presence(pin);
    writeByte(pin, 0xCC);
    writeByte(pin, 0xBE);
    int i;
    uint8_t data[9];
    for (i = 0; i < 9; i++) {
        data[i] = readByte(pin);
    }
    uint8_t crc = crc8(data, 9);
    if(crc!=0) return -2000;
    int t1 = data[0];
    int t2 = data[1];
    int16_t temp1 = (t2 << 8 | t1);
    float temp = (float) temp1 / 16;
    return temp;
}
```

```
int main()
{
    stdio_init_all();
    gpio_init(2);

    if (presence(2) == 1)
    {
        printf("No device \n");
    }
    float t;
    for (;;) {
        do {
            t = getTemperature(2);
        } while (t<-999);
        printf("%f\r\n",t);
        sleep_ms(500);
    };

    return 0;
}
```

A PIO DS18B20 Program

Implementing the 1-Wire protocol using a PIO is one of the most difficult tasks we tackle. It needs to both send and receive data and the master has to provide the start pulse for the slave to send data. The specification also makes it seem that we have to use a conditional to vary the timing of the data part of the pulse depending on sending a one or a zero. This is a lot of logic to fit into 32 instructions. In addition a 1-Wire device can send far more data than the FIFO can hold. At first appraisal the idea of implementing the 1-Wire protocol in a PIO program seems hopeless, but with a shift in emphasis it can be made easier.

The main operations that you need to work with a 1-Wire device is to send a set of bytes and receive a set of bytes. In general, the timing requirements of the 1-Wire bus are at the bit level. That is, when you read data the device will generally store the data until you are ready for it. This means that if you can implement a byte read/write in the PIO then the main program can get on with something else while the 1-Wire device processes data. If the main program is interrupted then no harm is done as it can expect the PIO to continue to process the next byte ready for when it returns.

What all of this implies is that all we really have to do is implement a bit send and a bit receive facility. Using the way that 1-Wire protocol is usually described, this would be very difficult. In other words, trying to implement the simple-minded bit-banging protocol as a PIO program isn't going to work. A slightly different interpretation of the protocol, however, makes it very possible. If you think of each bit frame as starting with a short low pulse which signals the start of the frame, then a zero sends a low after the initial pulse and a one sends a high. In other words, we can implement the write protocol as:

1) Send short "start bit" of about $6\mu s$

2) Send the data bit for the rest of the frame – about $60\mu s$

3) Set the line high for $10\mu s$ as a spacer between bit frames

The read protocol is much the same:

1) Send short "start bit" of about $6\mu s$

2) After about $9\mu s$ sample the line and use this as the read bit

3) Do nothing for about $55\mu s$ as a spacer between bit frames

In this form the protocol doesn't need conditionals as the sending of a zero or a one and the receiving of a zero or a one follows the same steps.

Using this version you could simplify the logic of the bit-banging example given earlier, but there is no real need to as there is plenty of space and computational power – using a PIO is a very different matter and regularity in the implementation of a protocol is important.

There is also the problem of how to implement the PIO program so that the C program can make use of it. One possibility is to use one state machine for send and other to receive, but it is possible to create a single program to to do both jobs.

Start a new PIO project and create a file called DS1820.c and DS1820.pio. The PIO program starts off with a presence pulse and, as this is long compared to the clock time, we use a loop set by the C program. As you generally don't need a presence pulse when reading data from a device, we can use a zero value to indicate that the operation is a read, not a write.

That is, you use the program by pushing data onto the FIFO – the first byte starts the program off and if it is zero it starts a read operation and otherwise starts a write operation with its value setting the length of the initialization pulse:

```
.program DS1820
.wrap_target
again:
        pull block
        mov x, osr
        jmp !x, read

write:  set pindirs, 1
        set pins, 0
loop1:
        jmp x--,loop1
        set pindirs, 0 [31]
        wait 1 pin 0 [31]
```

Once the write part of the code gets started, the non-zero value passed in via the FIFO is used to create a long, 500μs, low pulse which the slave responds to with a 120μs low presence plus. The final instruction waits for the end of the pulse so that we can start to send some data.

The second byte pushed onto the FIFO gives the number of bytes to send and these are pushed onto the stack to follow. Notice that if there are more than four or five then the program might stall until the FIFO has space.

```
        pull block
        mov x, osr
bytes1:
        pull block
        set y, 7
        set pindirs, 1
bit1:
        set pins, 0 [1]
        out pins,1 [31]
        set pins, 1 [20]
        jmp y--,bit1
        jmp x--,bytes1
        set pindirs, 0 [31]
        jmp again
```

You can see that the inner loop starting at bit1 takes the data byte in the OSR and sends it out to the GPIO line, a bit at a time. The first instruction in the loop generates the short start pulse and the second instruction sets the line high or low for 32 clock cycles. The final instruction in the loop provides the space between the bit frames. The loop repeats until all eight bits have been sent when the outer loop gets another byte to send, if there is one. If not, the program restarts and waits for the next set of data.

The read part of the program is very similar to the write:

```
read:
        pull block
        mov x, osr
bytes2:
        set y, 7
        bit2:
        set pindirs, 1
        set pins, 0 [1]
        set pindirs, 0 [5]
        in pins,1 [10]
        jmp y--,bit2
 jmp x--,bytes2
.wrap
```

In this case the only data we need from the FIFO is the number of bytes to read. This is stored in the X register and controls the number of bytes processed. The inner loop, starting at bit2, reads each bit in turn. The first three instructions change the line to output, send the short start pulse and sets the line back to input. The in instruction samples the line after a short delay and gets the data which is auto-pushed onto the FIFO ready for the C program to read. Notice that if the C program fails to read the data then the loop stalls, which is fine as long as the 1-Wire device can live with a pause – the DS18B20 can.

The entire program is 29 instructions, which does leave space for instructions to toggle another GPIO line for debugging purposes. It is very probable that it can be made shorter.

Next we move on the C program. We first need an initialization function:

```
uint DS18Initalize(PIO pio, int gpio)
{
    uint offset = pio_add_program(pio, &DS1820_program);

    uint sm = pio_claim_unused_sm(pio, true);
    pio_gpio_init(pio, gpio);

    pio_sm_config c = DS1820_program_get_default_config(offset);
    sm_config_set_clkdiv_int_frac(&c, 255, 0);
    sm_config_set_set_pins(&c, gpio, 1);
    sm_config_set_out_pins(&c, gpio, 1);
    sm_config_set_in_pins(&c, gpio);
    sm_config_set_in_shift(&c, true, true, 8);
    pio_sm_init(pio0, sm, offset, &c);
    pio_sm_set_enabled(pio0, sm, true);
    return sm;
}
```

The frequency is selected to allow the pulse times to be implemented using delays from 1 to 31.

The PIO program is fairly general in that you could use it to talk to almost any 1-Wire device, but we are interested in the DS18B20 and it is easy enough to implement a function to read the temperature along the lines of the previous function:

```
float getTemperature(PIO pio, uint sm)
{
```

First we send an initialization pulse followed by a Skip ROM and a Convert command. The first item sets a write operation with an initialization pulse:

```
pio_sm_put_blocking(pio, sm, 250);
pio_sm_put_blocking(pio, sm, 1);
pio_sm_put_blocking(pio, sm, 0xCC);
pio_sm_put_blocking(pio, sm, 0x44);
```

Next we should wait until the conversion is complete, but for simplicity we wait for 1s – after which time the conversion is either complete or the device is broken. Then we send another initialization pulse, a Skip ROM and a Read ScratchPad command:

```
sleep_ms(1000);
pio_sm_put_blocking(pio, sm, 250);
pio_sm_put_blocking(pio, sm, 1);
pio_sm_put_blocking(pio, sm, 0xCC);
pio_sm_put_blocking(pio, sm, 0xBE);
```

Finally we send a read command for nine bytes of data:

```
pio_sm_put_blocking(pio, sm, 0);
pio_sm_put_blocking(pio, sm, 8);
```

and read the nine bytes from the FIFO:

```
int i;
uint8_t data[9];
for (i = 0; i < 9; i++)
{
    data[i] = pio_sm_get_blocking(pio, sm) >> 24;
}
```

Now we have the same nine bytes of data as in the bit-banging example and the rest of the program is identical.

A better idea is to create two functions which read and write an array of bytes to the device:

```
void writeBytes(PIO pio, uint sm,uint8_t bytes[], int len){
    pio_sm_put_blocking(pio, sm, 250);
    pio_sm_put_blocking(pio, sm, len-1);
    for(int i=0;i<len;i++){
        pio_sm_put_blocking(pio, sm, bytes[i]);
    }
}
void readBytes(PIO pio, uint sm,uint8_t bytes[], int len){
    pio_sm_put_blocking(pio, sm, 0);
    pio_sm_put_blocking(pio, sm, len-1);
    for(int i=0;i<len;i++){
        bytes[i]=pio_sm_get_blocking(pio, sm) >> 24;
    }
}
```

Using these two functions the interaction with the 1-Wire device starts to look a lot like using the SPI or I2C bus.

This is about as complex a PIO program as you can implement. This raises the question of what to do if you need something more complex? You might think that using additional state machines might help, but you are still limited to 32 instructions in total. There are two possible practical solutions. You can use immediately executed instructions put directly into the state machine from the C program. This works for small tasks such as initialization. The second solution is more generally useful. If you can split your program into small, less than 32 instructions, modules then you can load one into one PIO and another into the second PIO. This, of course, occupies both PIOs and you can't use a PIO for another task. For example, you could use one PIO to send data to a 1-Wire bus device and the other to receive data. This approach is limited to just two modules, so a total of 64 instructions. You can extend this idea to any number of modules if they can be reloaded into the same PIO. For example, by splitting the 1-Wire code into a receive and a send module you could easily afford the time to load each module and set it up into the same PIO.

The current program can only work with a single device on the 1-Wire bus. If you want to support more, you could implement the search algorithm outlined in Chapter 15 of *Raspberry Pi IOT in C, Second Edition*, though this is complex. A simpler solution is to use one state machine and one GPIO line per device. This can support up to eight different 1-Wire devices.

The Complete Program

The C program using the read and write functions is:

```c
#include <stdio.h>
#include "pico/stdlib.h"
#include "hardware/gpio.h"
#include "DS1820.pio.h"

uint8_t crc8(uint8_t *data, uint8_t len)
{
    uint8_t i;
    uint8_t j;
    uint8_t temp;
    uint8_t databyte;
    uint8_t crc = 0;
    for (i = 0; i < len; i++)
    {
        databyte = data[i];
        for (j = 0; j < 8; j++)
        {
            temp = (crc ^ databyte) & 0x01;
            crc >>= 1;
            if (temp)
                crc ^= 0x8C;

            databyte >>= 1;
        }
    }
    return crc;
}
void writeBytes(PIO pio, uint sm, uint8_t bytes[], int len)
{
    pio_sm_put_blocking(pio, sm, 250);
    pio_sm_put_blocking(pio, sm, len - 1);
    for (int i = 0; i < len; i++)
    {
        pio_sm_put_blocking(pio, sm, bytes[i]);
    }
}
void readBytes(PIO pio, uint sm, uint8_t bytes[], int len)
{
    pio_sm_put_blocking(pio, sm, 0);
    pio_sm_put_blocking(pio, sm, len - 1);
    for (int i = 0; i < len; i++)
    {
        bytes[i] = pio_sm_get_blocking(pio, sm) >> 24;
    }
}
```

```c
float getTemperature(PIO pio, uint sm)
{
    writeBytes(pio, sm, (uint8_t[]){0xCC, 0x44}, 2);
    sleep_ms(1000);
    writeBytes(pio, sm, (uint8_t[]){0xCC, 0xBE}, 2);

    uint8_t data[9];
    readBytes(pio, sm, data, 9);

    uint8_t crc = crc8(data, 9);
    if (crc != 0)
        return -2000;
    int t1 = data[0];
    int t2 = data[1];
    int16_t temp1 = (t2 << 8 | t1);
    volatile float temp = (float)temp1 / 16;
    return temp;
}

uint DS18Initalize(PIO pio, int gpio)
{

    uint offset = pio_add_program(pio, &DS1820_program);

    uint sm = pio_claim_unused_sm(pio, true);
    pio_gpio_init(pio, gpio);

    pio_sm_config c = DS1820_program_get_default_config(offset);
    sm_config_set_clkdiv_int_frac(&c, 255, 0);
    sm_config_set_set_pins(&c, gpio, 1);
    sm_config_set_out_pins(&c, gpio, 1);
    sm_config_set_in_pins(&c, gpio);
    sm_config_set_in_shift(&c, true, true, 8);
    pio_sm_init(pio0, sm, offset, &c);
    pio_sm_set_enabled(pio0, sm, true);
    return sm;
}
```

```
int main()
{
    stdio_init_all();

    uint sm = DS18Initalize(pio0, 2);

    float t;
    for (;;)
    {
        do
        {
            t = getTemperature(pio0, sm);
        } while (t < -999);
        printf("temperature %f\r\n", t);
        sleep_ms(500);
    };

    return 0;
}
```

The PIO program is:

```
.program DS1820
.wrap_target
again:
  pull block
  mov x, osr
  jmp !x, read

write:  set pindirs, 1
  set pins, 0
loop1:
    jmp x--,loop1
set pindirs, 0 [31]
wait 1 pin 0 [31]

  pull block
  mov x, osr
bytes1:
  pull block
  set y, 7
  set pindirs, 1
bit1:
  set pins, 0 [1]
  out pins,1 [31]
    set pins, 1 [20]
    jmp y--,bit1
jmp x--,bytes1
set pindirs, 0 [31]
jmp again
```

```
read:
  pull block
  mov x, osr
bytes2:
  set y, 7
bit2:
  set pindirs, 1
  set pins, 0 [1]
  set pindirs, 0 [5]
  in pins,1 [10]
jmp y--,bit2
jmp x--,bytes2
.wrap
```

The CMakeLists file is:

```
cmake_minimum_required(VERSION 3.13)

set(CMAKE_C_STANDARD 11)
set(CMAKE_CXX_STANDARD 17)

include(pico_sdk_import.cmake)


project(ds18 C CXX ASM)
pico_sdk_init()
add_executable(ds18
 DS1820.c
)
pico_generate_pio_header(ds18 ${CMAKE_CURRENT_LIST_DIR}/DS1820.pio)
target_link_libraries(ds18  pico_stdlib hardware_gpio hardware_pio)
pico_add_extra_outputs(ds18)
```

Other Commands

As well as the commands that we have used to read the temperature, the DS18B20 supports a range of other commands. There are two commands concerned with when there are more devices on the bus. Search ROM, 0xF0, is used to scan the bus to discover what devices are connected and Match ROM, 0x55, is used to select a particular device.

You can also read the unique 64-bit code of a device using the Read ROM command, 0x33. In this case, the slave transmits eight bytes, comprised of a single-byte device family code, 0x28 for the DS18B20, six bytes of serial number and a single CRC byte.

As well as the Read ScratchPad command that we used to read the temperature, there is also a Write ScratchPad command, 0x4E.

The format of the scratchpad is:

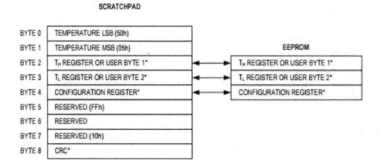

The first two bytes are the temperature that we have already used. The only writable entries are bytes 2, 3 and 4. The Write ScratchPad command transfers three bytes to these locations. Notice that there is no CRC and no error response if there is a transmission error. The datasheet suggests that you read the scratchpad after writing it to check that you have been successful in setting the three bytes.

The third byte written to the scratchpad is to the configuration register:

BIT 7	BIT 6	BIT 5	BIT 4	BIT 3	BIT 2	BIT 1	BIT 0
0	R1	R0	1	1	1	1	1

Essentially the only thing you can change is the resolution of the temperature measurement.

Configuration Register	Resolution	Time
0x1F	9 bits	93ms
0x3F	10 bits	175ms
0x5F	11 bits	375ms
0x7F	12 bits	750ms

The time quoted is the maximum for a conversion at the given precision. You can see that the only real advantage of decreasing precision is to make conversion faster. The default is 0x7F and 12 bits of precision.

The first two bytes of the write scratchpad set a high and low temperature alarm. This feature isn't much used, but you can set two temperatures that will trigger the device into alarm mode. Notice you only set the top eight bits of the threshold temperatures. This is easy enough, but the alarm status is set with every read so if the temperature goes outside the set bounds and then back in the alarm is cleared.

The second problem is that, to discover which devices are in alarm mode, you have to use the Alarm Search command, 0xEC. This works like the Search ROM command, but the only devices that respond are the ones with an alarm state. The alarm feature might be useful if you have a lot of devices and simply want to detect an out-of-band temperature. You could set up multiple devices with appropriate temperature limits and then simply repeatedly scan the bus for devices with alarms set.

You may notice that the scratchpad also has an EEPROM memory connected. You can transfer the three bytes of the scratchpad to the EEPROM using Copy Scratchpad, 0x48, and transfer them back using the Recall EEPROM command, 0xB8. You can use this to make the settings non-volatile.

Finally there is the Read Power Supply command, 0xB4. If the master reads the bus after issuing this command a 0 indicates that there are parasitic powered devices on the bus. If there are such devices the master has to run the bus in such a way that they are powered correctly.

If you restrict yourself to a single slave device on the bus, this is more or less all there is to the DS18B20, and the 1-Wire bus in general. If you want to have multiple slave devices, however, while you don't need any more hardware, you do need some more software. Multidrop working as it is called is beyond the scope of this introduction, but you should find it possible to follow the description in Chapter 15 of *Raspberry Pi IOT in C, Second Edition* and implement your own version.

Summary

- The 1-Wire bus is a proprietary, but widely-used, bus. It is simple and very capable.

- As its name suggests it makes use of a single data wire and usually a power supply and ground.

- It is possible to dispense with the power line and the connected device will draw power from the data line.

- Implementing the 1-Wire protocol is mostly a matter of getting the timing right.

- There are three types of interaction: presence pulse, read and write.

- The presence pulse simply asks any connected devices to reply and make themselves known.

- The 1-Wire protocol is easier to implement than you might think because each bit is sent as a "slot" and while timing is critical within the slot, how fast slots are sent isn't and the master is in control of when this happens.

- The DS18B20 temperature sensor is one of the most commonly encountered 1-Wire bus devices. It is small, low-cost and you can use multiple devices on a single bus.

- After a convert command is sent to the device, it can take 750ms before a reading is ready.

- To test for data ready you have to poll on a single bit. Reading a zero means data not ready and reading a one means data ready.

- When the data is ready you can read the scratchpad memory where the data is stored.

- The DS18B20 has other commands that can be used to set temperature alarms etc, but these are rarely used.

- With a shift in viewpoint it is just possible to squeeze a 1-Wire bus protocol into a 32 instruction PIO program.

Chapter 16

The Serial Port

The serial port is one of the oldest of ways of connecting devices together, but it is still very useful as it provides a reasonably fast communication channel that can be used over a longer distance than most other connections such as USB. Today, however, its most common and important use is in making connections with small computers and simple peripherals. It can also be used as a custom signal decoder, see later.

Serial Protocol

The serial protocol is very simple. It has to be because it was invented in the days when it was generated using electromechanical components, motors and the like. It was invented to make early teletype machines work and hence you will often find abbreviations such as TTY used in connection with it. As the electronic device used to work with serial is called a Universal Asynchronous Receiver/Transmitter, the term UART is also often used.

The earliest standards are V24 and RS232. Notice, however, that early serial communications worked between plus and minus 24V and later ones ±12V. Today's serial communications work at logic, or TTL, levels of 0V to 5V or 0V to 3.3V. This voltage difference is a problem we will return to later. What matters is that, irrespective of the voltage, the protocol is always the same.

For the moment let's concentrate on the protocol. As already mentioned, the protocol is simple. The line rests high and represents a zero. When the device starts to transmit it first pulls the line low to generate a start bit. The width of this start bit sets the transmission speed - all bits are the same width as the start bit. After the start bit there are a variable number, usually seven or eight, data bits, an optional single parity bit, and finally one or two stop bits.

Originally the purpose of the start bit was to allow the motors etc to get started and allow the receiving end to perform any timing corrections. The stop bits were similarly there to give time for the motors to come back to their rest position. In the early days the protocol was used at very slow speeds; 300 baud, i.e. roughly 300 bits per second, was considered fast enough.

Today the protocol is much the same, but there is little need for multiple stop bits and communication is often so reliable that parity bits are dispensed with. Transmission speeds are also higher, typically 9600 or 115200 baud.

To specify what exact protocol is in use, you will often encounter a short form notation. For example, 9600 baud, 8 data bits, no parity, one stop bit, will be written as 9600 8n1. Here you can see the letter 0 (01101111 or 0x6F) transmitted using 8n1:

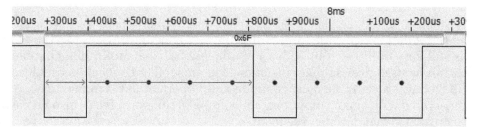

Notice that the signal is sent least significant bit first. The first low is the start bit, then the eight dots show the ideal sampling positions for the receiver. The basic decoding algorithm for receiving serial data is to detect the start of the start bit and then sample the line at the center of each bit time. Notice that the final high on the right is the stop bit.

Notice also that the sampling points can be put to use on custom protocols. As long as the data is transmitted in fixed time "cells" indicated by a start bit, you can use a serial port to read individual bits.

For a serial connection to work, it is essential that the transmitter and the receiver are set to the same speed, data bits and parity. Serial interfaces most often fail because they are not working with the same settings.

A logic analyzer with a serial decoder option is an essential piece of equipment if you are going to do anything complicated with serial interfacing.

What is a baud? Baud rate refers to the basic bit time. That is, 300 baud has a start bit that is 1/300s wide. This means that for 9600 baud a bit is 1/9600 wide or roughly 104μs and at 115200 baud a bit is 1/115200 or roughly 8.6μs. Notice that baud rate doesn't equate to speed of sending data because of the overhead in stop, start and perhaps parity bits to include in the calculation.

UART Hardware

A simple serial interface has a transmit pin, TX, and a receive pin, RX. That is, a full serial interface uses two wires for two-way communications. Typically you connect the TX pin on one device to the RX pin on the other and vice versa. The only problem is that some manufacturers label the pins by what they should be connected to not what they are and then you have to connect RX to RX and TX to TX. You generally need to check with a scope, logic probe or meter which pin is which if you are in any doubt.

In addition to the TX and RX pins, a full serial interface also has a lot of control lines. Most of these were designed to help with old fashioned teleprinters and they are not often used. For example, RTS - Request To Send is a line that it used to ask permission to send data from the device at the other end of the connection, CTS - Clear To Send is a line that indicates that it is okay to send data and so on. Usually these are set by the hardware automatically when the receive buffer is full or empty.

You can use RTS and CTS as a hardware flow control. There is also a standard software flow control involving sending XON and XOFF characters to start and stop the transmission of data. For most connections between modern devices you can ignore these additional lines and just send and receive data. If you need to interface to something that implements a complex serial interface you are going to have to look up the details and hand-craft a program to interact with it.

The Pico has two UARTs which can be used in addition to the USB interface. Both UARTs support buffered (32-character) and unbuffered modes and RTS/CTS hardware flow control. The UARTs can be connected to a group of four GPIO pins:

UART0			
TX	GP0	GP12	GP16	GP28
RX	GP1	GP13	GP17	GP29
CTS	GP2	GP14	GP18	
RTS	GP3	GP15	GP19	

UART1			
TX	GP4	GP8	GP20	GP24
RX	GP5	GP9	GP21	GP25
CTS	GP6	GP10	GP22	GP26
RTS	GP7	GP11	GP23	GP27

To set a GPIO line to its UART function use:

```
gpio_set_function(UART_TX_PIN, GPIO_FUNC_UART);
```

You can select any combination of pins and if you don't want to use the RTS/CTS lines they can be used for some other purpose.

There is a problem with making the connection to the Pico's RX and TX pins in that devices work at different voltages. PC-based serial ports usually use +13V to -13V and all RS232-compliant ports use a + to - voltage swing, which is completely incompatible with most microprocessors which work at 5V or 3.3V.

If you want to connect the Pico to a PC or other standard device then you need to use a TTL-to-RS232 level converter. In this case it is easier to use the PC's USB port as a serial interface with a USB-to-TTL level converter. All you have to do is plug the USB port into the PC, install a driver and start to transmit data.

Remember when you connect the Pico to another device that TX goes to the other device's RX and RX goes to the other device's TX pin. Also remember that the signaling voltage is 0V to 3.3V.

Setting Up the UART

There are two basic ways to use the serial interface, directly or via the `stdio` library. In most cases you need to know how to work with both so we start with the SDK functions that control the UART.

In all of these functions the UART is specified as the address of the hardware, but there are two constants you can use, `uart0` and `uart1`, and there is a function that converts the hardware address to a 0/1 index:

```
static uint uart_get_index (uart_inst_t *uart)
```

The simplest initialization function is:

```
uint uart_init (uart_inst_t *uart, uint baudrate)
```

and to stop using the UART:

```
void uart_deinit (uart_inst_t *uart)
```

The function:

```
static bool uart_is_enabled (uart_inst_t *uart)
```

can be used to find out if a UART is enabled.
You can also set the baud rate separately:

```
uint uart_set_baudrate (uart_inst_t *uart, uint baudrate)
```

If the baud rate cannot be achieved using the current clock frequency and available dividers then the nearest rate is used and returned as the result.

To set the complete configuration of the UART, other than baud rate, you need to use:

```
uart_set_format (uart_inst_t *uart, uint data_bits,
                        uint stop_bits, uart_parity_t parity)
```

You can set 5, 6, 7 or 8 data bits and 1 or 2 stop bits. Parity can be any of:

```
UART_PARITY_NONE
UART_PARITY_EVEN
UART_PARITY_ODD
```

These are the main configuration functions, but there are two others that are occasionally useful. If you want to make use of hardware flow control, i.e. RTS/CTS lines, then you need to enable them using:

```
uart_set_hw_flow (uart_inst_t *uart, bool cts, bool rts)
```

If you set `cts` to true then the CTS line has to be high to allow the UART to send data and if the `rts` is true then the RTS line is set high if there is data to send.

By default 32-element FIFO buffers are used on RX and TX. This is usually what you want, but if you need to react to immediate input, and can risk losing data, then you can turn the buffering off. Notice that with buffering off only a single character is stored while another is being received:

```
uart_set_fifo_enabled (uart_inst_t *uart, bool enabled)
```

Finally you can enable interrupts:

```
uart_set_irq_enables (uart_inst_t *uart, bool rx_has_data,
                                        bool tx_needs_data)
```

either on the need to read or write data or both.

To set up the interrupt handler you need to use:

```
irq_set_exclusive_handler(uartIRQ, handler);
irq_set_enabled(uartIRQ, true);
```

where `uartIRQ` is `UART0_IRQ` or `UART1_IRQ` and you also have to enable the interrupt.

Data Transfer

After you have set up the UART you can start sending and receiving data using SDK functions.

There are two general-purpose read/write functions:

```
uart_write_blocking(uart_inst_t *uart,const uint8_t *src,size_t len)
```

```
uart_read_blocking(uart_inst_t *uart, uint8_t *dst, size_t len)
```

In both cases data is stored in a byte array. In the case of the write function the number of bytes indicated by len are written – it is up to you to make sure that the array has enough data. If the data isn't read the buffer might fill up and the function will block until all of the data has been sent. In the case of the read function the len parameter gives the number of bytes to read and the function blocks until it has read that number of bytes.

For example:

```c
#include <stdio.h>
#include "pico/stdlib.h"
#include "hardware/gpio.h"

int main()
{
    stdio_init_all();
    uart_init(uart1, 9600);
    gpio_set_function(4, GPIO_FUNC_UART);
    gpio_set_function(5, GPIO_FUNC_UART);
    uart_set_format(uart1, 8, 1, UART_PARITY_EVEN);
    uint8_t SendData[] = "Hello World";
    uint8_t RecData[20];
    uart_write_blocking(uart1, SendData, 11);
    uart_read_blocking(uart1, RecData, 11);
    RecData[11]=0;
    printf("%s",RecData);

}
```

In this case it is assumed that GP4 and GP5 are used for UART1 and they are connected together to form a loopback test. Notice that we are using UART1 because UART0 is used by default for the stdio functions such as printf, more on this later. The write function sends 11 bytes of data which are received and stored in the FIFO buffer ready for the read function to retrieve. Notice that if the FIFO buffer became full, the write function would hang until it was cleared. As this is a loopback test, the receiver automatically accepts data until it is full when it stops receiving data. What this means is that if you try this program with more than 64 characters it will never finish as the write function will hang with a full buffer and the read function will never get a chance to clear it.

The problem of stalling when trying to read or write a serial interface is serious as you can never know if the outside world is going to behave as you expect. The usual approaches to tackling the problem are polling or using interrupts.

To poll for serial I/O you need to use one of:

```
static bool uart_is_writable (uart_inst_t *uart)
static bool uart_is_readable (uart_inst_t *uart)
```

which returns true if you can safely send or receive a single item of data. Notice that it isn't safe to assume that you can send or receive more than one item of data.

It you want to set a timeout for a read then use:

```
bool uart_is_readable_within_us (uart_inst_t *uart, uint32_t us)
```

which returns true if there is data to read in the buffer or false if it times out after us microseconds. Despite returning a bool, this gives the number of characters waiting in the queue.

In the case of transmit you can test to see if there is space in the FIFO buffer for a single element using:

```
static bool uart_is_writable (uart_inst_t *uart)
```

There are two less-used functions:

```
uart_tx_wait_blocking (uart_inst_t *uart)
uart_default_tx_wait_blocking (void)
```

which wait until the TX FIFO is empty, i.e. all of the data has been sent and presumably received. The second function tests the default UART, see later.

It is easy to see that you can use these functions to write polling loops which test to see if there is anything to read or any space to send data. For example:

```
uint8_t RecData[1];
while (true)
    {
        if (uart_is_readable(uart1))
        {
            uart_read_blocking(uart1, RecData, 1);
            printf("%c", RecData[0]);
        }
    };
```

The advantage of this loop is that you can do other work within the while loop and check that reading hasn't been waiting too long.

Alternatively you can set an interrupt to send or receive data when the hardware is ready. For example to read data using an interrupt, the equivalent of the polling loop in the last example, the interrupt handler simply has to read the data until there is no more and return:

```
void uartIRQ()
{
    uint8_t RecData;
    while (uart_is_readable(uart1))
    {
        uart_read_blocking(uart1, &RecData, 1);
        printf("%c", RecData);
    }
}
```

Setting up the handler is just a matter of three lines of code:

```
irq_set_exclusive_handler(UART1_IRQ, uartIRQ);
irq_set_enabled(UART1_IRQ, true);
uart_set_irq_enables(uart1, true, false);
```

After this the interrupt handler is called every time there is at least one character waiting to be read.

Reading and Writing Characters and Strings

In the previous examples we have used a byte array to read and write data. A more basic method of working is to read and write a single character at a time. The functions:

```
uart_putc (uart_inst_t *uart, char c)
static char uart_getc (uart_inst_t *uart)
```

read and write a single char or byte. They are simply more equivalent to using the usual blocking read or write functions. There is also:

```
uart_putc_raw (uart_inst_t *uart, char c)
```

which puts a character without applying carriage return line feed translation. Some systems need a carriage return to start a new line and some a line feed. You can set automatic translation of line feed to carriage return using:

```
void uart_set_translate_crlf (uart_inst_t *uart, bool translate)
```

A bigger problem for which there is no easy solution is that some systems need a line feed and a carriage return for a new line.

So far we have used read and write and put and get to work with arrays and characters. There is also a function which allows you to work with strings. Recall that a C string is just a byte or character array that is null- or zero-terminated. That is, the end of a string is indicated by a zero and not by the length of the array. You can send a string to the serial interface using:

```
uart_puts (uart_inst_t *uart, const char *s)
```

This is blocking and there is no equivalent to get a string, but it isn't difficult to create one.

This is an appropriate place to point out the, hopefully well-known, fact that null strings are dangerous in that it is far too easy to create a buffer overrun by not having a null termination in a supposed string. The standard C library has functions which allow you to work with strings, but with a maximum length indicated as a parameter to avoid such overruns.

Finally, it is worth mentioning that there is a function that will send a break signal. The break signal doesn't correspond to any character that you can send in the usual way – it corresponds to holding the TX line low for more than the time to transmit a single character. It is not often used today, but there are serial-based protocols that use the break to synchronize data transfer. You can send a break using:

```
uart_set_break (uart_inst_t *uart, bool en)
```

Stdio

The Pico supports the C Stdio library and this can be used to send and receive data via a UART or via the USB port. It also has some non-standard extensions designed to make it easier to work with the hardware. The main advantage of using stdio is the availability of printf. Notice that there can be multiple devices connected to either stdin or stdout. In this section the focus is on using the UART – there are similar functions for using the USB as a serial interface:

To initialize all devices use:

```
stdio_init_all (void)
```

To initialize just the default UART:

```
void stdio_uart_init (void)
```

and to initialize it as just stdout or stdin use:

```
void stdout_uart_init (void)
void stdin_uart_init (void)
```

If you want to configure the UART then use:

```
stdio_uart_init_full (uart_inst_t *uart, uint baud_rate,
                                 int tx_pin, int rx_pin)
```

To flush any buffers in use call:

```
stdio_flush (void)
```

The default UART is also set up via defines in a header file:

```
#define PICO_DEFAULT_UART 0
#define PICO_DEFAULT_UART_TX_PIN 0
#define PICO_DEFAULT_UART_RX_PIN 1
```

You can redefine this if you want to.

The important thing to realize about stdio is that by default its printf function is a simplified implementation of the one in the full stdio. You can find out more at https://github.com/mpaland/printf

As well as printf you also get implementations of:

```
int sprintf(char* buffer, const char* format, ...);
int snprintf(char* buffer, size_t count, const char* format, ...);
int vsnprintf(char* buffer, size_t count,
                          const char* format, va_list va);
```

which can be used to format a list of variables into a string. You can think of them as working exactly like printf but sending their output to a string. You can ignore vsnprintf and avoid sprintf and always use the safer snprintf where you have to specify the length of the buffer and so avoid any chance of buffer overflow.

Working With Small Buffers

If you have used serial communications under an operating system such as Linux, you may be familiar with how it works with the help of a large buffer. The Pico's serial interface has a very small buffer and this makes a lot of difference. For example, you have to restrict any processing of data to the time it takes to empty or fill the 32-element FIFO buffers. This can be more difficult and tricky than you might think. Consider the problem of echoing the input on one UART to another.

```
int count = 0;
while(true){
 while (count < len - 1)
 {
   buf[count++] = uart_getc(uart1);
 }
 buf[count] = 0;
 printf("%s",buf);
}
```

This looks harmless – simply collect characters from uart1 until the buffer is full then print it as a string. In a system with a large serial buffer the printf would be complete in a few microseconds and the outer while loop would restart ready to read the next block of data. However, with a buffer of only 32 elements, things don't work in the same way. After the first 32 characters are sent to the default UART the printf stalls and has to wait for free space in the FIFO. This means that the time it takes to send the data using the printf is only just a little shorter than the time it took to receive it. If there is any other data being sent at the same time, it will be lost during the time the printf is sending data. A better solution, although it depends on the exact nature of the problem, is to use uart_putc to send one character as one character is received so that neither FIFO buffer is ever allowed to fill:

```
int count = 0;
while(true){
  while (count < len - 1)
  {
    buf[count] = uart_getc(uart1);
    uart_putc(uart0,buf[count++]);
  }
}
```

The point is, when buffers are small sending lots of data can take more time that you expect. You can implement a larger buffered system using interrupts or you can simply break down serial operations into smaller, blocking operations.

Summary

- The serial port is one of the oldest ways of connecting devices together, but it is still very much in use.

- The serial protocol is asynchronous, but simple. A start bit gives the timing for the entire exchange.

- There are many control lines once used with telephone equipment that are mostly ignored in computer use. Similarly, the original ±12V signaling has been mostly replaced by 5V, and even 3.3V, signaling.

- The standard hardware that implements a serial connection is usually called a UART.

- The Pico contains two UARTs in addition to the USB serial connection.

- The SDK provides functions for initializing and sending and receiving data.

- Each UART has a 32 element FIFO send and receive buffer which can be disabled.

- You can use the read and write blocking functions to send and receive byte buffers of data.

- There are also functions to work with single characters and strings.

- The stdio library provides an efficient implementation of printf.

- As the UART buffers are small all transactions should be in terns of amounts of data that do not fill the buffers.

Chapter 17

WiFi Using The ESP8266

The Pico currently lacks WiFi which severely limits its utility as an IoT device. The ESP8266 provides a low cost and relatively easy way to remedy this. As we will make a lot of use of the Pico's serial ports, it is assumed that you know roughly how these work. In particular, it is assumed that you are familiar with the material in the previous chapter.

The Amazing ESP8266

Before we get on to the details of using the ESP8266 we need to find out what makes it special. It is remarkably low cost, $5 or less, but it is a full microprocessor with GPIO lines, RAM and built-in WiFi. It is built by a Chinese company Espressif Systems, but there are a number of copies on the market. The proliferation of devices and software revisions makes it difficult to work with, but it is well worth the effort.

While you can set up a development system yourself and program the ESP8266 to do almost anything, it comes with built-in software that allows it to be used as a WiFi module for other processors. This is how we are going to use it to give WiFi capability to the Pico.

The ESP8266 connects to the outside world using the serial port. The Pico controls it and transfers data using a system of AT commands. These were commonly used to control modems and other communication equipment and they still are used in mobile phone modems. In essence the ESP8266 looks like a modem that connects to WiFi. The module that is used in this chapter is the ESP-01, which is widely available from many different sources, but they all look like this:

There is another version, the ESP-07, which comes with a screen RF stage and other advantages, and this should also work. A bigger problem is that there are new versions of the firmware and some of these might not work in exactly the same way. However, it should be easy to make the changes necessary.

Connecting the ESP8266 ESP-01

There a number of minor problems in using the ESP8266. The first is that it comes with an 8-pin male connector which is not prototype board friendly. The best solution to this is to use some female-to-male jumper cables to connect it to the prototype board or use female-to-female cables to connect directly to the Pico. Note that for high baud rates cables should be kept as short as possible.

You can power the ESP8266 directly from the Pico's 3.3V supply pin, but if possible it is better to use an alternative as, when transmitting, the ESP8266 takes a lot of current, 300mA or so, and this means there isn't a lot left over to power other things. The maximum current for the Pico's 3.3V isn't given, but the chip used claims to be happy at 1200mA and it worked to run all of the examples in this chapter.

The pinout of the ESP-01 is usually shown from the component side, but in fact the pins that you want to connect to are on the other side. To make things easier, the two views are given in the diagram:

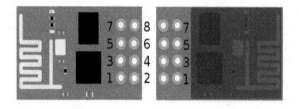

The pin functions are:

        1 Ground   connect to ground
        2 TXO   the serial tx pin
        3 GPIO2   ignore
        4 CHPD   chip enable connect to 3.3V
        5 GPIO0   ignore
        6 RST   reset leave unconnected
        7 RXI   the serial rx pin
        8 VDD   supply voltage connect to 3.3V

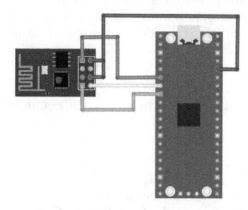

From the pinouts you should be able to work out the way the ESP8266 has to be connected. If we use GP4 as Tx from the Pico and GP5 as Rx to the Pico we have to connect ESP-01 pin 7 to GP4, pin 2 to GP5 and pins 8 and 4 to the power supply. To make it all work we also have to connect pin 1 to the ground.

AT Commands

The key idea in using the ESP8266 is that the Pico has to send an AT command, literally the characters AT, followed by other command strings. The command has to end with \r\n for the ESP8266 to take notice of it.

You can find a fill list of commands at the Espressif web site, but the most important are:

AT	Attention
AT+RST	Reset the board
AT+GMR	Firmware version
AT+CWMODE=	Operating Mode
	1 - Client, 2 -Access Point, 3 - Client and Access Point
AT+CWJAP=	Join network
AT+CWLAP	View available networks
AT+CWQAP	Disconnect from network
AT+CIPSTATUS	Show current status as socket client or server
AT+CIPSTART=	Connect to socket server
AT+CIPCLOSE	Close socket connection
AT+CIFSR	Show assigned IP address when connected to network
AT+CIPMUX=	Set connection
	0 - Single Connection, 1 - Multi-Channel Connection
AT+CIPSERVER=	Open the Socket Server
AT+CIPMODE=	Set transparent mode
AT+CIPSTO=	Set auto socket client disconnect timeout from 1s to 28800s
+IPD	Data

This is just a very general overview and omits the commands that allow the device to work as an access point. It is assumed that client mode is the more common application, but it isn't difficult to extend this example to access point operation.

Setup

We need a function to set up the hardware ready to communicate with the device:

```
int initWiFi()
{
    uart_init(uart1, 115200);
    gpio_set_function(4, GPIO_FUNC_UART);
    gpio_set_function(5, GPIO_FUNC_UART);
    uart_set_format(uart1, 8, 1, UART_PARITY_NONE);
    uart_set_translate_crlf(uart0,true);

    sleep_ms(100);
    return 0;
}
```

The model of ESP8266 used worked at 115200 baud by default. Newer models and updated firmware are reported to work at 9600 baud. If this is the case you need to modify the data rate and/or change the ESP8266's baud rate.

The entire program is hard coded to use UART1 as this leaves UART0 free for use as a debug port. The 100ms delay at the end is needed to allow the ESP8266 time to initialize. The uart_set_translate_crlf call is only needed to make web pages display correctly as HTML tends to use lf in place of cr.

Attention!

To start with the easiest, but possibly least useful, command let's implement some functions that test that we have a connection to the device - always a good idea at the beginning of a project.

In this section we develop the first of a number of functions that send a command to the device and get back a response. To do this we need a few other functions to help and these are reused in other AT functions. Once you have one AT function, the rest are very similar, so it is worth spending some time following how this most simple AT function works.

There isn't much point in moving on until you have tested that the connection works. To do this send the string AT\r\n and the ESP8266 should reply with a single "OK", which proves that the serial interface is working.

The most basic AT function is simply:

```
int ATWiFi()
{
    uint8_t SendData[] = "AT\r\n";
    uart_write_blocking(uart1, SendData, 4);
    return 9;
}
```

This is the most basic form of function that will do the job, but it isn't really practical. We need to check that it works and get some feedback by reading the data from the device.

The following function attempts to read a block of data from the device:

```
int getBlock(uint8_t buf[], int len)
{
    int count = 0;
    while (count < len - 1)
    {
        if (uart_is_readable_within_us(uart1, 10000))
        {
            buf[count++] = uart_getc(uart1);
            if (Debug)
            uart_putc(uart0,buf[count-1]);
        }
        else
        {
            break;
        }
    }
    buf[count] = 0;
    return count;
}
```

The uart_is_readable_within_us function is used to set an inter-character timeout of 0.1s. That is, if no data is received after 0.1s it is assumed that this is the end of the transaction. The timeout is enough for more than 500 characters at 115200 baud and 100 at 9600 baud. Typical responses are a few hundred bytes, so using a buffer 512 bytes in size is reasonable.

Next the read function attempts to read a full buffer of data. Notice that there might not be a full buffer when the call is made, but as long as the data is coming in with gaps shorter than 0.1s between characters it will continue reading until the buffer is full. Notice that a zero byte is added to the end of the buffer so that it can be treated like a valid C string and count gives the length of the string, not including the zero.

The return value is the number of bytes read which could be zero. If the constant `Debug` is a 1 then the string is printed to UART0 and you can examine it. Notice that the function can come to an end for two different reasons – the time between characters is long enough to suggest that the transmission is finished or the buffer is full. If the buffer is full there may well be more data to be received and, as it stands, this data is lost.

If the AT command has been successful it returns a string containing "OK". One of the problems of working with AT commands is that they don't have an exact syntax and there is no formal "end of message" signal. By observation, any successful command does end with "OK" and if you can't find "OK" in the response then you either haven't read it all or there has been an error.

With all of this we can now create an `ATWiFi` function that returns its response:

```
int ATWiFi(uint8_t buf[], int len)
{
    uint8_t SendData[] = "AT\r\n";
    uart_write_blocking(uart1, SendData, 4);
    return getBlock(buf,len);
}
```

A complete program is:

```
#include <stdio.h>
#include "pico/stdlib.h"
#include "hardware/gpio.h"

#define Debug true
int initWiFi()
{
    uart_init(uart1, 115200);
    gpio_set_function(4, GPIO_FUNC_UART);
    gpio_set_function(5, GPIO_FUNC_UART);
    uart_set_format(uart1, 8, 1, UART_PARITY_NONE);
    sleep_ms(100);
    return 0;
}
```

```
int getBlock(uint8_t buf[], int len)
{
    int count = 0;
    while (count < len - 1)
    {
        if (uart_is_readable_within_us(uart1, 10000))
        {
            buf[count++] = uart_getc(uart1);
             if (Debug)
             uart_putc(uart0,buf[count-1]);
        }
        else
        {
            break;
        }
    }
    buf[count] = 0;
    return count;
}

int ATWiFi(uint8_t buf[], int len)
{
    uint8_t SendData[] = "AT\r\n";
    uart_write_blocking(uart1, SendData, 4);
    return getBlock(buf, len);
}

int main()
{
    stdio_init_all();
    initWiFi();
    uint8_t buf[512];
    ATWiFi(buf, 512);
    sleep_ms(1000);
}
```

When you run this program you should see:

```
AT
OK
```

printed on the serial console. If you don't there are five possible reasons:

1. You have connected the wrong pins – check
2. You haven't connected enable to +V
3. The power supply you are using is inadequate - check/replace
4. The serial console isn't working - check you can see any message
5. The baud rate is wrong - try 9600
6. The ESP8266 is broken - try another

Some Utility Functions

Assuming that you have managed to make the AT command work, it is time to move on to other AT commands. The first useful command is to find the Version number of the firmware. This is more or less the same as the AT function, but the command is AT+GMR:

```
int getVersionWiFi(uint8_t buf[], int len)
{
    uint8_t SendData[] = "AT+GMR\r\n";
    uart_write_blocking(uart1, SendData, 8);
    return getBlock(buf, len);
}
```

The device in use returned:

```
AT+GMR
AT version:1.3.0.0(Jul 14 2016 18:54:01)
SDK version:2.0.0(5a875ba)
v1.0.0.3
Mar 13 2018 09:35:47
OK
```

The manual says that it should return AT, SDK and the time it was compiled, so we get a little extra with this third-party device.

Reset is another useful function. The device often gets stuck and then a reset is all that you can try. This is a software reset; another option is to use a GPIO line to connect to reset pin 6. By controlling this line you can force the device to hard reset. The soft reset command is AT+RST and all you get back in theory is "OK", but in practice what the device sends varies:

```
int resetWiFi(uint8_t buf[], int len)
{
    uint8_t SendData[] = "AT+RST\r\n";
    uart_write_blocking(uart1, SendData, 8);
    return getBlock(buf, len);
}
```

The final utility function is to set the serial connection parameters to 115200, 8 bits, 1 stop bit, no parity, no flow control:

```
int setUARTWiFi(uint8_t buf[], int len)
{
    uint8_t SendData[] = "AT+UART_CUR=115200,8,1,0,0\r\n";
    uart_write_blocking(uart1, SendData, 28);
    return getBlock(buf, len);
}
```

If you change the baud rate to something other than what is in use you will, of course, lose communication with the device until you reconfigure the serial connection.

Configuring WiFi

The first thing we need to configure is the operating mode. The ESP8266 can operate as an access point, i.e. it can allow other devices to connect to it. However, in most cases you will want it to work in client mode, i.e. connecting to your existing WiFi.

Mode

A function to set its operating mode is:

```
int modeWiFi(uint8_t buf[], int len, int mode)
{
    uint8_t command[32];
    int count = snprintf(command, 32, "AT+CWMODE_CUR=%d\r\n", mode);
    uart_write_blocking(uart1, command, count);
    return getBlock(buf, len);
}
```

In this case the command is:

AT+CWMODE_CUR = n

where n is 1 for client, 2 for access point and 3 for both. If you want to make the change permanent then change CUR to DEF and the setting is stored in flash memory. Older devices do not support CWMODE_CUR. Simply change it to CWMODE, which is deprecated.

To set client you would call:

modeWiFi(buf, 512, 1);

and see OK sent back.

Scan

The scan function is one that everyone wants to try out, but in practice it isn't very useful. Why would you want a list of WiFi networks? There are some applications for this function, but not as many as you might think. In most cases, you simply want to connect to a known WiFi network, which is what we do in the next section.

The scan command is easy - just send AT+CWLAP and the device sends you a complete list of WiFi networks. The problem is that scanning takes a long time and often hangs for a few seconds. Clearly we can't simply read a single block of data using the getBlock function as it will time out due to the long pauses. We need a more powerful reading function that retrieves multiple blocks with an overall timeout.

While it is doing this it might as well also scan the incoming data for a target like "OK" to use as a signal that it can stop reading blocks:

```
int getBlocks(uint8_t buf[], int len, int num, char target[])
{
    for (int i = 0; i < num; i++)
    {
        if (uart_is_readable_within_us(uart1, 1000 * 1000));
        getBlock(buf, len);
        if (strstr(buf, target))
            return i;
    }
    return -1;
}
```

Notice that we try to retrieve a maximum of num blocks and wait 1 second between trying each. If a block contains the target string then we return with the number of blocks read. The getBlock function is used to get each block and it displays what it has retrieved if Debug is set to 1. In a more sophisticated application you would probably want to concatenate the received blocks into a single larger buffer for further processing – as written it simply throws this data away.

Now we can retrieve multiple blocks we can implement the scan function:

```
int scanWiFi(uint8_t buf[], int len)
{
    uint8_t SendData[] = "AT+CWLAP\r\n";
    uart_write_blocking(uart1, SendData, 18);
    return getBlocks(buf, len, 20, "OK");
}
```

In this case the function is set to retrieve a maximum of 20 blocks, which could mean waiting as long as 20 seconds for the function to exit. However, in most cases it exits after only a small number of blocks because it detects an "OK".

The getBlocks function is so useful that you might as well go back and change the call to getBlock to getBlocks(buf,len,20,"OK"), which will improve the reliability of the program.

Connecting to WiFi

Our final, and most useful, functions connect the device to a known WiFi network. All you have to do is supply the SSID and password. There are other versions of the command that allow you to specify the connection more precisely, but this general form is the most useful. Connection to a network takes a while and there is quite a lot of data sent back, so we need to use a long timeout in the getBlocks function introduced in the scan function:

```
int connectWiFi(uint8_t buf[], int len, char ssid[], char pass[])
{
    uint8_t command[128];
    int count = snprintf(command, 128,
                "AT+CWJAP_CUR=\"%s\",\"%s\"\r\n", ssid, pass);
    uart_write_blocking(uart1, command, count);
    return getBlocks(buf, len, 20, "OK");
}
```

Notice the way the snprintf function is used to insert the SSID and password into the command. If you have an older device you might need to change CWJAP_CUR to the deprecated CWJAP command. There is also a CWJAP_DEF command that will save the connection in the flash memory.

The connection is made with:

```
connectWiFi(buf, 512,"myWiFi","myPassword");
```

After a few seconds you should see:

```
        AT+CWJAP_CUR="myWiFi","myPassword"
        WIFI CONNECTED
        WIFI GOT IP
        OK
```

Once you are connected and the "WIFI GOT IP" message has been received you can ask what the IP address is:

```
int getIPWiFi(uint8_t buf[], int len)
{
    uint8_t SendData[] = "AT+CIFSR\r\n";
    uart_write_blocking(uart1, SendData, 10);
    return getBlocks(buf, len, 20, "OK");
}
```

Of course, if you really need to know the IP address within a program you need to extract it from the string. The device replies with:

```
        AT+CIFSR
        +CIFSR:STAIP,"192.168.253.4"
        +CIFSR:STAMAC,"5c:cf:7f:16:97:ab"
        OK
```

This makes it very easy to get the IP address, even without the help of a regular expression.

Getting a Web Page

Now we have enough functions to tackle the two standard tasks in using the TCP stack - getting and sending data as a client and as a server.

First we tackle the problem of acting as a client. This isn't as common a requirement as you might expect because most of the time devices like the Pico are used to supply data to other servers, not the other way round. However, it is worth seeing how it is done.

It doesn't matter if you are implementing a client or a server, either way you make use of sockets which represent the basic TCP connection. What you do with this connection is up to you. For example, if you send HTTP headers on an appropriate port, you can fetch or deliver a web page, i.e. HTTP over TCP.

The first thing we have to do is set up a socket connection between the client, i.e. the Pico, and the server.

```
int getWebPageWiFi(uint8_t buf[], int len, char URL[], char page[])
{
    uint8_t command[128];
    int count = snprintf(command, 128,
                     "AT+CIPSTART=\"TCP\",\"%s\",80\r\n", URL);
    uart_write_blocking(uart1, command, count);
    if (getBlocks(buf, len, 20, "OK") < 0)
        return -1;
}
```

You pass the URL to the function as an IP address or as a full URL, but the device looks up domain names using a fixed set of DNS servers. It is recommended that you use an IP address, especially when testing. The CIPSTART command opens a socket to the specified IP address and port.

You can also specify a TCP or UDP connection in the AT command:

```
AT+CIPSTART=type, IP, port
```

In this case we open port 80 on the specified IP address or URL. If it works you will get back a message something like:

```
Connect
AT+CIPSTART="TCP","192.168.253.23",80
CONNECT
OK
```

Now we have a socket open we can send some data to the server and wait for some data to be sent back to us. This can be a problem as you can't anticipate the amount of data you get back from the web server.

For this example, the web page is served by a small sensor that returns a JSON temperature and Humidity reading. The sensor is another Pico running the web server as described in the next section.

To send data over a socket you use `CIPSEND`, which will send any data you specify to the server. As already made clear, what you send is a matter of what protocol you are using over the socket. In this case it is HTTP and we are going to send headers corresponding to a `GET` request for `index.html`

```
char http[150];
sprintf(http, "GET %s HTTP/1.1\r\nHost:%s\r\n\r\n", page, URL);
```

This time we can't just send the string using `uart_write_blocking` because we need to include the length of the string in the header we send to the server.

The headers we are sending are:

```
GET /index.html HTTP/1.1
Host:192.168.253.23
```

Remember, an HTTP request always ends with a blank line.

To send this request we use the `CIPSEND` command which specifies the number of characters that are to follow:

```
count = snprintf(command, 128, "AT+CIPSEND=%d\r\n", strlen(http));
 uart_write_blocking(uart1, command, count);
```

Now we have to send the number of bytes/ characters that we specified in the `CIPSEND`. but first we wait for a ">" to indicate that the device is ready to receive the data:

```
if (getBlocks(buf, len, 20, ">") < 0)
    return -1;
uart_write_blocking(uart1, http, strlen(http));
return getBlocks(buf, len, 20, "</html>");
```

What happens next depends on the server. As a result of the HTTP GET the server will now send data over the WiFi link and the device will send this over the serial connection as soon as it gets it. Notice that this data is not a direct response to a command and so the device prefixes it with:

`+IPD,len:`

The +IPD makes it clear to the client that is a packet of data sent from the server. The len value gives the number of characters sent after the colon. You could use this to work out when to stop reading data, but for simplicity we scan for "</html>" which is usually, but not always, the final tag at the end of a web page.

In principle what your program should do next is sit in a polling loop looking for +IPD. It should then read the digits between the comma and the colon and convert this to an integer. Finally it should then read exactly that number of characters from the serial port:

```
+IPD,1440:HTTP/1.1 200 OK
Accept-Ranges: bytes
Age: 223181
Cache-Control: max-age=604800
Content-Type: text/html; charset=UTF-8
Date: Sun, 11 Apr 2021 06:40:22 GMT
Etag: "3147526947+gzip"
Expires: Sun, 18 Apr 2021 06:40:22 GMT
Last-Modified: Thu, 17 Oct 2019 07:18:26 GMT
Server: ECS (dcb/7F83)
Vary: Accept-Encoding
X-Cache: HIT
Content-Length: 1256
+IPD,127:<html><head><title>Temperature</title></head>
<body><p>{"humidity":0,"airtemperature":0}
       </p></body></html>CLOSED
```

You can see that there are three "packets" of data – 1440 characters and 127 characters. In principle you could process the +IPD characters as they come in and work out how many characters to read. However, you still wouldn't know how many packets to expect.

The complete function and a more general main program is:

```
int getWebPageWiFi(uint8_t buf[], int len, char URL[], char page[])
{
    uint8_t command[128];
    int count = snprintf(command, 128,
                    "AT+CIPSTART=\"TCP\",\"%s\",80\r\n", URL);
    uart_write_blocking(uart1, command, count);
    if (getBlocks(buf, len, 20, "OK") < 0)
        return -1;
    char http[150];
    sprintf(http, "GET %s HTTP/1.1\r\nHost:%s\r\n\r\n", page, URL);
    count = snprintf(command, 128,
                        "AT+CIPSEND=%d\r\n", strlen(http));
    uart_write_blocking(uart1, command, count);
    if (getBlocks(buf, len, 20, ">") < 0)
        return -1;
    uart_write_blocking(uart1, http, strlen(http));
    return getBlocks(buf, len, 20, "</html>");
}
```

```
int main()
{
    stdio_init_all();
    initWiFi();
    uint8_t buf[512];
    modeWiFi(buf, 512, 1);
    connectWiFi(buf, 512, "ssid", "password");
    getWebPageWiFi(buf, 512, "example.com", "/index.html");
    sleep_ms(1000);
}
```

This program makes use of some of the functions given earlier: `initWiFi`, `modeWiFi`, `getBlocks` and `getBlock`. It starts with:

```
#include <stdio.h>
#include "pico/stdlib.h"
#include "hardware/gpio.h"
#include <string.h>

#define Debug true
```

A Web Server

The most common use for an internet connection on a small device like the Pico is to allow another device to request data. It is fairly easy to create a web server running on the ESP8266, but don't expect Apache or anything advanced. All you can reasonably do is accept a connection and send a web page or two back to the client.

The key differences between client and server mode is that in server mode the device is constantly "listening" for clients to make TCP connections on the port. When the device receives a connection it reads all of the data the client sends and passes it on via the serial port to the Pico. This means that in server mode the Pico has to be constantly on the lookout for new data from the ESP8266. You can do this using an interrupt, but for simplicity this example uses a polling loop.

There is another difference between client mode and server mode - there can be multiple TCP connections from as many clients as try to connect. The solution to this problem is that the ESP8266 assigns each TCP socket connection an id number and this is what you need to use to make sure you send the data to the right place.

Let's see how it all works. Assuming we are already connected to WiFi and have an IP address, we can set up a server quite easily. First we need to use the command `CIPMUX=1` to set the device into multiple connection mode. You cannot start a server if `CIPMUX=0`, the default single connection mode. Once multiple connections are allowed you can create a server using `CIPSERVER=1,port`.

In this example we are using port 80. the standard HTTP port, but you can change this to anything you want:

```
int startServerWiFi(uint8_t buf[], int len)
{
    char temp[256];
    char id[10];
    uart_write_blocking(uart1, "AT+CIPMUX=1\r\n", 13);
    if (getBlocks(buf, len, 10, "OK") < 0)
        return -1;
    uart_write_blocking(uart1, "AT+CIPSERVER=1,80\r\n", 19);
    if (getBlocks(buf, len, 10, "OK") < 0)
        return -1;
    return 0;
}
```

If you run just this part of the program you will see the response:

```
AT+CIPMUX=1
OK
AT+CIPSERVER=1,80
OK
```

Now we just have to wait for a client to make a connection and send some data. This is done simply by reading the serial input and checking for "+IPD" in an infinite polling loop:

```
for (;;) {
  if (getBlocks(1, "+IPD") < 0)continue;
```

If we don't get a block containing "+IPD" we simply move on to the next iteration, i.e. there is nothing to do.

If we have received a block containing "+IPD", the body of the loop processes it. Note that all of the following instructions are inside the loop and are repeated for each request for the web page. We need to remove the IPD information. As this is C, string processing it is not elegant. The received data has the format:

```
+IPD,id, rest of data
```

We need to extract the ID, as a string, so we can use it to communicate with the client. This is just some standard string handling, but it is still messy:

```
char *b = strstr(buf, "+IPD");
b += 5;
strncpy(temp, b, sizeof (temp));
char *e = strstr(temp, ",");
int d = e - temp;
memset(id, '\0', sizeof (id));
strncpy(id, temp, d);
```

The algorithm is:

1. Find "+IPD" and trim the string to remove it and the comma
2. Find the next comma and extract the characters from the start of the string to the next comma.

Now we have the ID we can communicate with the client, but first we need something to send. As with all HTTP transactions, we have to send some headers and then some data. There are a lot of possible headers you could send, but a reasonable minimum that works with most browsers is:

```
char data[] = "HTTP/1.0 200 OK\r\nServer: Pico\r\nContent-
type:
text/html\r\n\r\n<html><head><title>Temperature</title></head
><body><p>{\"humidity\":81%,\"airtemperature\":23.5C}</p></
body></html>\r\n";
```

Note that this is a single string with no spaces between the elements that have been split over different lines for presentation.

Of course, in a real application, the HTML part of the data would be generated by the program or read from a file. You can include timestamps and lots of other useful information, but this is simple and it works. Remember to include a blank line at the end of the headers. This is vital as the browser will ignore everything sent to it if you don't.

Now we want to send the data to the client. This is just a matter of using the `CIPSEND` command again, only this time with `id` specified as the first parameter:

```
CIPSEND=id,data length
```

and we wait for the response ">" before sending the data.

Notice that we don't have to open a TCP socket as we did in the case of acting as a client. The TCP socket has already been opened by the client connecting to the server and when the transaction is complete we can close it:

```
uint8_t command[128];
int count = snprintf(command, 128,
        "AT+CIPSEND=%s,%d\r\n", id, strlen(data));
uart_write_blocking(uart1, command, count);
```

Now, at last, we can send the data to the client:

```
uart_write_blocking(uart1, data, strlen(data));
if (getBlocks(buf, len, 10, "OK") < 0)
            return -1;
```

and wait for it to complete.

Finally we close the connection and complete the loop to wait for another connection:

```
count = snprintf(command, 128, "AT+CIPCLOSE=%s\r\n", id);
uart_write_blocking(uart1, command, count);
if (getBlocks(buf, len, 10, "OK") < 0)
            return -1;
}
```

Try it out with a main program something like:

```
int main()
{
    stdio_init_all();
    uint8_t buf[512];
    initWiFi();
    modeWiFi(buf, 512, 1);
    connectWiFi(buf, 512, "laribina1", "hawkhawk");
    getIPWiFi(buf, 512);
    startServerWiFi(buf, 512);
    sleep_ms(1000);
}
```

You should now be able to connect to the IP address that is displayed and retrieve the web page that displays:

```
{"humidity":81%,"airtemperature":23.5C}
```

There are a lot of WiFi commands that haven't been covered here, but now that you have seen examples of most of the basic types and encountered the typical problems that occur you should be able to implement any that you need.

There is still going to be the occasional unexplained crash and in this case the best solution is to use the soft reset command introduced earlier. It is also worth mentioning that the server program as presented does not actually handle multiple simultaneous connections. It has to finish dealing with one connection before it can deal with a second. To make it deal with multiple connections would mean checking for another connection while processing the first.

Complete Listing Of Web Server

The following listing also includes all of the functions presented in the chapter even if they aren't used.

```c
#include <stdio.h>
#include "pico/stdlib.h"
#include "hardware/gpio.h"
#include <string.h>
#define Debug true
int initWiFi()
{
    uart_init(uart1, 115200);
    gpio_set_function(4, GPIO_FUNC_UART);
    gpio_set_function(5, GPIO_FUNC_UART);
    uart_set_format(uart1, 8, 1, UART_PARITY_NONE);

    uart_set_translate_crlf(uart0, true);
    sleep_ms(100);
    return 0;
}
int getBlock(uint8_t buf[], int len)
{
    int count = 0;
    while (count < len - 1)
    {
        if (uart_is_readable_within_us(uart1, 10000))
        {
            buf[count++] = uart_getc(uart1);
            if (Debug)
                uart_putc(uart0, buf[count - 1]);
        }
        else
        {
            break;
        }
    }
    buf[count] = 0;
    return count;
}
```

```c
int ATWiFi(uint8_t buf[], int len)
{
    uint8_t SendData[] = "AT\r\n";
    uart_write_blocking(uart1, SendData, 4);
    return getBlock(buf, len);
}

int getVersionWiFi(uint8_t buf[], int len)
{
    uint8_t SendData[] = "AT+GMR\r\n";
    uart_write_blocking(uart1, SendData, 8);
    return getBlock(buf, len);
}

int resetWiFi(uint8_t buf[], int len)
{
    uint8_t SendData[] = "AT+RST\r\n";
    uart_write_blocking(uart1, SendData, 8);
    return getBlock(buf, len);
}

int setUARTWiFi(uint8_t buf[], int len)
{
    uint8_t SendData[] = "AT+UART_CUR=115200,8,1,0,0\r\n";
    uart_write_blocking(uart1, SendData, 28);
    return getBlock(buf, len);
}

int modeWiFi(uint8_t buf[], int len, int mode)
{
    uint8_t command[32];
    int count = snprintf(command, 32, "AT+CWMODE_CUR=%d\r\n", mode);
    uart_write_blocking(uart1, command, count);
    return getBlock(buf, len);
}

int getBlocks(uint8_t buf[], int len, int num, char target[])
{
    for (int i = 0; i < num; i++)
    {
        if (uart_is_readable_within_us(uart1, 1000 * 1000))
        {
            getBlock(buf, len);
            if (strstr(buf, target))
                return i;
        }
    }
    return -1;
}
```

```c
int scanWiFi(uint8_t buf[], int len)
{
    uint8_t SendData[] = "AT+CWLAP\r\n";
    uart_write_blocking(uart1, SendData, 18);
    return getBlocks(buf, len, 20, "OK");
}

int connectWiFi(uint8_t buf[], int len, char ssid[], char pass[])
{
    uint8_t command[128];
    int count = snprintf(command, 128,
                    "AT+CWJAP_CUR=\"%s\",\"%s\"\r\n", ssid, pass);
    uart_write_blocking(uart1, command, count);
    return getBlocks(buf, len, 20, "OK");
}

int getIPWiFi(uint8_t buf[], int len)
{
    uint8_t SendData[] = "AT+CIFSR\r\n";
    uart_write_blocking(uart1, SendData, 10);
    return getBlocks(buf, len, 20, "OK");
}

int getWebPageWiFi(uint8_t buf[], int len, char URL[], char page[])
{
    uint8_t command[128];
    int count = snprintf(command, 128,
                    "AT+CIPSTART=\"TCP\",\"%s\",80\r\n", URL);
    uart_write_blocking(uart1, command, count);
    if (getBlocks(buf, len, 20, "OK") < 0)
        return -1;
    char http[150];
    sprintf(http, "GET %s HTTP/1.1\r\nHost:%s\r\n\r\n", page, URL);
    count = snprintf(command, 128,
                    "AT+CIPSEND=%d\r\n", strlen(http));
    uart_write_blocking(uart1, command, count);
    if (getBlocks(buf, len, 20, ">") < 0)
        return -1;
    uart_write_blocking(uart1, http, strlen(http));
    return getBlocks(buf, len, 20, "</html>");
}
```

```c
int startServerWiFi(uint8_t buf[], int len)
{
    char temp[256];
    char id[10];
    uart_write_blocking(uart1, "AT+CIPMUX=1\r\n", 13);
    if (getBlocks(buf, len, 10, "OK") < 0)
        return -1;
    uart_write_blocking(uart1, "AT+CIPSERVER=1,80\r\n", 19);
    if (getBlocks(buf, len, 10, "OK") < 0)
        return -1;
    for (;;)
    {
        if (getBlocks(buf, len, 1, "+IPD") < 0)
            continue;

        char *b = strstr(buf, "+IPD");
        b += 5;
        strncpy(temp, b, sizeof(temp));
        char *e = strstr(temp, ",");
        int d = e - temp;
        memset(id, '\0', sizeof(id));
        strncpy(id, temp, d);

        char data[] = "HTTP/1.0 200 OK\r\nServer: Pico\r\n
         Content-type: text/html\r\n\r\n
           <html><head><title>Temperature</title></head>
            <body><p>
             {\"humidity\":81%,\"airtemperature\":23.5C}
            </p></body>
           </html>\r\n";

        uint8_t command[128];
        int count = snprintf(command, 128,
                        "AT+CIPSEND=%s,%d\r\n", id, strlen(data));
        uart_write_blocking(uart1, command, count);
        if (getBlocks(buf, len,  10, ">") < 0)
            return -1;

        uart_write_blocking(uart1, data, strlen(data));
        if (getBlocks(buf, len,  10, "OK") < 0)
            return -1;
        count = snprintf(command, 128, "AT+CIPCLOSE=%s\r\n", id);
        uart_write_blocking(uart1, command, count);

        if (getBlocks(buf, len, 10, "OK") < 0)
            return -1;
    }
    return 0;
}
```

```c
int main()
{
    stdio_init_all();
    uint8_t buf[512];
    initWiFi();
    modeWiFi(buf, 512, 1);
    connectWiFi(buf, 512, "SSID", "password");
    getIPWiFi(buf, 512);
    startServerWiFi(buf, 512);
    sleep_ms(1000);
}
```

Summary

- Adding WiFi to the Pico is fairly easy using the low-cost ESP8266 ESP-01, which connects via the serial port and makes use of AT style commands to control the device as if it was a WiFi modem.

- In addition to an ESP8266, you also need a power supply capable of running it. The Pico seems able to do the job from its 3.3 output.

- You can use AT commands to set the device into client mode and connect to a WiFi network.

- While it is possible to use ad-hoc protocols, there are advantages in using TCP, HTTP and HTML so that other devices can work with the Pico.

- The Pico can use client mode to download data from web servers.

- It can also emulate a server to deliver data to any web browser or HTML-using client.

Chapter 18

Direct To The Hardware

The SDK provides functions to let you access most of the hardware features of the Pico. They are very simple wrappers around the basic mechanism of working with the hardware – memory mapped registers. You might think that bypassing the SDK and doing the job directly via hardware access would be attractive because it is more efficient – it isn't. The SDK is such a light wrapper over the hardware there is very little point in trying to gain the few fractions of a microsecond that direct access provides. The obvious reason for knowing how to use memory-mapped registers is if the SDK doesn't provide a function that does what you want – perhaps a better reason is just to know how things work!

In this chapter we take a look at how the Pico presents its hardware for you to use and how to access it via basic software.

Registers

Some processors have special ways of connecting devices, but the Pico's processor uses the more common memory-mapping approach. In this, each external device is represented by a set of memory locations or "registers" that control it. Each bit in the register controls some aspect of the way the device behaves. Groups of bits also can be interpreted as short integers which set operating values or modes.

How do you access a register? Simply by storing the values in it or by assigning its value to a variable. This is nothing new in C. The big difference is that you now have to refer not to a memory location provided by the system, but to a fixed address provided by the documentation. You still use a pointer, but one that is initialized by a constant or literal. For example, if you look in the documentation you will find that the GPIO registers start at address 0x40014000. The registers are defined by their offset from this starting address.

So for example the table of GPIO registers starts:

Offset	Register Name	Description
0x000	GPIO0_STATUS	GPIO status
0x004	GPIO0_CTRL	GPIO control including function select and overrides
0X008	GPIO1_STATUS	GPIO status
0x00c	GPIO1_CTRL	GPIO control including function select and overrides
... and so on down to		
0x0ec	GPIO29_CTRL	GPIO control including function select and overrides

You can see that there are two registers for each GPIO line from GP0 to GP29, one control register and one status register.

Each register has the same format for each GPIO line. For example the status register is:

Bits	Name	Description	Type	Reset
31:27	Reserved		-	-
26	IRQTOPROC	Interrupt to processors, after override applied	RO	0x0
25	Reserved		-	-
24	IRQFROMPAD	Interrupt from pad, before override applied	RO	0x0
23:20	Reserved		-	-
19	INTOPERI	Input signal to peripheral, after override applied	RO	0x0
18	Reserved		-	-
17	INFROMPAD	Input signal from pad, before override applied	RO	0x0
16:14	Reserved		-	-
13	OETOPAD	Output enable to pad, after override applied	RO	0x0
12	OEFROMPERI	Output enable from selected peripheral, before override applied	RO	0x0
11:10	Reserved		-	-
9	OUTTOPAD	Output signal to pad after override applied	RO	0x0
8	OUTFROMPERI	Output signal from selected peripheral, before override applied	RO	0x0
7:0	Reserved		-	-

You can see that many of the 32 bits in the register are not used, but bit 9 is OUTTOPAD which is the final state of the GPIO line after register overrides have been applied. You can read its current value using:

```
#include <stdio.h>
#include "pico/stdlib.h"
int main()
{
    stdio_init_all();
    uint32_t *addrGP0Status=(uint32_t*) 0x40014000;
    uint32_t value=*addrGP0Status;
    printf("%b",value);
}
```

This prints the current status of GP0 in binary. If you want to find the status of GPn you need to use address 0x40014000+2n.

This is the general way you work with peripheral devices such as the PWM units or I2C hardware, but the GPIO is special in that it has another set of registers that control it.

Single-Cycle IO Block

At this point you might think that we are ready to access the state of the GPIO lines for general input and output. This isn't quite the whole story. To accommodate the fact that the processor has two cores, and to make access faster to important devices, there is a special connection, the SIO or Single-cycle IO Block, between the cores and, among other things, the GPIO. The SIO connects directly to the two cores and they can perform single-cycle 32-bit reads and writes to any register in the SIO. Notice that the SIO is not connected via the general address bus.

You can see the general structure of the SIO in the diagram below. You can find out about the other devices it connects to from the documentation - our focus is on the GPIO lines.

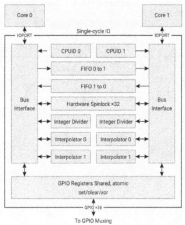

Notice that the GPIO lines are multipurpose and to use a GPIO line via the SIO you have to set its mode to SIO either via direct access to its control register or using the SDK function:

```
gpio_set_function(pin,GPIO_FUNC_SIO);
```

In this sense the SIO is just another peripheral that can take control of a GPIO line. The SDK `gpio_init` function automatically sets the GPIO line to use the SIO, so you are using the SIO even if you don't realize it.

The SIO provides a set of registers that makes using the GPIO much faster and much easier. The basic registers are:

GPIO_OUT Sets all GPIO lines to high or low
GPIO_IN   Reads all GPIO lines
GPIO_OE   Sets any GPIO line to output driver or high impedance

There are also three registers – SET, CLR and XOR - that make working with GPIO_OUT and GPIO_OE easier. Each of these can be thought of as a mask that sets, clears or XORs bits in the corresponding register.

For example, GPIO_OUT_SET can be used to set just those bits in GPIO_OUT that correspond to the positions that are set high.

The locations of these registers are as offsets from `0xd0000000` (defined as `SIO_BASE` in the SDK):

Offset	Name	Description
0x004	GPIO_IN	GPIO Input value
0x010	GPIO_OUT	GPIO output value
0x014	GPIO_OUT_SET	GPIO output value set
0x018	GPIO_OUT_CLR	GPIO output value clear
0x01c	GPIO_OUT_XOR	GPIO output value XOR
0x020	GPIO_OE	GPIO output enable
0x024	GPIO_OE_SET	GPIO output enable set
0x028	GPIO_OE_CLR	GPIO output enable clear
0x02c	GPIO_OE_XOR	GPIO output enable XOR

Now we can re-write Blinky again, but this time using direct access to the SIO GPIO registers.

```
#include "pico/stdlib.h"
#include "hardware/gpio.h"

int main()
{
    gpio_init(25);
    gpio_set_dir(25, GPIO_OUT);

    uint32_t *SIO = (uint32_t *)0xd0000000;
    while (true)
    {
        *(SIO + 0x014 / 4) = 1ul << 25;
        sleep_ms(500);
        *(SIO + 0x018 / 4) = 1ul << 25;
        sleep_ms(500);
    }
}
```

This program uses the SDK to set the GPIO line to SIO control and output. If you think that this is cheating, it is an exercise to set the line correctly using the GPIO control register and the SIO. The only possible confusion is the use of the offset divided by 4. The reason for this is that the pointer to the start of the registers is declared as uint32_t and, by the rules of pointer arithmetic, adding one to it adds the size of a uint32_t, i.e. 4. To keep the address as a byte address we have to divide the offset by 4 and rely on the pointer arithmetic to multiply it by 4 before use.

The SDK Set Function

The single instruction in our previous program:

```
 *(SIO + 0x018 / 4) = 1ul << 25;
```

is equivalent to the SDK's gpio_set function. Now that we know how things work, it is worth looking at the way the SDK does the job:

```
static inline void gpio_put(uint gpio, bool value) {
    uint32_t mask = 1ul << gpio;
    if (value)
        gpio_set_mask(mask);
    else
        gpio_clr_mask(mask);
}
```

This doesn't really tell us much about how things work because the put function simply passes the job onto the set or clr function. You can at least see that the function creates a bit mask in the same way our function did. Let's look at set and see how it completes the job:

```
static inline void gpio_set_mask(uint32_t mask) {
    sio_hw->gpio_set = mask;
}
```

The key to understanding this is that sio_hw is a struct that has fields for each of the SIO registers and its starting address is set to the start of the SIO. This is a fairly standard way of getting easy access to registers specified as offsets from a base address without having to do pointer arithmetic or defining lots of constants. If you take a look at the start of the sio_hw definition, it should make sense:

```
typedef struct {
 io_ro_32 cpuid;
 io_ro_32 gpio_in;
    io_ro_32 gpio_hi_in;
    uint32_t _pad;

    io_wo_32 gpio_out;
    io_wo_32 gpio_set;
    io_wo_32 gpio_clr;
    io_wo_32 gpio_togl;

      rest of the registers
      .    .    .
} sio_hw_t;
```

To set this struct so that its fields correspond to the registers we simply set its starting location to the address of SIO_BASE:

```
#define sio_hw ((sio_hw_t *)SIO_BASE)
```

Following this, when you set and retrieve values from the struct's fields you are working with the registers.

Example I - Events

The SDK does a fairly good job of covering all of the possible ways you might want to access the hardware but there are some omissions. In Chapter 7 the idea of events was introduced, but the SDK doesn't provide any access to events. The solution is to add our own function that accesses the GPIO register that records interrupts. This is a register in the GPIO set of registers rather than the SIO as GPIO interrupts aren't specific to what is controlling the GPIO line.

Now that we know about using structs to gain access to registers it makes sense to use the struct that the SDK defines to access the GPIO registers:

```
typedef struct {
    struct {
        io_rw_32 status;
        io_rw_32 ctrl;
    } io[30];
    io_rw_32 intr[4];
    io_irq_ctrl_hw_t proc0_irq_ctrl;
    io_irq_ctrl_hw_t proc1_irq_ctrl;
    io_irq_ctrl_hw_t dormant_wake_irq_ctrl;
} iobank0_hw_t;
```

The struct is set to start at the base of the GPIO registers and you can see that it starts off with the status and control registers for each GPIO line and then the four raw interrupt registers. The format of the raw interrupt registers is more complicated than the previous one bit to one GPIO line arrangement we have encountered before. In this case there are four bits per GPIO line and they record different interrupt types. The first four bits of the first register record interrupts on GP0:

3	GPIO0_EDGE_HIGH	WC	0x0
2	GPIO0_EDGE_LOW	WC	0x0
1	GPIO0_LEVEL_HIGH	RO	0x0
0	GPIO0_LEVEL_LOW	RO	0x0

This pattern is repeated for each of the GPIO lines and, when all of the bits in the first register have been used, the pattern continues in the second register with GP8 and so on. Each register records the event data for eight GPIO lines. Notice that each of the bits is set if the event that would cause the interrupt occurs – the interrupt itself only occurs if it is enabled. What this means is that the level bits track the current level of the GPIO line and the edge bits are set if an edge of that type has occurred. The WC in the third column indicates that the bit is cleared if you write to it and this is how the event is cleared.

We now know how to check for an event. All we have to do is read the value of the four bits corresponding to the GPIO line. If we are interested in GPIO line gpio then it is easy to see that the register that has its information is gpio/8. A mask for the correct four bits within the register is more difficult to devise, but you have to shift 0xFF, i.e. 1111, left by 4*(gpio%8). To see that this works try it out with a few values.

Using this we can now get the four bits:

```
iobank0_hw->intr[gpio/8] & mask
```

However, this gives the bits in their original position within the word. To get a right-aligned four bits we need to shift them down by 4*(gpio%8). Putting all this together gives the function introduced in Chapter 7:

```
uint32_t gpio_get_events(uint gpio)
{
  int32_t mask = 0xF << 4 * (gpio%8);
  return (iobank0_hw->intr[gpio / 8] & mask) >> 4 * (gpio%8);
}
```

To clear the raw interrupt bit you simply have to write a zero to it and there is already an SDK function that will do this.

Example II PAD - Pull, Drive and Schmitt

Each GPIO line has an identical input output stage, called a PAD, which is the connection to the outside world, no matter what mode the GPIO line is being used in. This is fundamental to the workings of the GPIO line and you might be wondering why it is being introduced so late? The answer is that the SDK doesn't fully support it and the aspects of the PAD that it does support, Pull Up and Pull Down, are simple enough. If you are interested in the finer details then you are going to have to implement functions that work with them.

The structure of the PAD can be seen below:

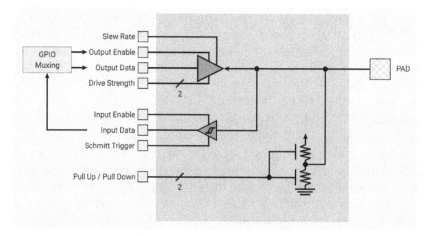

358

You can see that under program control you can set the Pull Up/Pull Down configuration and enable the input/output. The input also has a Schmitt trigger that can be enabled to clean up noisy inputs. The output can be customized by slew rate, how fast it changes and drive strength.

Before moving on to the software, it is worth explaining the basic ideas of the options.

The Schmitt trigger adds hysteresis to the input line. This means that before the state changes from high to low it has to cross a threshold, but to change back to a low state it has to cross a lower threshold. This acts like a limited debounce mechanism in that it stops the line from going low because the input drops a little after going high. The Pico's Schmitt trigger uses thresholds of 0.2V difference if the processor supply voltage is 2.5V to 3.3V and 0.18V if the voltage is 1.8V. What this means is that at 3.3V the input has to be greater than 2V to be a one, but after this the voltage has to fall to 1.8V before it changes back to a zero. For a zero the thresholds are 0.8V to change a zero and 2V to change back to a one.

The output drive strength isn't to do with how much current the GPIO line can source, it is about the voltage output at different currents. It is the effective output resistance. Each time the drive current is increased by 2mA another transistor is used in the drive, so lowering the output resistance. This has the effect of increasing or decreasing the voltage at the pin. For example, if you set the drive to 1 then if you want to keep the output voltage at or above 2.62V, i.e. a logic 1, then you can't draw more than 2mA. Put more simply, if you want the output to maintain voltages that are within the threshold for a logic 1 or 0 then you can only draw 2, 4, 8 or 12mA from the GPIO line depending on the setting of the drive strength. If you draw more current then this is fine, but the voltage will fall below the standards for 3.3V logic.

The final option is to change the slew rate. There is no information on this in the data sheet, but slowing the rate of change of the GPIO line can be useful when driving long lines or reactive loads. How useful this is in practice is a matter of experimentation.

If you want to work with the PAD directly then you need to know the location and format of the PAD control registers. These start at 0x4001c000 (defined as PADS_BANK0_BASE in the SDK) and the first, controlling the GP0 PAD is at offset 0x04 and in general the register for GPn PAD is at offset 4(n+1).

The format of the PAD register is:

Bits	Name	Description	Type	Reset
31:8	Reserved.	-	-	-
7	OD	Output disable. Has priority over output enable from peripherals	RW	0x0
6	IE	Input enable	RW	0x1
5:4	DRIVE	Drive strength. 0x0 → 2mA 0x1 → 4mA 0x2 → 8mA 0x3 → 12mA		
	RW	0x1		
3	PUE	Pull up enable	RW	0x0
2	PDE	Pull down enable	RW	0x1
1	SCHMITT	Enable Schmitt trigger	RW	0x1
0	SLEWFAST	Slew rate control. 1 = Fast, 0 = Slow	RW	0x0

Using this information it is fairly easy to write functions to set each of the characteristics of the PAD. For example, to read the slew rate:

```
uint32_t pad_get_slew(uint gpio){
  return padsbank0_hw ->io[gpio] &0x01;
}
```

where we are using the SDK-defined struct `padsbank0_hw` which is defined in:

```
#include "hardware/structs/padsbank0.h"
```

To set the same bit we need to use a mask that only changes the bit in question. This sort of operation is so commonly required that the SDK provides some functions to do the job:

```
hw_set_bits (io_rw_32 *addr, uint32_t mask)
hw_clear_bits (io_rw_32 *addr, uint32_t mask)
hw_xor_bits (io_rw_32 *addr, uint32_t mask)
hw_write_masked (io_rw_32 *addr, uint32_t values,
                                 uint32_t write_mask)
```

These are not only convenient to use, they are also atomic in the sense that if both cores attempt to modify the same register the two operations will not interfere with one another – one will complete before the other begins.

Using the set_bits function, we can easily set the skew rate:

```
void pad_set_slew(uint gpio, bool value)
{
    if (value)
        hw_set_bits(&padsbank0_hw->io[gpio],1ul);
    else
        hw_set_bits(&padsbank0_hw->io[gpio],1ul);
}
```

Getting and setting the Schmitt trigger is just as easy:

```
void pad_set_schmitt(uint gpio, bool value)
{
    uint32_t mask = 1ul << 1;
    if (value)
        hw_set_bits(&padsbank0_hw->io[gpio],mask);
    else
        hw_set_bits(&padsbank0_hw->io[gpio],mask);
}
```

Setting the drive is slightly more complicated as it is a three-bit value:

```
uint32_t pad_get_drive(uint gpio)
{
    return (padsbank0_hw->io[gpio] & 0xE0) >> 5;
}

void pad_set_drive(uint gpio, uint8_t value)
{
    uint32_t mask = 0xE0ul;
    hw_write_masked(&padsbank0_hw->io[gpio],value<<5,mask);
}
```

Of course we, don't need to deal with the pull-ups or pull-downs as there are SDK functions that do the job.

Digging Deeper

There is so much more to explore, but now we have covered the details that make things difficult to get started. From here you can read the SDK functions to find out how they work and you should be able to modify them and add to them. If you find that you need to create a program that doesn't include the SDK you can also use this knowledge to create slimmed-down versions of the code that does exactly what you want. Knowledge is never superfluous.

Summary

- All of the peripherals, including the GPIO lines, are controlled by registers – special memory locations that you write and read to configure and use the hardware.

- Exactly where the registers are positioned in address space is given in the documentation as a base address used for all of the similar registers and an offset that has to be added to the base to get the address of a particular register.

- The SIO block provides a more convenient way to access the GPIO lines and it has a different set of addresses and registers to the GPIO lines.

- You can learn a lot about how things work by reading the code for the relevant SDK functions.

- With knowledge of how things work you can add functions that are missing from the SDK such as events and PAD control.

- Each GPIO line connects to the outside world via a PAD which has a number of configurable elements such as pull-up, Slew rate and so on.

Index

1-Wire...235, 282
2N2222..18, 67, 69, 147
2N7000...71
775 motor...145
8n1..316

ADC..199, 211
address...225
aliasing...87
AM2302...261
armature...144
AT command...329
AT commands...327
automatic project creation...39
autopull..250
autopush...277

base...66
baud..315
baud rate...318
beta...66
bidirectional...150
bipolar...164
Bipolar Junction Transistor..66
bit banging..235
BJT...66, 67, 70, 77, 147
Blinky..46, 47
BME280...190
braked..148, 150
breakout board...223
breakpoints...35
brushed...143
brushed motor..144
brushes...144
brushless motor..143, 161, 163
busy_wait...54
busy_wait_until..55, 57
button...74, 81, 90, 101

C...20
C#..20
C++...20
checksum..231, 291
CIE 1931...135
clock divider...203
clock speed...215

clock stretching..223
CMake..28, 29
CMakeLists.txt..28, 115
collector..66
command..225
commutator..144
compiler collection..30
CoreMeltdown..90
counter..127
CPHA..181
CPOL..181
CRC..231, 291
critical section..110
CS line..189
CTS..318
current-limiting resistor..47, 64, 68
cyclic redundancy checksum..231

D-to-A..131
Darlington pair..146
data bits..319
DC motors..141, 143
debounce..83
DHT11..261
DHT22..235, 261, 270
dip relay..69
drain..70
Drain-Source On-State Resistance..70
drive strength..359
DS18B20..282, 305, 313
Dupont wires..18
duty cycle..114, 126, 130

EEPROM..313
Electronic Speed Controller..162
EMF..148
emitter..66
ESC..162
ESP-01..327
ESP-07..328
ESP8266..14, 327
Espressif Systems..327
event..98, 357
event queue..97

fast mode..215
FET..67, 70, 77
Field Effect Transistor..70
FIFO..97, 202, 245, 271, 277, 304

finite state machine..88
fixed time delay..57
floating-point...131, 298
forward voltage drop...64
fractional divider..120
FSM...88, 91, 94
FSM Button...89
FSM Hold Button...91
FSM Ring Counter..92

gate..70
gearbox...144, 163
GPIO..28, 43, 49, 90, 113, 352
gpio_pull_down...74
gpio_pull_up..74
gpio_set_pulls..74

H-bridge..147, 152, 153, 171
half bridge...156
hfe..68
hold..84
Hold master..227
HTTP..338
HTU21..224
humidity..230, 267
hysteresis...359

I2C...213
infinite loops...87
input..79
integration..76
internal pull-up..81
interrupt service routine...98
interrupts...97, 98, 104, 128, 129, 357
inverting buffer..77
IoT...14
IRLZ44..72, 147
IRQ...204
ISR...98, 253, 271, 277

L298 Dual H-bridge..152
launch.json...34, 38
LED.........................18, 47, 58, 64, 65, 66, 67, 134, 135, 136, 141, 241
level..117
logic analyzer...19, 47
loopback..186
low-pass filter..130

mask..50, 116, 360
MAX14870...156
MCP3008...204
Mealy machine..88
memory-mapping..351
micro-steps...165
MicroPython..16
middle C...134
MISO...179
MOSFET...70, 72, 147, 150, 152, 166
MOSI...179
motor..59, 143
multibyte transfer..186
multimeter..19
mutex..110

N-channel...70
No Hold master...227, 230
non-linear..64
NPN..66
Nyquist..131

Ohm's law..63, 64
ohmic..64
open collector bus..214
OpenOCD...33
oscilloscopes..19
OSR..246, 249, 253
OUT group..237
out instruction...237
Output Shift Register...246
override..60

P-channel...70
PAD...358
parasitic...282
parity...319
parity bits...316
password...337
permanent magnet..163
phase-correct...117, 118, 125
phased pulses..58
Pi 4..16, 24
Pi 400..24
Pi OS...24
Pi Zero...13
PicoProbe...17, 35, 37, 40
Picotool..40
PIO...13, 235, 270, 282, 307

PIO clock..241
PM stepper...163
PNP...67
pointer..351
polling is wasteful...88
polling loop....................................79, 85, 87, 88, 89, 94, 99, 222
potential divider..76
potentiometer...157
power consumption...63
press..84
printf...324
prototyping...44
pull-down...72, 73
pull-up...72, 73, 75, 214, 284
Pulse Width Modulation...113
push-pull...72
PWM...113, 126, 134, 141, 146, 153, 158
PWM applications...130
PWM generator..115, 116, 138
PWM Input...137
Python...20

race conditions..108
Read ROM...311
reading from a register...221
registers...351, 357
repeated start bit...221
resistors..18
rotor..143
round-robin..201, 202
RP2040..15
RS232...315, 318
RTS..318

sample-and-hold..205
Schmitt trigger..359
SCL..214
SCLK..179, 180
ScratchPad...312
SDA..214
SDK..15
Search ROM...311
semaphore..110
serial bus..213
serial port...315
servos..157
SET group...237
set instruction...237
Si7021...223

side effect...251
SIDESET...237, 251, 254
Single-cycle IO..353
SIO..353
sio_hw...356
sleep_ms..54
sleep_until..55, 57
slew rate...359
slow read...222
SN754410...153
snprintf...324
SoC..13
software interrupt..99
solderless prototype board...18
source..70
SPI bus..179, 199
SPI controllers...182
split ring...144
sprintf...324
SSID...337
Stack Overflow..20
starvation..108, 109
state machines..236
states...90
stator,...143
stepForward...168
stepper motor..163
stepReverse..168
stop bits..316, 319
strong pull-up...282
successive approximation converter..........................200, 205
surface-mount...223
SWD..32, 33, 35
switch..74, 81, 90
synchronization...126
synchronous...59

TCP..338
temperature...229, 267, 297
timeout...321
timers..172
timing..79
TIP120..146
torque...144
transistor...67
trap...99
tri-state...196
TTY..315
TX FIFO..244

UART..85, 315
unidirectional driver...164
unipolar...164

V24...315
Variable Reluctance...163
variable resistor..157
VGS(th)..70, 71
Visual Studio..26
Visual Studio Code...24
VR...163
VS Code..16, 24

web client...338
web server..341
Weber-Fechner..135
WiFi...327
wrap..116, 128
write..219
writing to a register..219

XOR...292

Zadig...37

Other Books by Harry Fairhead

Programming The Raspberry Pi Pico in Python
ISBN: 978-1871962697

The MicroPython version of this book explains the many reasons for wanting to use Python with the Pico, not least of which is the fact that it is simpler and easier to use. This makes it ideal for prototyping and education. It is slower than using C and programs use more memory, but sometimes this is a worthwhile trade off to get the sophistication of a higher-level language. What is surprising is how much you can do with Python plus I2C, SPI, PWM and PIO.

Raspberry Pi IoT in C, Second Edition
ISBN: 978-1871962635

In Raspberry Pi IoT in C you will find a practical approach to understanding electronic circuits and datasheets and translating this to code, specifically using the C programming language. The main reason for choosing C is speed, a crucial factor when you are writing programs to communicate with the outside world. If you are familiar with another programming language, C shouldn't be hard to pick up. This second edition has been brought up-to-date and focuses mainly on the Pi 4 and the Pi Zero. There is new material on the recently introduced GPIO character driver and using the Pi 4's additional ports and scheduling.

The main idea in this book is to not simply install a driver, but to work directly with the hardware using the Raspberry Pi's GPIO (General Purpose Input Output) to connect with off-the-shelf sensors. It explains how to use its standard output with custom protocols, including an in-depth exposition of the 1-Wire bus. You will also discover how to put the Internet into the IoT using sockets.

Although NetBeans is used to develop programs, VS Code is now considered an alternative remote development environment and all the book's code, which is available for download, has been tested with VS Code.

Applying C For The IoT With Linux
ISBN: 978-1871962611

If you are using C to write low-level code using small Single Board Computers (SBCs) that run Linux, or if you do any coding in C that interacts with the hardware, this book brings together low-level, hardware-oriented and often hardware-specific information.

It starts by looking at how programs work with user-mode Linux. When working with hardware, arithmetic cannot be ignored, so separate chapters are devoted to integer, fixed-point and floating-point arithmetic. It goes on to the pseudo file system, memory-mapped files and sockets as a general-purpose way of communicating over networks and similar infrastructure. It continues by looking at multitasking, locking, using mutex and condition variables, and scheduling. Later chapters cover managing cores, and C11's atomics, memory models and barriers and it rounds out with a short look at how to mix assembler with C.

Fundamental C: Getting Closer To The Machine
ISBN: 978-1871962604

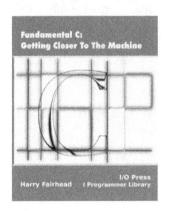

At an introductory level, this book explores C from the point of view of the low-level programmer and keeps close to the hardware. It covers addresses, pointers, and how things are represented using binary and emphasizes the important idea is that everything is a bit pattern and what it means can change.

For beginners, the book covers installing an IDE and GCC before writing a Hello World program and then presents the fundamental building blocks of any program - variables, assignment and expressions, flow of control using conditionals and loops.

When programming in C you need to think about the way data is represented, and this book emphasizes the idea of modifying how a bit pattern is treated using type punning and unions and tackles the topic of undefined behavior, which is ignored in many books on C. A particular feature of the book is the way C code is illustrated by the assembly language it generates. This helps you understand why C is the way it is. And the way it was always intended to be written - close to the metal.

Raspberry Pi IoT in Python With GPIO Zero
ISBN:978-1871962666

Python is an excellent language to learn about the IoT or physical computing. It might not be as fast as C, but it is much easier to use for complex data processing. The GPIO Zero library is the official way to use Python with the GPIO and other devices. This book looks at how to use it to interface the Raspberry Pi 4 and Raspberry Pi Zero to IoT devices and at how it works so that you can extend it to custom devices. Studying GPIO Zero is also a great way to improve your Python.

Raspberry Pi IoT in C With Linux Drivers
ISBN:978-1871962642

There are Linux drivers for many off-the-shelf IoT devices and they provide a very easy-to-use, high-level way of working. The big problem is that there is very little documentation to help you get started. This book explains the principles so that you can tackle new devices and provides examples of using external hardware via standard Linux drivers with the Raspberry Pi 4 and Raspberry Pi Zero in the C language, which provides optimal performance.

Raspberry Pi IoT in Python With Linux Drivers
ISBN:978-1871962659

If you opt to use Linux drivers to connect to external devices then Python becomes a good choice, as speed of execution is no longer a big issue. This book explains how to use Python to connect to and control external devices with the Raspberry Pi 4 and Raspberry Pi Zero using the standard Linux drivers.

Micro:bit IoT In C, Second Edition
ISBN: 978-1871962673

The new V2 version of the micro:bit is fully covered in this fully updated second edition which now uses VS Code for offline development.

It covers how to get started the easy way with two downloadable templates. Next it looks how to control the micro:bit's I/O lines and explores using the GPIO. For speed we need to work directly with the raw hardware and also master memory-mapping and pulse width modulation. Sensors are connected using first the I2C bus, then by implementing a custom protocol for a 1-Wire bus, and eventually adding eight channels of 12-bit ADC. The micro:bit lacks WiFi connectivity, but can become an Internet server via its serial port.

The book concludes with a look at the micro:bit's LED display and how it can be used in C for the classic game of Commando Jump, and a new chapter on the micro:bit's radio and the V2's sound capabilities.

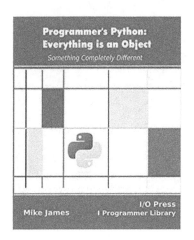

Programmer's Python: Everything is an Object: *Something Completely Different*
by Mike James
ISBN: 978-1871962581

This book sets out to explain the deeper logic in the approach that Python 3 takes to classes and objects. The subject is roughly speaking everything to do with the way Python implements objects. That is, in order of sophistication, metaclass; class; object; attribute; and all of the other facilities such as functions, methods and the many "magic methods" that Python uses to make it all work. This is a fairly advanced book in the sense that you are expected to know basic Python. However, it tries to explain the ideas using the simplest examples possible. As long as you can write a Python program, and you have an idea what object-oriented programming is about, it should all be understandable and, as important, usable.

www.ingramcontent.com/pod-product-compliance
Lightning Source LLC
LaVergne TN
LVHW062302060326
832902LV00013B/2022